REASSESSING RUDOLPH

Edited by
Timothy M. Rohan

Published by:
Yale School of Architecture
180 York Street
New Haven, Connecticut 06511
www.architecture.yale.edu

Distributed by:
Yale University Press
302 Temple Street
New Haven, CT 06511
Yalebooks.com

Editors:
Timothy Rohan
Nina Rappaport, publications director
Ann Holcomb, copy editor

Design:
Amy Kessler
to concept by MGMT.Design

Library of Congress Control Number:
2017953230

ISBN 978-0-300-22586-0

Printed in the USA

Contents

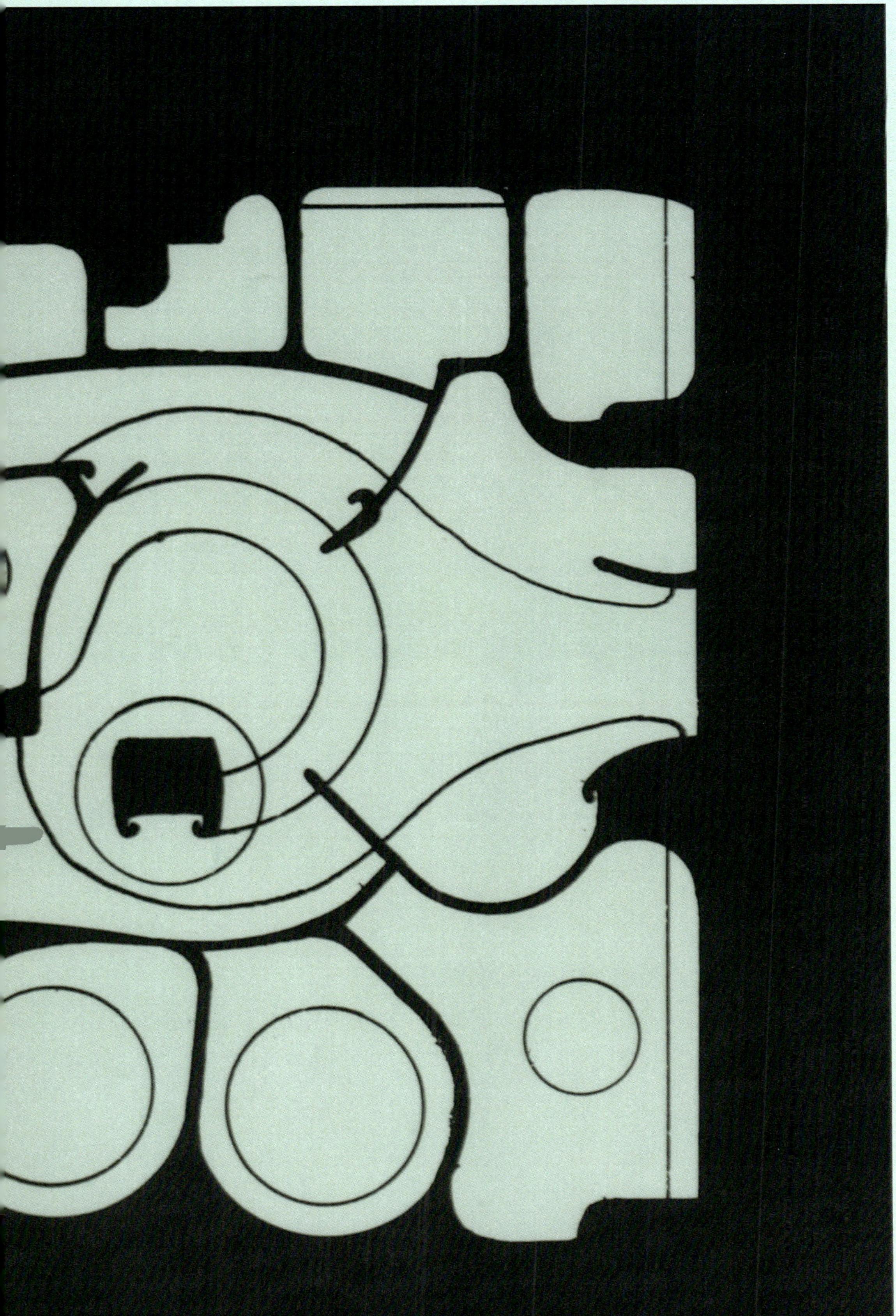

0.1 [previous spread]
Paul Rudolph, Dental office for Dr. Nathan Shore, New York City, conceptual plan, 1967

INTRODUCTION

Timothy M. Rohan

Paul Rudolph (1918–1997) was one of the most significant architects of postwar America, and yet he has been overlooked by scholarship, compared to contemporaries such as Louis Kahn and Eero Saarinen. This book addresses this situation with eleven articles by scholars organized in four categories: "Urbanism and Place," "Materials and Technology," "The Interior" and "Discourse." By considering Rudolph in light of these themes, these essays broaden our understanding not just of Rudolph but of architecture and society in the second half of the twentieth century, and all that shaped it.

Interest in Rudolph's architecture has fluctuated greatly over the years. Scores of descriptive articles about Rudolph's inventive Florida beach houses and Brutalist institutional buildings appeared in print from the late 1940s until the end of the 1960s, a time when he was most productive, admired, and discussed. Few had much depth, though critics provided some valuable analysis. In the 1970s, Rudolph's reputation and practice declined precipitously, as did the number of publications about him. The vicissitudes of Rudolph's buildings and career at that time fascinated architectural journalism and the popular press more than his new work or its content. Since Rudolph's death in 1997, interest in his architecture has grown as part of the revival of interest in postwar Modernism. Newspapers, architecture and design magazines, and many online sites often report on the fortunes of Rudolph's buildings, several of which have been demolished or altered. Preservationist groups, such as DOCOMOMO and the Paul Rudolph Foundation, raise awareness of Rudolph's buildings through their advocacy efforts. As a result, interest in Rudolph continues to grow, especially as the postwar revival shifts its attention to Brutalism.

However, scholarship, for the most part, has still not caught up with Rudolph. Academics have not quite known what to make of this prolific architect who left over three hundred buildings behind him, but few clues about their development and meaning. Little is known about this very contradictory and private man who was both egotistical and self-deprecating, sociable and shy, serious and witty, but above all committed to architecture. Ranging from the rational to the mannered, laced with hubris and redolent of failure, Rudolph's architecture is as difficult to reckon with as he was, much less interpret or canonize. Consequently, his buildings remain nearly absent from the primary textbooks about Modern architecture. Their authors do not know how to fit Rudolph into their narratives. And yet scholars realize that Rudolph is significant because the primary texts of the postwar era are littered with references to him and his buildings. New academic work of recent years about postwar Modernism often refers to him obliquely, or, more appropriately, depicts him as a character in a broader narrative, as in Robert A.M. Stern and Jimmy Stamp's history of architectural education at Yale.[1] The first of its kind about Rudolph, this volume of essays devoted entirely to him and his architecture makes up for the lacuna of academic analysis. The essays were originally papers given at the first scholarly conference about Rudolph's architecture that I organized at Yale University between January 23 and 24 of 2009. The conference was part of the events held to celebrate the restoration and rededication in Fall 2008 of Rudolph's Yale Art & Architecture Building as Rudolph Hall. Arriving in a timely fashion for Rudolph's centenary in 2018, these essays suggest new possibilities for the investigation of Rudolph's work in relationship to the discipline of architecture, its history, and all else that shapes them. Its tone and methods are academic, but it is also a book intended to be accessible to any reader with some knowledge of Modern architecture.

To further assist readers, the story of Rudolph's rise and fall is outlined here. Until recently, Rudolph's architecture and his trajectory were mostly known from the accounts scattered across the many profiles and articles published about him during his heyday. My research pieced together Rudolph's story and resulted in a monograph

[1] Robert A. M. Stern and Jimmy Stamp, *Pedagogy and Place: 100 Years of Architecture Education at Yale* (New Haven and London: Yale University Press, 2016)

about his work, *The Architecture of Paul Rudolph* (2014), again, the first of its kind on the subject.[2] The book confirmed in print the following account of Rudolph's career, which the essayists of this volume engage with fruitfully.

Paul Rudolph was born in 1918 the son of a Methodist minister and grew up in Depression-era Alabama. From an early age, he was ambitious. Recognized as being architecturally gifted during his undergraduate years at Alabama Polytechnic (now Auburn University) in the late 1930s, he was admitted to Harvard's Graduate School of Design, America's premier training ground for Modern architecture. He briefly studied with Walter Gropius who became his mentor, but left Harvard after World War II began in December 1941. During the war years, he supervised ship repair in the Brooklyn Navy Yard where he learned about so-called "new materials," such as plywood and plastics. After the war, he employed these materials to build structurally expressive beach houses in Sarasota, Florida with architect Ralph Twitchell that quickly attracted international attention in architectural periodicals, in part because of Rudolph's superlative drawings of them. His use of new materials and technology gave him a reputation for being daring and progressive. By the mid-1950s, Rudolph had established his own practice in Sarasota and begun to produce bigger buildings in and beyond Florida, such as the well-received Jewett Arts Center at Wellesley College (1955–1958) where Rudolph experimented with sensitive approaches to urbanism and place. He regularly taught and lectured at architecture schools across America, positioning himself as a maverick foe of the International Style, then at its zenith. As an alternative, he advocated a Modernism with greater urban, historical, and contextual qualities and more expressive and emotional content.

Admired as a rising star for architecture, Rudolph at the age of 39 in 1958 became chairman of the architecture department at Yale University. He transformed it into the most lively, interesting, and important place to study architecture in the 1960s, attracting students who became leading practitioners for the next several decades, such as Charles Gwathmey and Robert A.M. Stern. In their history of architectural education at Yale, Stern and Stamp have remarked that " . . . Rudolph ran the department as ringmaster of an ever-changing circus of visitors."[3] Guests came from opposite ends of the ideological spectrum, from Jane Jacobs to Mies van der Rohe, making Yale a place where new and established thinking clashed productively. The paradigm of the postwar hero-architect, Rudolph occupied a place near the center of architectural discourse at this time. Showing a keen awareness of developing tendencies abroad, Rudolph established a strong Anglo-American axis by inviting British architects to Yale, such as James Stirling, who joined the faculty, and Alison and Peter Smithson, who visited briefly to critique student work. He taught talented British students who later achieved international prominence, namely Richard Rogers and Norman Foster. A gifted pedagogue, Rudolph felt passionately about architecture. One of the worst criticisms Foster remembered receiving from Rudolph was, "You don't care enough."[4]

To house his department, Rudolph designed the Yale Art & Architecture Building (1958–1963), his masterwork discussed by many of the essays in this book. Known as the A&A Building and well received in America when it was completed, it helped establish concrete monumentality—which became known as Brutalism—as the preferred way of rendering institutional and civic buildings during the 1960s. That decade was Rudolph's heyday. He built several Brutalist complexes for American schools and cities, such as the Boston Government Service Center (1962–1971). In pursuit of technological innovation, he experimented with mass-produced modules to build a housing complex made of mobile-home-like units: Oriental Masonic Gardens (New Haven, 1968–1971).

However, the decisive cultural, political, and economic shifts of the late 1960s challenged Rudolph's ceaselessly innovative,

[2] Timothy M. Rohan, *The Architecture of Paul Rudolph* (New Haven and London: Yale University Press, 2014).
[3] Stern and Stamp: 203.
[4] Ibid: 181.

heroic approach to architecture. His Yale Art & Architecture Building fell out of favor with a younger generation who found it uncomfortable and who associated monumentality with authority. In New Haven, they protested against the Vietnam War and against the injustices of established society. Though never proven, many believed student protestors set the fire that consumed the A&A Building in 1969. The repairs were unsympathetic towards Rudolph's original intentions and made the structure even more uncomfortable, providing further evidence for those who saw its shortcomings as representative of Modernism's failures. Rudolph had left Yale in 1965 to pursue his practice in New York, but he was so associated with the A&A Building that its perceived failures were seen as his own. During the 1970s, Rudolph's reputation and practice declined along with Modernism's fortunes and those of the American economy. He was at odds with postmodernism as it had developed out of the ideas of Robert Venturi and Denise Scott Brown. Consequently, Rudolph became increasingly introverted and isolated from the architectural community, concentrating on making fascinating if perplexing domestic interiors for himself and his clients. He built a series of tall buildings in Asia in his final decades, but never regained his position at the forefront of the discipline. He was a marginal figure for architecture during his final years and little of note was written about him. When Rudolph died in 1997 at the age of 78, he was rarely discussed, though a small group admired his commitment to Modernist ideals.

By the first decade of the twenty-first century, appreciation for Rudolph rebounded and new opportunities for research about his work developed. The Library of Congress accessioned and catalogued Rudolph's extensive archive, making materials available for scholarship, exhibitions, and the preservation of his buildings. At the same time, at Yale, new interest in Rudolph developed. One of Rudolph's students, Robert A.M. Stern, became dean of the Yale School of Architecture and saved the Yale A&A Building from further physical decline. Charles Gwathmey restored the structure and designed an addition for it. As part of the events for the rededication of the building as Rudolph Hall in Fall 2008, I curated an exhibition, "Model City, Buildings & Projects by Paul Rudolph for Yale and New Haven," about Rudolph's projects for New Haven featuring many drawings from the Rudolph Archive at the Library of Congress.[5] Several of the unbuilt structures had never been seen, published, or exhibited before. To make even more primary sources available, the Yale School of Architecture also published a collection of Rudolph's writings from the 1950s to the 1990s.[6]

The essays presented in this volume emerged from the culminating event of the rededication, the symposium held in January 2009 entitled, "Reassessing Rudolph: Architecture and Reputation." It attracted a full house and lively, critical discussions. In the spirit of that event, these essays do not celebrate Rudolph. In fact, they question and interrogate him and his work and challenge some of the basic preconceptions about him. They reveal networks of relationships and affiliations that help in understanding Rudolph's engagement with postwar society, architecture, and culture. The articles are thematic and analytical. No attempt has been made to cover all works and periods in Rudolph's career. Subjects useful for thinking about Rudolph provide the four subheadings for the chapters.

In the first group, titled, "Urbanism and Place," Lizabeth Cohen and Brian D. Goldstein show that Rudolph's career declined not just because of changing tastes and the rise of postmodernism, but because of the decline of government support for urban renewal in the 1970s. Revealing important relationships for postwar Modernism, they explain how Rudolph had shifted his practice to federally financed civic and housing projects during the 1960s, which were often received through his friendship with Edward J. Logue, respectively director of redevelopment for New Haven, Boston, and New York State. Other authors also question

[5] A catalog with an essay about the projects and checklist exists for this exhibition. Timothy M. Rohan, *Model City, Buildings & Projects by Paul Rudolph for Yale and New Haven,* Yale School of Architecture, 2008. Exhibit held Nov. 3 – Feb. 6, 2009.
[6] Paul Rudolph, *Writings on Architecture: Paul Rudolph,* edited by Nina Rappaport, foreword by Robert A.M. Stern (New Haven: Yale School of Architecture, 2008).

established notions about Rudolph. In his essay, Eric Mumford demonstrates that, though Rudolph has often been considered a producer of idiosyncratic, stand-alone buildings as individual as himself, his urbanism relates to concepts promulgated by the International Congress of Modern Architecture (CIAM). Mumford explains how Rudolph's Jewett Arts Center at Wellesley College meditated on history and place in light of those contemporary discussions about urban space. In a complete departure from the places with which Rudolph is usually associated, namely Florida and New Haven, Kazi K. Ashraf takes the reader to Bangladesh for a little-known and curious postcolonial episode in Rudolph's career during the 1960s when he designed a master plan and buildings for a university campus in that newly independent nation at the behest of Muzharul Islam, one of Rudolph's Yale students. Ashraf considers the ambiguities of Rudolph's encounters with this place and his brushes there with other American architects also working in Bangladesh at that time, Stanley Tigerman and Louis Kahn.

During Rudolph's early years, the architectural press extolled Rudolph's use of "New Materials and Technology," which is the title for the next group of essays. Pat Kirkham and Tom Tredway show that Rudolph's experiments in his Florida houses and later residential projects were not his own inventions, but actually drew upon far broader investigations of the properties of plastics and plywood underway during the twentieth century. The other authors in this section of the book also contribute to a better understanding of Rudolph's experiments by relating them to contemporary efforts. Réjean Legault carefully traces Rudolph's development of textured concrete surfaces in relationship to the postwar culture of materials. He assesses the troubled, intertwined legacy of concrete and Brutalism left by Rudolph. Ken Tadashi Oshima surveys Rudolph's development of the mass-produced housing modules that he called "twentieth-century bricks." He explains their relationship to Modernism's long-term investigations of prefabricated units and highlights connections between Rudolph and postwar Japanese architecture.

Though most remembered for his Florida houses and Brutalist buildings, Rudolph devoted a surprising amount of time to interiors, which are explored in a section with that name. Sylvia Lavin proposes that Rudolph's nearly hallucinatory New York residences of the '60s and '70s should be considered in a category beyond architecture, one of liberating "speculation" and "experimentation." Rudolph intrigues Lavin, who believes that his range of scales and forms—from Christmas tree lights to megastructures,—do not add up to one single coherent body of work. In my own essay, I too look at Rudolph's interiors, but I find a key to understanding his spatial strategies in his consistent use of the perspective section to depict the complex insides of his buildings. The perspective section is one of Rudolph's many signature gestures that both cohere his architecture and yet also open up the fissures and rents in his imagery and buildings to reveal the wonder and agony of his project. Despite all the concrete, Rudolph's architecture is not as solid as it seems.

The final section of the book, entitled "Discourse," further complicates our understanding of Rudolph by examining his relationships with postwar architectural tendencies. Louis Martin helps us to better understand the Anglo-American axis in architecture by explicating Rudolph's fraught relationship with British architects, critics, and their Brutalism, which was quite different from the Brutalism practiced by Rudolph. Emmanuel Petit enhances our awareness of the roles that architects play within their disciplinary discourse when he explains how the definers of postmodernism, namely Robert Venturi and Denise Scott Brown, cast Rudolph as the paradigm of the postwar, Modernist, hero-architect whom "anti-hero" jesters like themselves would supersede in order to make a more inclusive, ordinary architecture. Unwittingly, Rudolph played a foundational role in launching the postmodernism he opposed. The final essay by Eeva-Liisa Pelkonen relates Rudolph's images, spaces, and draftsmanship to the phenomenology of Henri Focillon, whose thinking greatly shaped art and architecture at Yale after World War II. She concludes with a description of how the 2008 renovation of the A&A restored to the building its porous, open-ended qualities.

The unblocking of internal and external vistas and the creation of new ones in the building rededicated as Rudolph Hall is a fitting analogue for what these essays accomplish in reassessing Rudolph. The articles help readers to view Rudolph's career, architecture, urbanism, and engagement with materials, technology, and architectural discourse from different perspectives. The passage of time has allowed the writers to assess Rudolph and his approach to Modernism in a more balanced manner than in the past, distanced from twentieth-century Modernism's prejudices while remaining critical of him and his work. At times virtually absent from these texts, Rudolph emerges from them not as one subject, but as many. Individually and collectively, these essays therefore prepare the way for future investigations not just about Rudolph and his architecture, but about the world that made both. It is a world that we inherited and transform today as we read this book.

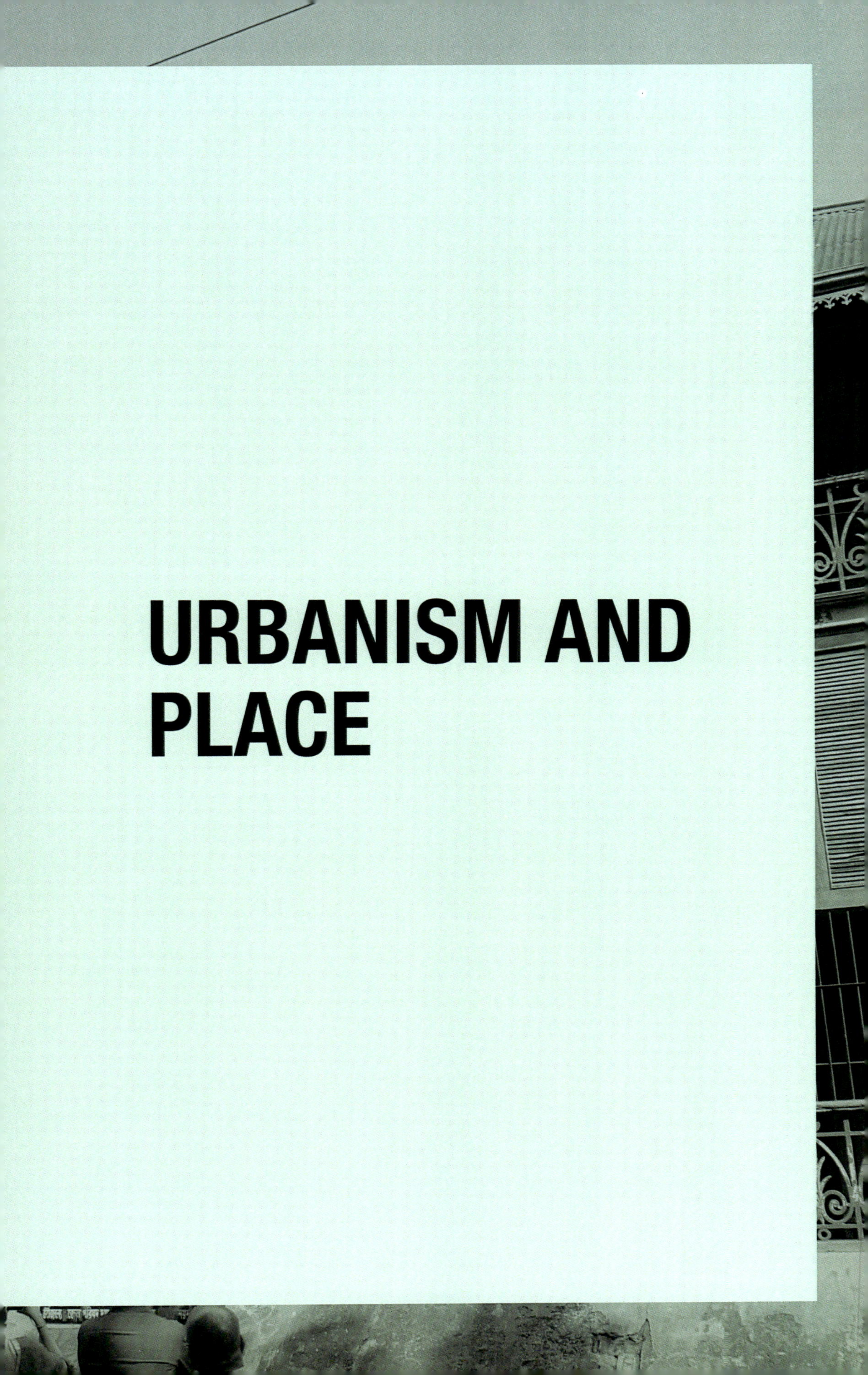

URBANISM AND PLACE

Paul Rudolph and the Rise and Fall of Urban Renewal

Lizabeth Cohen and Brian D. Goldstein

This is a tale of two men—an architect, Paul Rudolph, and an urban redeveloper, Edward J. Logue—who met in New Haven, Connecticut in 1958 as reshapers of this city's downtown in the heyday of federally funded urban renewal. They would go on to collaborate in Boston, Washington, D.C., and across New York State **[Figure 1.1, 1.2]**. In their work redeveloping cities, they not only built important urban buildings, but they also forged many of the design principles—for good or ill—that came to define urban renewal from the 1950s through the mid-1970s. By the mid-1970s, the federal government essentially withdrew from the kind of direct funding and oversight that had shaped urban redevelopment since the passage of the Housing Act of 1949. This was due to the twin assaults of a staggering economic crisis and Richard Nixon's intentional abandonment of Lyndon Johnson's Great Society for his own New Federalism. In many ways, the careers of both Paul Rudolph and Ed Logue would never recover from this federal shift—a retreat from big spending, but also from big thinking about the form of modern American cities in an age of intense competition for resources and residents with flourishing suburbs.

Examining the work that Rudolph and Logue did together over the almost two decades preceding this decline, however, helps illuminate four major design commitments underlying federally funded urban renewal, some more successfully implemented than others. Reestablishing urban monumentality, unwaveringly promoting Modernism, acknowledging the importance of the automobile in the next-generation city, and applying the latest technological tools to make housing affordable—particularly through prefabrication—were concerns that Rudolph and Logue shared and time and again addressed in their projects.

Recognizing how important urban renewal was to Rudolph's architectural career explains why his public buildings—arguably his most important commissions—were clustered in the period from the mid-1950s to the mid-1970s **[Figure 1.3]**. It

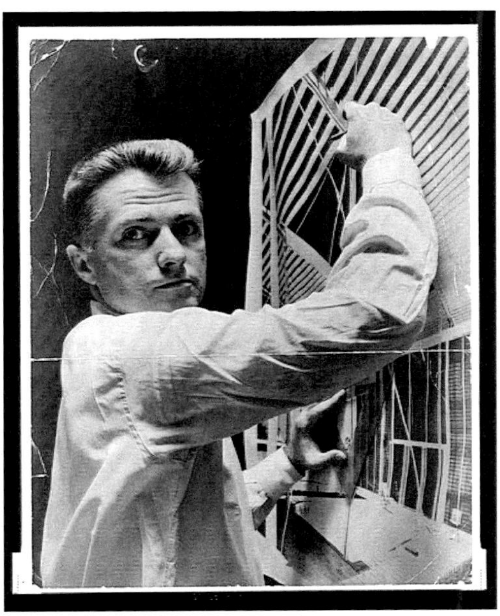

1.1
Paul Rudolph, Portrait, Drafting

1.2
Edward J. Logue, Portrait overlooking New Haven, Connecticut

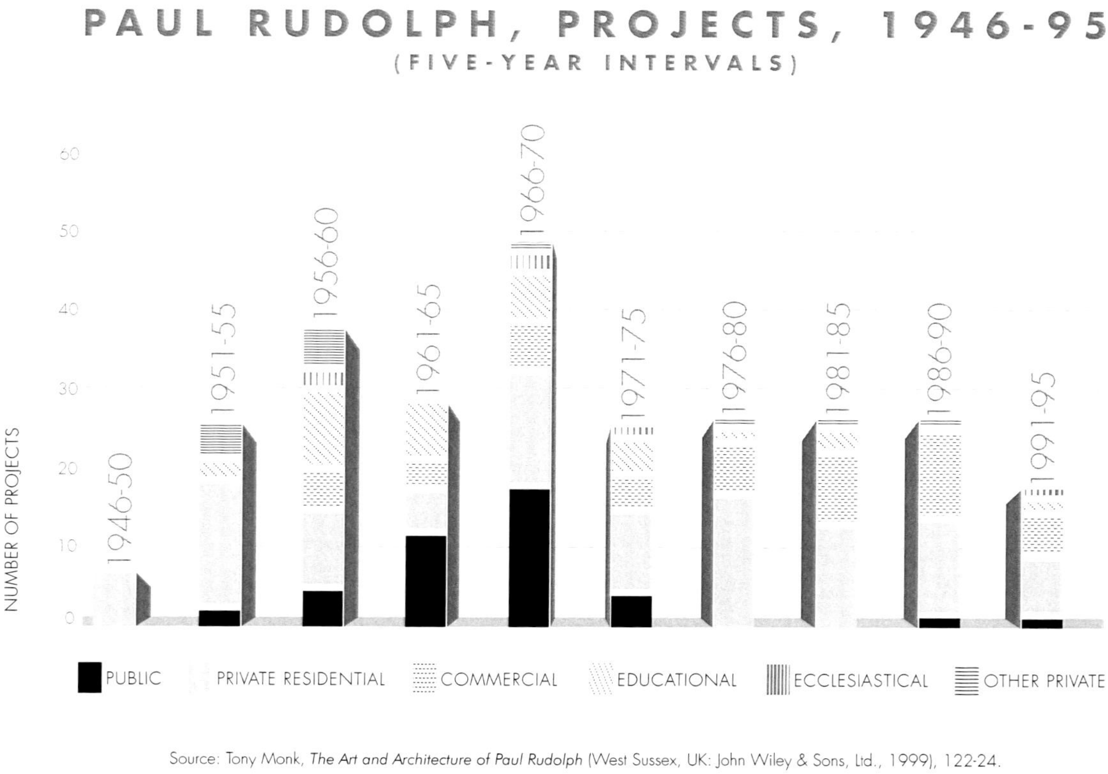

1.3
Graph showing the typological breakdown of Rudolph's projects

1.4
Paul Rudolph, Church Street Redevelopment, New Haven, Connecticut, perspective with corner pavilion, looking south from Green, 1958

likewise suggests a new reason why his career slid into decline thereafter. The government patronage underlying a quarter century of urban renewal not only empowered urban planners and redevelopment administrators. It also promoted the careers of an elite group of architects, to which Rudolph belonged, who gained the opportunity to reinvent civic architecture thanks to subsidies from Washington bureaucrats—the Medicis of mid-twentieth-century urbanism. As I. M. Pei later recollected in an interview, "There was a difficult time [after the war] . . . what little building . . . was probably all captured by SOM [Skidmore, Owings & Merrill] . . . Those of us who were outside had to pick up [what government made possible] . . . urban redevelopment, low-cost housing."[1]

For Rudolph, this opportunity first came during his tenure as both architect and educator in New Haven. In the 1950s, the urban redevelopment of New Haven gained national significance as the "Elm City" became the nation's "model city" of urban renewal, receiving more federal dollars per capita than any other American city. Soon after the election of reform Democratic mayoral candidate Richard Lee in November 1953, a Yale College- and Yale Law-educated stalwart in his campaign—Ed Logue—took the reins of the New Haven Redevelopment Agency. He quickly turned it into an agency so powerful and so independent that it became known locally as "the Kremlin." With the eyes of Washington and the nation on New Haven, the city undertook to revitalize itself, in the face of declining local industries and the departure of middle-class residents, as a laboratory for urban renewal. Strategies developed here, such as cutting a highway through a deteriorating low-income neighborhood to whisk suburbanites downtown, enticing middle-class residents into high-rise luxury apartments instead of suburban housing developments, and remaking the heart of downtown with suburban-style department stores and a shopping mall attached to a massive parking garage, would later appear in cities from Baltimore to Sacramento.[2]

By the time Rudolph arrived in New Haven to chair the Architecture Department of Yale's School of Art and Architecture in February 1958, work was already underway on the Oak Street Connector highway, the first new apartment tower downtown, and renewal projects in the Wooster Square and Dixwell neighborhoods. The city was also working closely with a New York developer, Roger L. Stevens, to reconstruct downtown New Haven through the ambitious Church Street Redevelopment Project. This was the first federal urban renewal project to focus on a commercial district, and it was trendsetting in using federal dollars to restructure land use, parking, and traffic circulation in order to recentralize a region's retail activities in its major city's downtown core. By that summer, however, Logue was having deep reservations about the design of the project. "The final reputation of the Stevens project as well as its commercial success will depend a good deal on the architectural quality of the finished product. The project will have a much greater impact on New Haven than even Rockefeller Center has on New York," Logue wrote Stevens.[3] By mid-September, with little improvement in sight, Logue insisted on hiring a design consultant to the city "who would assist with our review and who would be a man of such outstanding reputation that the question of our competence [to criticize the initial design] could not be raised again."[4] After considering a wide range of possibilities, including Hugh Stubbins, Eero Saarinen, Harry Weese, Carl Koch, Norman Fletcher, and Minoru Yamasaki, Logue settled on Rudolph, whom he described as "young (39) and of very flexible and practical temperament." This new architecture chairman at Yale, Logue asserted, was not only "the best man in New Haven, but the best man in the United States."[5] It did not hurt that Rudolph fulfilled Mayor Lee's injunction to hire local architects—"insiders"—while still offering the expertise of a prominent "outsider" architect.[6]

As design consultant to the Church Street Redevelopment Project, Rudolph did not merely review existing designs but also drafted extensive

[1] Interview with I.M. Pei, by Lizabeth Cohen, June 20, 2007, in possession of author, 60–61.

[2] See Richard Longstreth, *The American Department Store Transformed, 1920–1960* (New Haven: Yale University Press, 2010), Chapter 9: "Stores in the City," 219–245 for details.

[3] Edward J. Logue to Roger Stevens, September 19, 1958, Edward J. Logue Papers, Yale University Manuscripts & Archives (EJL), box 88, folder 926, 1.

[4] Draft of letter by Edward J. Logue to Roger Stevens, September 12, 1958, EJL, box 88, folder 826, 1.

[5] Edward J. Logue to Roger Stevens, September 19, 1958, EJL, box 88, folder 826.

[6] Memo from Richard Lee to Edward Logue, May 21, 1958, EJL, box 81, folder 732.

1.5
Paul Rudolph, Temple Street Parking Garage, New Haven, Connecticut, perspective looking north, 1959–1963

conceptual plans and elevations **[Figure 1.4]**. The greatest prize he walked away with, however, was the commission to design the 1,500-car Temple Street Parking Garage (1959–1963), which has probably become his best-known urban renewal project. In this, his first independent undertaking in redevelopment, Rudolph began to articulate the architectural language that he and Logue would promote for many years thereafter **[Figure 1.5]**. That Rudolph strived—and achieved—monumentality through his Temple Street garage is undeniable, even though his original design, which stretched across the Oak Street Connector to rejoin the divided parts of downtown New Haven, was scaled back. He conceptualized the building as much more than a garage, rather as a new "gateway to the city," and one of the civic "focal points" that he had argued in his theoretical treatise of 1956, "The Six Determinants of Architectural Form," required massive scale and a bold Modernist architectural statement.[7] Ed Logue's wife Margaret later recalled how excited Logue was about the Modern form of the parking garage. "[H]e loved the line created and was excited by beauty used in such a utilitarian way. That sort of structure was very unusual then."[8] For Rudolph, Logue, and Mayor Lee, it was totally appropriate that a garage serve as the foundational building for the new New Haven, given how important the automobile would be to the city's economic rebirth. A 1963 promotional brochure entitled, "New Haven: New England's Newest City," proclaimed "The Pulling Power of 9,850 Parking Spaces" beside a photo of Rudolph's garage, dramatically lit. For the city's most recent founding fathers, the garage's

[7] Paul Rudolph, "The Six Determinants of Architectural Form," *Architectural Record* 120 (October 1956): 183–90.
[8] Margaret Logue, email to Lizabeth Cohen, January 11, 2009.

1.6 [above]
Paul Rudolph, Government Service Center, Boston, Massachusetts, model showing planned but unbuilt tower, 1962–1971
© Ezra Stoller/Esto

1.7 [below]
Paul Rudolph, Government Service Center, Boston, Massachusetts, perspective, 1962–1971

prominence—spatially massive, stylistically Modernist, and car-oriented—conformed perfectly to the message they hoped to send, that, in the mayor's words, "In Connecticut, all roads lead to New Haven."[9]

Logue left for Boston towards the end of 1960, hired by another new mayor to bring his skills as an urban renewer to a larger but also long-depressed city. In New Haven, he had forged a strong relationship with Rudolph through their collaboration in the Church Street Redevelopment Project. Logue's wife Margaret attributes it to "the chance occurrence of the two living in the same university community and sharing a focus on urban problems early in their careers and early in the recognition of urban decay."[10] Throughout his life, Logue would refer to Rudolph as "one of my favorite architects and mentors," a "good friend," and someone who had educated him in design.[11] Logue arrived in Boston aware that Rudolph's Blue Cross/Blue Shield Building (1960) was one of only three new buildings constructed in downtown Boston since the Great Depression (and admired it as the best of them).[12] Now head of the newly invigorated Boston Redevelopment Authority (known as the BRA), Logue had his work cut out for him. As Logue's plans for the redevelopment of Boston took shape, with the Government Center project at its heart, he intervened to ensure that Rudolph was once again his partner in some of this endeavor, specifically in designing one of the key buildings in the complex, the Government Service Center (1962–71), intended to house combined facilities for the State of Massachusetts, including agencies for health, welfare, and education.

The details of how Rudolph became the chief architect of the project, overseeing the four firms hired to design its various components, are circuitous, but led once again to Rudolph's characteristic vision of monumentality and particular brand of Modernism winning out. The State of Massachusetts contributed two buildings to the Government Center complex, an office building and the Government Service Center, but had not initially planned on tapping federal funding for their construction. The State was required to confer with Logue's Boston Redevelopment

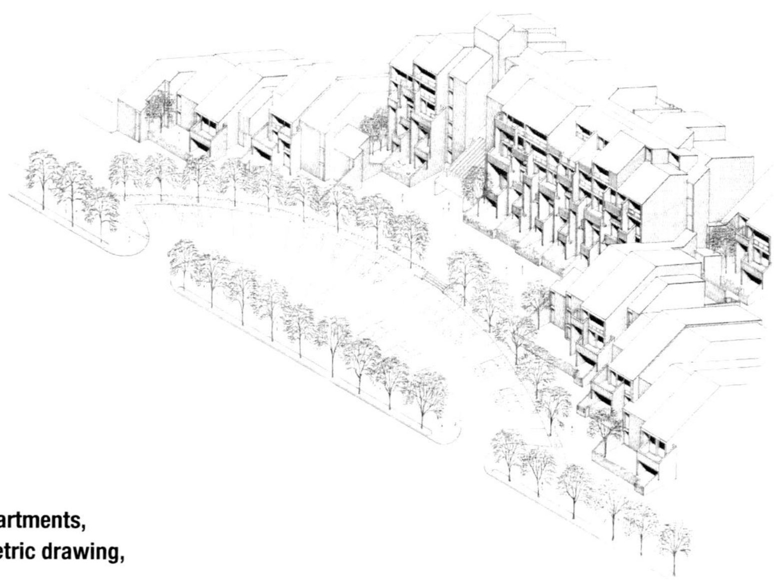

1.8
Paul Rudolph, Shoreline Apartments, Buffalo, New York, axonometric drawing, 1969–1977

[9] City of New Haven, *New Haven: New England's Newest City* (New Haven: City of New Haven, 1963), n.p., Richard Lee Papers, box 60, folder 1,183.
[10] Margaret Logue, email to Lizabeth Cohen, January 11, 2009.
[11] Interview with Edward J. Logue by Frank Jones, April 1999, transcript in possession of author (original recordings in EJL, accession 2012-M-027, boxes 69-76); interview with Edward Logue by Ivan Steen, April 9, 1990, EJL, accession 2002-M-001, box 21, folder "EJL Rockefeller Oral History," 20. Also see Edward J. Logue to Paul Rudolph, May 17, 1965, EJL, box 150, folder 443.

Authority before acquiring any land, however, and this opened a debate over whether to allow the State to take and clear the necessary land itself or have the BRA do so with federal support. The State's decision in late 1960 to follow the second route represented more than a procedural detail.[13] As an official part of the Government Center Urban Renewal Project, the state buildings came under the purview of the BRA, meaning that the BRA and its Design Advisory Committee could now dictate their design.[14]

The BRA lost little time using its oversight power to better coordinate the work of the four architectural firms involved, each of which was assigned to handle a different part of the Government Service Center.[15] The "Service Center," Logue said with typical frankness, "was poking along with a collection of architects who were sort of sniffing around at each other."[16] The design on the table, according to a young architect who worked for Desmond & Lord, the firm responsible for the portion housing mental health agencies, was "a kind of Italianate hill town." The BRA, armed with newfound authority over the project and dissatisfied with its direction, rejected this plan in April 1962, proposing "more land coverage and much less building fragmentation." Rudolph, only a minor player at this stage as design consultant to Desmond & Lord, grasped that the project had a program "too small for the site."[17]

Likely with his old friend Logue's support, Rudolph seized the opening created by the BRA's dissatisfaction and reconceptualized the project, proposing to push the complex out to the street to gain the massiveness its social importance required **[Figure 1.6]**. He also integrated the three separate buildings into a single textured concrete structure bordering the perimeter of the triangular site, creating a bowl-like stepped plaza in the interior, and designed a dramatic 26-story tower to mark the building's entrance and give the courtyard a focus.[18] Later, he would explain how key the Government Service Center's large scale was to people's recognition of the building's public role: "The manipulation of scale is the most important tool in the hands of an architect."[19] Rudolph's design solution was so compelling that the four firms involved, the client Government Center Commission, and the BRA's Design Advisory Committee, headed by Hugh Stubbins, all enthusiastically accepted it.[20] Despite this unanimity, however, budget constraints continued to haunt the project, compelling Logue and Stubbins to push to ensure Rudolph's continued involvement as coordinating architect until the project neared completion.[21] To Rudolph and Logue's regret, the tower, such an essential part of the Government Service Center's design and intended to announce the building from afar, was never constructed due to cost **[Figure 1.7]**. However, an underground parking garage, a necessity in Rudolph and Logue's conception of a renewed city, was completed.

The Government Service Center finally began construction in 1967, the same year that Ed Logue decided to tackle Boston's problems from the mayor's suite, rather than the back offices of the BRA, and announced his candidacy for mayor. Paul Rudolph—together with other architects

[12] Interview with Edward J. Logue by Ivan Steen, December 13, 1983, EJL, accession 2002-M-001, box 21, Folder "EJL Rockefeller Oral History," 21.

[13] See "1961 Government Center Commission Yearly Report," PMR Papers, box PMR-3022-2, file "Excerpts from Gov't Center Commission Yearly Reports," 10–11 for discussion of the land acquisition for the state's buildings.

[14] "Project Review: Health, Welfare & Education Service Center," January 27, 1965, PMR, box PMR-3022-2, folder "Project Review/ Health, Welfare and Education Service Center/Boston MA 16 Dec 1964 Office Copy," 5.

[15] Shepley, Bulfinch, Richardson and Abbott was to design the Division of Employment Security Building, M.A. Dyer Company was to design the Health, Welfare and Education Building, Desmond & Lord, Inc. was to design the Mental Health Center, and Pedersen and Tilney was to coordinate the efforts of all firms and develop a site plan for the multi-building project. See "1962 Government Center Commission Yearly Report," PMR, box PMR-3022-2, folder "Excerpts from Gov't Center Commission Yearly Reports."

[16] Edward J. Logue, "Work of the Boston Renewal Administration in the Urban Core," address to the Harvard Graduate School of Design 8th Urban Design Conference ("The Role of Government in the Form and Animation of the Urban Core"), May 1, 1964, 5.

[17] Interview with James McNeely by Lizabeth Cohen, May 31, 2007, in possession of author; "1st Draft, Health, Welfare and Education Building," PMR, box PMR-3022-4, folder "Governor's Report."

[18] "1st Draft, Health, Welfare and Education Building," PMR, box PMR-3022-4, folder "Governor's Report."

[19] Paul R. Kramer, "Summary of an Interview with Paul Rudolph, New York," *Werk* 60.4 (1973): 457.

[20] There is material in both the Rudolph and Logue Papers on the evolution of this project. See also Charles Hilgenhurst, "Evolution of Boston's Government Center," *Architectural Design* (January 1971): 14; and interview with James McNeely by Lizabeth Cohen, 31 May 2007.

[21] Hugh Stubbins to Edward J. Logue, March 14, 1963, EJL box 168, folder 688; Edward J. Logue to Paul Rudolph, March 19, 1963, EJL, box 168, folder 688; Paul Rudolph, "Project Review Memorandum," November 18, 1964, PMR, box PMR-3022-1, folder "Project Reviews."

who had worked closely with Logue—declared loyalty to their patron by forming "Architects for Logue." As they wrote in a letter, "He has fought for architecture and architects and in turn we have been made more aware of our responsibilities for improving design in the urban center." Each member contributed $500 (equivalent in today's dollars to about $3,600) to Logue's campaign.[22]

Having resigned from the BRA to run for mayor and then having lost the race, in 1968 Logue moved on to an even more powerful job, wooed by New York Governor Nelson Rockefeller to head a new statewide urban renewal agency, the New York State Urban Development Corporation (known nationwide as the UDC). Frustrated with the obstacles to building badly needed subsidized housing and other civic infrastructure, Rockefeller pushed through the New York State Legislature a semi-autonomous redevelopment agency, empowered to issue its own bonds, employ eminent domain, override local zoning and building codes, and make its projects tax-exempt. Over its frenetic seven-year life, Logue's UDC would put up 33,000 units of housing across the state, construct three new towns (two upstate—Radisson outside Syracuse and Audubon Village near Buffalo—and his prized Roosevelt Island in New York City's East River), and develop dozens of industrial parks and downtown renewal projects.

Not surprisingly, within months of taking the job, Logue hired his favorite architect, Paul Rudolph, to design an important mixed-use project for Buffalo's Lake Erie waterfront, an early statement of the UDC's commitment to upstate, not just downstate, New York, and an early test of the UDC's ability. A sign of the project's significance was Rudolph's almost $1,000,000 contract to plan 2,750 units of housing—much of it low- and moderate-income, community and commercial facilities, a school, and a marina, all aimed at reintegrating unused land near Buffalo's downtown into the city's urban fabric. As in his earlier redevelopment work, Rudolph took the Buffalo Waterfront Development project as a chance to experiment with his particular approach to architectural Modernism **[Figure 1.8]**. John Stainton, the UDC's regional director in western New York, recalls that after Logue selected Rudolph, the architect spent the day talking with Buffalo officials, who were upset that the firm with which they had previously been working did not get the project. After hours of politely listening to their hopes for a traditional design and materials, Rudolph "went off and designed another split block project."[23] Logue would soon make the case to jurors at the American Institute of Architects (AIA) that Rudolph's design for this project, completed in 1974, along with Crawford Manor, housing designed for the elderly in New Haven (1962–1966), soundly qualified him for nomination as an AIA fellow by virtue of offering "fresh, imaginative and most importantly, exciting" alternatives to the "banal and mediocre" low-rent housing in this country.[24]

Rudolph also brought his orientation towards the automobile to the 115-acre Buffalo project, the completed portion of which came to be known as the Shoreline Apartments **[Figure 1.9]**. A UDC staffer assured Logue, "The fact that an elevated expressway bisects this site is viewed by Mr. Rudolph as a design opportunity rather than an adverse liability."[25] The New York State Thruway challenged Rudolph to explore more deeply issues he had pondered since his early redevelopment work in New Haven: how to incorporate into the landscape people's attraction to the car "for unmatched freedom and convenience," as well as how to define the "new dimensions of scale... introduced by a quickly moving vehicle."[26] Rather than "cut up our cities," Rudolph insisted to an interviewer, thruways "are the first step towards building megastructures, which I see as a great unifying element in the cityscape."[27] In Buffalo, Rudolph allowed automobiles to remain visible and planned pedestrian ramps over the Thruway to the lakeshore.[28]

[22] Peter Lucas, "Can Architects Have Forgotten," *Boston Herald,* ca. August 1967; Peter Lucas, "Architect Rapped for Aiding Logue," *Boston Herald,* August 22, 1967; untitled article beginning "The disclosure," *Boston Globe,* August 23, 1967, all in PMR, box PMR-3022-3, folder "Clippings." For conversion of 1967 dollars, see http://www.bls.gov/data/inflation_calculator.htm.
[23] Email from John Stainton to Lizabeth Cohen, January 12, 2009.
[24] Edward Logue to Jury of Fellows, December 3, 1969, EJL, box 239, folder 84.
[25] Herbert Tessler to Edward J. Logue, January 20, 1969, EJL, box 300, folder 596.
[26] John W. Cook and Heinrich Klotz, "Paul Rudolph" in *Conversations with Architects* (New York: Praeger Publishers, 1973), 105; Rudolph, "Six Determinants," 189.
[27] Cook and Klotz, "Paul Rudolph," 107.
[28] Ann Stagg Belle, "New Way to Live—A Village in the Heart of the City," *House & Garden* (April 1973): 199.

1.9
Paul Rudolph, Shoreline Apartments, Buffalo, New York, site plan, 1969–1977

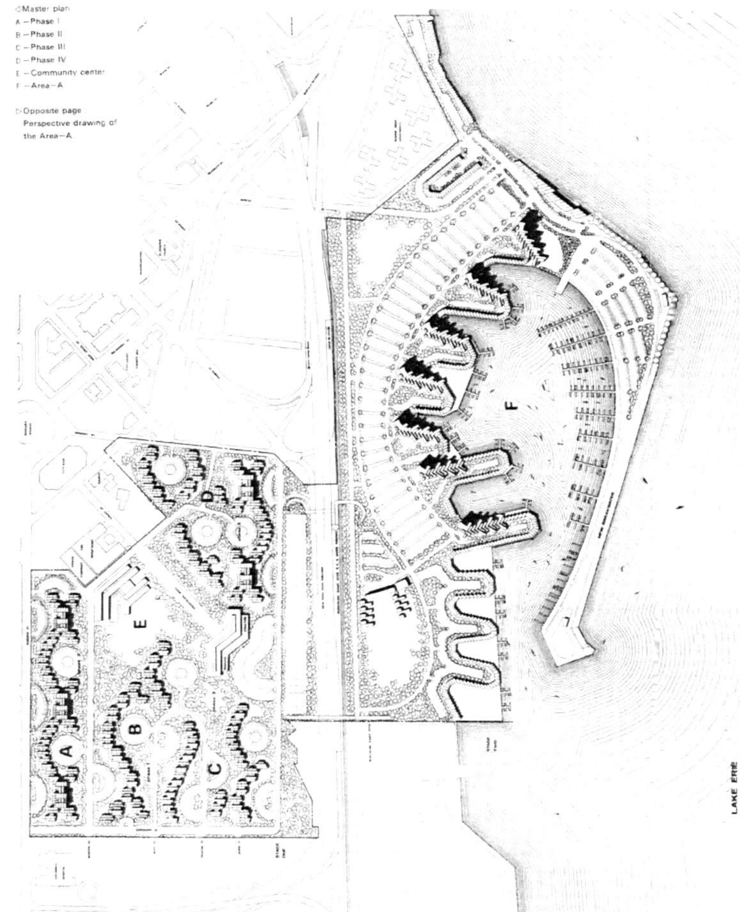

1.10
Paul Rudolph, Shoreline Apartments, Buffalo, New York, model of prefabricated units mounted on columns, 1969–1977

1.11
Paul Rudolph, Oriental Masonic Gardens, New Haven, Connecticut, perspective, 1968–1971

Shortly after designing the Buffalo Waterfront Development, Rudolph would push his thinking about automobility in the modern city even further with his schematic urban highway plan for the Lower Manhattan Expressway, where megastructures filled with housing, schools, stores, and offices hung from the vehicular route. Rudolph insisted that here, too, his scheme would "knit together existing accommodations on either side of the proposed route, rather than . . . cut the city."[29] Though that project never came to fruition, it became an iconic representation of ideas he had worked out with Logue's support over more than a decade.

Rudolph's efforts in Buffalo also provided him with the opportunity to develop a fourth element of his urban renewal vision that he had previously experimented with but had never been able to build: the prefabrication of housing using the trailer modules that he labeled "twentieth-century brick." Rudolph proposed 12-by-60-foot housing units that, after arriving at the site by truck, would be mounted on columns **[Figure 1.10]**. "Diagonal walls within the module fold out to become cantilevered floors for a three-level low-rise unit," *Progressive Architecture* wrote of the design in 1974.[30] Despite Logue's shared interest in prefabrication as a means to make housing more affordable, he became frustrated as Rudolph's explorations delayed groundbreaking and ran up the cost. In an exasperated tone, he scolded Rudolph: "My report on your first design for Phase III Buffalo Waterfront is that it will win a *P/A* Award and that is about it. After the length of time you have been working on this job, it seems to me that we ought to be able to get down to the real world without a waste of time, money, and your own unique talents."[31] Unfortunately, Logue's UDC would collapse in financial crisis in 1975 before this third phase (and the resort-like portion on the other side of the Thruway) could be built.

Notwithstanding Logue's frustrations with Rudolph's procrastinations in Buffalo, he continued to depend on him to articulate in design their shared commitments to monumentality, Modernism, automobility, and prefabrication. Whether for low-income housing at Fifth Avenue and 106th Street in 1969, or on the site of the Morgan Annex Post Office in 1974 (both unbuilt), Logue trusted Rudolph to propose the appropriate design solution, often in order to rescue a project that had gone awry. Logue's last gesture as president of the UDC was to hand-pick Rudolph as a juror for the 1975 Roosevelt Island Housing Competition for the second stage of the island's development, an event rendered purely theoretical by the UDC's collapse, but whose four winning designs included one by former Rudolph students Robert A.M. Stern and John S. Hagmann.[32]

Although prefabrication never made it into Rudolph's Buffalo Waterfront Development project, both he and Logue tried throughout their careers to apply its promised technical advantages and cost savings to construct decent and affordable housing for ordinary Americans. Rudolph expressed even loftier goals—that "these twentieth-century bricks will be a truly important material in creating a truly human city."[33] Surely, they must have shared their hopes. Despite all the work they did together, however, it was separately that each finally succeeded in constructing a prefabricated modular project. Both developments employed factory-produced structures and both, coincidentally, were labeled as "gardens." Rudolph's chance came when he was hired by the New Haven Redevelopment Authority in the late 1960s to design a townhouse project for a 12-acre site along Wilmot Road and Wintergreen Avenue, northwest of the city's downtown. Richard Lee, still the city's mayor and ever its booster, wanted New Haven to be the first with a city-sponsored "modular project." "Oriental Masonic Gardens" opened in 1970, with 148 two- to five-bedroom units scattered across the site in pinwheels that created small yards for each **[Figure 1.11]**. Rudolph added vaulted roofs to the trailer modules to create variety and greater interior space. Despite his innovation, however, the project soon failed. The homes were burdened with leaks and unpopular with tenants. Indeed, Rudolph

[29] Peter Wolf, *The Evolving City, Urban Design Proposals by Ulrich Franzen and Paul Rudolph* (New York: American Federation of Arts, 1974); Paul Rudolph, "Enigmas of Architecture," *A+U* 49.1 (Special Issue on Paul Rudolph), n.p.
[30] Suzanne Stephens, "Standing by the Twentieth-Century Brick," *Progressive Architecture* (October 1974): 81.
[31] Edward J. Logue to Paul Rudolph, October 21, 1971, EJL, box 300, folder 597.
[32] Memos from September and October 1974, EJL, box 312, folder 894. Also see Deborah Nevins, Ed., *The Roosevelt Island Housing Competition, The Architectural League of New York* (New York: Wittenborn Art Books, Inc., 1975).
[33] Paul Rudolph, "The Nature of Prefabricated System Design," *Japan Architect* (January–February 1971): 20.

later acknowledged that "people hated it," which he attributed to the fact that "psychologically, the good folk who inhabited these dwellings thought they were beneath them." The City of New Haven tore down Oriental Masonic Gardens in 1981.[34]

Ed Logue's most extensive experience with prefabricated dwellings took place in his last major position, when, three years after the failure of the UDC, he became head of the South Bronx Development Organization. Here he channeled his years of urban redevelopment experience into the nearly impossible job of turning around the devastated South Bronx, but with fewer financial resources and less political backing than he had ever before had at his disposal. Best known of his South Bronx work is his Charlotte Gardens project (1983–1986), an unorthodox plan to repopulate the abandoned, rubble-strewn Charlotte Street neighborhood with owner-occupied, single-family, prefabricated ranch-style houses, offered for sale at highly subsidized prices **[Figure 1.12]**. He decided that despite his personal Modernist sympathies, working-class New Yorkers would be most attracted to investing in the community if they had the opportunity to buy conventional suburban-type homes with private yards. The scheme worked and the project is often cited as having had a critical role in the remarkable turnaround of the South Bronx.

These two men—architect and urban redeveloper—came together at a moment in the nation's history when government invested heavily in rebuilding American cities. The rise and fall of that support shaped the reputation of each. Clearly, they had different talents and used different tools, and their projects left complex legacies behind. But their joint authorship of urban renewal design principles created an architectural vocabulary that demonstrated the dynamically interwoven contributions of both planners and architects in this era. Together they took the credit and together they deserve whatever blame we choose to assign them. Logue and Rudolph were friends, colleagues, and promoters of each other's careers; each of their personal papers are littered with clippings about the other. At their last known public meeting, a 1992 conference at the New School on "Rethinking Design of the '60s" that they both attended, Logue spoke of Rudolph with affection: "I had a long interest in design, but when I realized how ignorant I was, I called a friend, head of the Yale Architecture School, one Paul Rudolph. He is responsible for a lot of the sins I've committed I guess ever since."[35] An even more poignant tribute was Logue's effort in 1988, after he returned to Boston as a private redeveloper, to assemble a development project that would make possible the completion of Rudolph's Government Service Center as the two men had originally envisioned it, with its tower. The *Boston Herald* reported that "Logue...sees himself as attempting to finish a project he started. He has arranged for Paul Rudolph, the architect of those buildings, to design the rest of the complex."[36] Yet that project never happened. Rudolph's pinwheeling tower never closed the Service Center's open corner. The urban renewal moment had passed.

[34] Peter Braestrup, "U.S. Tests Modular Housing," *Washington Post,* July 20, 1970; J.V., "A Module That Stacks," *Design and Environment* 3 (Spring 1972): 48; "Modular Co-ops for New Haven," *New York Times,* 31 August 1969; "Thanks to Prefabs, Out of the Slums and Into Their Own Co-Ops," *New York Times,* February 11, 1972; "Paul Rudolph's '20th-Century Brick' Used in Cluster Apartments," *Architectural Record* (September 1970): 148; "Rethinking Designs in the '60s," *Perspecta* 29 (1998), 62.

[35] Edward J. Logue, remarks in "Rethinking Design of the '60s," *Perspecta* 29 (1998): 11.

[36] "'New Boston' Planner Comes Back for More," *Boston Herald,* January 12, 1988.

1.12
Edward Logue, Charlotte Gardens Project, South Bronx, New York, prefabricated houses, 1983–1986

1.13 [next spread]
Paul Rudolph, Oriental Masonic Gardens, New Haven, Connecticut, perspective, 1968–1971

ORIENTAL MASONIC
GARDENS
GAS

Paul Rudolph and CIAM's Postwar “Heart of the City”

Eric Mumford

In 1958, Sigfried Giedion wrote a "friendly warning" to Oscar Niemeyer, his Brazilian colleague in the International Congress of Modern Architecture (CIAM), about the winning design for Brasilia: "Change, change the plan!" The students in his Harvard Graduate School of Design (GSD) seminar, "The Human Scale," which Giedion was then teaching with Dean Josep Lluís Sert and the historian Eduard Sekler, had analyzed Lúcio Costa's project for the new national capital of Brazil, along with various historical examples of pedestrian urban design, including central Paris and Washington, D.C. They had found the length of the Monumental Axis at Brasilia "rather dangerous," and questioned whether a "one-street city can ever be filled with life."[1] While the doubts that Giedion, a former secretary-general of CIAM, expressed about the design of one of the quintessential examples of Modernist urbanism may seem surprising today, they were entirely in keeping with the urban design ideas that were the focus of the GSD during Sert's deanship, from 1953 to 1969. These concepts had grown out of Sert's own emphasis, while president of CIAM, on the pedestrian "heart of the city," the theme of the CIAM 8 meeting held near London in 1951.[2] For Sert, urban pedestrian life and the exchanges and encounters it made possible were central to both cultural life and democracy, and he and Giedion saw continuities between the postwar work of CIAM and the tradition of urban spaces that went back to Greek agoras and Roman fora, ideas that had largely been rejected in the design of the new capital, which was scaled to the automobile. The now canonical reading of this period as one where a reductive or, sometimes, expressionistic Modernism triumphed over classicism, as exemplified by Brasilia, has obscured the important effort by Modernists in the 1950s to come to terms with *history* and *urbanism*—words that entered mainstream architectural discourse around this same time.

Although not a CIAM member, Paul Rudolph was one of the most successful American practitioners who attempted to engage American historical contexts with new forms of Modern architecture. He never seems to have referenced Sert or Giedion in his published writings, but Rudolph was aware of these postwar CIAM ideas when, at Sert's invitation, he taught as a visitor at the GSD in the spring of 1954, while Sert was still president of CIAM. While Rudolph's GSD scholarship to travel in

2.1
Paul Rudolph, Jewett Arts Center, Wellesley College, aerial view from the northwest, 1955–1958

[1] Eric Mumford, *The CIAM Discourse on Urbanism, 1928–60* (Cambridge: MIT Press, 2000), 340, n. 11.
[2] Jaqueline Tyrwhitt, J. L. Sert, and E. N. Rogers, *CIAM 8: The Heart of the City* (New York: Pellegrini and Cudahy, 1952).

2.2
Paul Rudolph, Jewett Arts Center, Wellesley College, rendering, 1955–1958

Europe in 1948–1949 had introduced him to a world of architecturally rich pedestrian urban spaces and surfaces, it was only after teaching at the GSD that he began to pursue this new direction. As Timothy M. Rohan has shown, it was around the time that Rudolph's work changed significantly in scale and type, from his early, "Harvard box" Florida houses to an intense engagement in larger commissions, with issues of public space and historical context.[3] This was clearly evident in his first large institutional commission, the Jewett Arts Center at Wellesley College in Wellesley, Massachusetts. To what extent this new direction in Rudolph's work was encouraged by Sert's nascent urban design program at the GSD has never been documented, but there are striking parallels between the issues Rudolph addressed at the Jewett Arts Center and those that Sert and Giedion had emphasized since CIAM 7, held in Bergamo, Italy, in 1949.[4]

At the Jewett Arts Center (1955–1958), Rudolph attempted to reconcile the influence of Frank Lloyd Wright, particularly his Florida Southern College campus (1938) in Lakeland, Florida, which Rudolph knew well, with various directions associated with the GSD and CIAM,[5] including CIAM concepts of the pedestrian "core," now introduced into an existing American campus context. **[Figure 2.1]** His design process also suggests that he was concerned about relating the building to an existing historic context, in a way that paralleled the revisionist Modern design direction that would soon be dubbed "neo-liberty" in Italy. This direction, later strongly criticized by both Reyner Banham[6] and Team 10, was part of the effort led by Italian CIAM members to respond architecturally to the strong "preexisting conditions" of their historic urban environments. Its parallels to Sert's development of the discipline of urban design at Harvard in the

[3] Timothy M. Rohan, *The Architecture of Paul Rudolph* (New Haven: Yale University Press, 2014).

[4] Sert's introduction of these ideas to CIAM can be found in the transcription of the "Séance d'ouverture," *CIAM 7 Bergamo 1949 Documents* (Nendeln/Liechtenstein: Krauss Reprint, 1979), 1–2. Sert elaborated on the ideas in his opening remarks at CIAM 8, published as "Centres of Community Life" in Tyrwhitt, Sert, and Rogers, *CIAM 8: The Heart of the City*, 3–16. The text does not follow Sert's more incisive opening remarks as transcribed in the CIAM documents. For a transcript of those remarks, from the CIAM Archives at the ETH Zurich, see Eric Mumford, ed., *The Writings of Josep Lluís Sert* (New Haven and London: Yale University Press and the Harvard Graduate School of Design, 2015), 59-68.

[5] The many links between the GSD and CIAM have never been fully traced, but CIAM members who taught there after 1937 included Walter Gropius, chair of architecture from 1937–1951. Gropius was also a vice president of CIAM until its dissolution in 1956, though he chose not to publicize this role after he arrived in the United States. After Gropius's forced retirement in 1951, he was succeeded by Sert, who was appointed by Harvard President Nathan Pusey as both dean of the GSD and chair of architecture. CIAM members at the GSD then included Sigfried Giedion, Ernesto

1950s have been forgotten, but Rudolph's Wellesley building itself suggests that not only Wright's work, but also the concept of urban design, had a significant influence on him at this key point in his career.

Rudolph was a successful residential practitioner in Sarasota, Florida when Sert invited him to be a visiting studio critic at Harvard. His time at the GSD overlapped with that of Italian CIAM member Ernesto Rogers, and it seems probable that Sert, Rogers, and Giedion had some influence on Rudolph's subsequent urbanistic preoccupations. Along with Jaqueline Tyrwhitt (who would join the faculty at Sert's invitation in 1955), they had all strongly advocated a focus on the "heart of the city" at CIAM 8. At that event, Sert had stressed the political and cultural importance of urban places for collective meeting and face-to-face discussion, and in his work with BBPR, Rogers had begun to relate new buildings to the strong existing contexts of Italian cities.[7]

In his speech to the national convention of the American Institute of Architects in Boston in 1954 (published as "The Changing Philosophy of Architecture"[8]), Rudolph echoed the talks that Sert, Rogers, and Giedion had given at CIAM 8,[9] which emphasized the perceptual-psychological

2.3
Paul Rudolph, Jewett Arts Center, Wellesley College, photo of library screen and stair, 1955–1958

Nathan Rogers (teaching in 1954), and in the following year, Serge Chermayeff, Jaqueline Tyrwhitt, and Eduard Sekler. Design visitors at the GSD with CIAM ties included Wells Coates (English MARS group), Alvaro Ortega (Colombia), and Mario Romañach (Cuba).

[6] Reyner Banham, "Neoliberty: the Italian retreat from Modern Architecture," *Architectural Review* 125 (April 1959): 230–35.

[7] Ernesto Nathan Rogers was an influential figure in the development of Italian architectural culture from the formation of his firm BBPR in Milan in 1932 through his brief editing of the magazine *Domus* (1946–1947) to his editorship at *Casabella Continuità* (1954–1964). Aldo Rossi was one of his best-known students at the Milan Polytechnic. See Ezio Bonfanti and Marco Porta, *Città, Museo e Architettura: il gruppo BBPR nella cultura architettonica italiana 1932–1970* (Florence: Vallecchi, 1973).

[8] Paul Rudolph, "Changing Philosophy of Architecture," *Architectural Forum* 101 (July 1954), 120–21; republished in Paul Rudolph: *Writings on Architecture* (New Haven: Yale University Press, 2008), 14–20.

[9] See Sert, "Centres of Community Life"; Sigfried Giedion, "The Historical Background of the Core"; Ernesto Rogers, "The Heart: Human Problem of Cities," in *CIAM 8: The Heart of the City,* 3–16; 17–25; 69–73.

importance of enclosed spaces for social interaction. Rudolph called for "outer spaces which encourage social contact" by using "piazzas, courtyards, squares, freestanding sculptures," as well as manipulating "the approaches and sequences of space."[10] **[Figures 2.2, 2.3, 2.4]** Citing Camillo Sitte's work, and, like Sert and Giedion at this time, Rudolph defined the task of postwar Modern architects as the creation of such public spaces, although he put more emphasis on purely "visual delight" than CIAM had. This speech marked Rudolph's turn towards pedestrian urbanism, which coincided with his commission for the Jewett Arts Center that year. The larger scale and Collegiate Gothic context of the project allowed him to begin to put forward a possible new direction for American Modern architecture.

As Timothy M. Rohan has documented in detail, Rudolph was chosen for the Jewett commission from a short list of architects that included Eero Saarinen, Walter Gropius and his firm The Architects Collaborative (TAC), Edward Durell Stone, Marcel Breuer, and Hugh Stubbins.[11] Like them, Rudolph was strongly identified with Modern architecture and its rejection of the classical tradition. The short list was selected by a Wellesley advisory committee led by Professor John McAndrew, who had been closely associated with the Museum of Modern Art's promotion of the International Style. McAndrew had been nominated for the role by Philip Johnson's sister, Jeanette Johnson Dempsey, who was a Wellesley trustee.

Rudolph knew Johnson well from their student days at the GSD in the early 1940s, and this may have been a factor in the then relatively unknown Florida residential architect being considered alongside more established firms for such a major commission, although Rudolph had also just been commissioned for a new United States Embassy in Amman, Jordan (1954). When Rudolph submitted his first scheme for Jewett in 1955, both McAndrew and Agnes Abbot, another faculty member on the committee, were taken aback. The first scheme included a literal reworking of the facade of the Doge's Palace in Venice, and was perhaps also inspired by Wright's Masieri Memorial project in Venice of the previous year. While Rudolph's initial project may seem anomalous for a Modern architect in the Miesian and Corbusian-influenced 1950s, it also reflected his effort to effectively synthesize some of the most advanced design currents of the time with his own American Modernist leanings. For Sert, Rogers, and the Italian CIAM, for example, the historical and cultural importance of urban life was of paramount importance for Modern architecture, which they saw as entering a new, formative phase after the dry functionalism of the prewar period.[12]

Ernesto Rogers is mainly remembered today for the Italian urban contextual work of his firm BBPR, and for the Team 10 attacks on that work in the late 1950s, which led to the breakup of CIAM at Otterlo in 1959. Along with other Italian CIAM members, Rogers had developed an influential approach to relating works of Modern architecture to their urban contexts, emphasizing the importance of "continuity" between the history of the city and Modern architecture. This direction, though formally different, had close affinities to Sert's vision of urban design, and both had attempted to shift CIAM towards an engagement with urbanism during a postwar era of massive, American-led suburban development.

While Rogers's work had its roots in the progressive industrial environment of prewar northern Italy, which fell to some extent under the shadow of Mussolini's regime—though Rogers himself went into exile in Switzerland in 1943—Sert's urban design approach had grown out of his and Giedion's earlier wartime efforts in New York, initially done with the French painter Fernand Léger, to articulate the need for a "new monumentality." In their 1943 manifesto, "Nine Points on Monumentality," Sert, Giedion, and Léger evoked the new scale of large highways and engineering works then being built by the American New Deal, and suggested combining such works of vast scale with the new visual language of

[10] Rudolph, "Changing Philosophy," 16.
[11] Timothy M. Rohan, "The Dangers of Eclecticism: Paul Rudolph's Jewett Arts Center at Wellesley," in Sarah Goldhagen and Réjean Legault, eds., *Anxious Modernisms: Experimentation in Postwar Architectural Culture* (Cambridge: MIT Press, 2000), 191–211.
[12] See, for example, Josep Lluís Sert, "Architectural Fashions and the People," unpublished lecture, April 7, 1959 (Josep Lluís Sert Collection, Frances Loeb Library, Harvard Graduate School of Design, Folder D0050), reprinted in Eric Mumford, ed., *The Writings of Josep Lluís Sert* (New Haven and London: Yale University Press and the Harvard Graduate School of Design, 2015), 91-98.

2.4
Paul Rudolph, Jewett Arts Center, Wellesley College, view of site model, 1955–1958

modern artists like Picasso. It was in this same wartime context that Sert would argue—in his 1944 lectures at Yale—for more human-scaled, pedestrian-oriented cities. This call paralleled Le Corbusier's less vehement focus on similar issues in his own postwar project for the urban reconstruction of St. Dié, exhibited in New York after the end of the war in 1945. In that same postwar era of optimism about planning and social progress, Sert and his partner Paul Lester Wiener began to propose various pedestrian "cores" in their Latin American town plans of the late 1940s.

After Sert's elevation to the presidency of CIAM in 1947, he began to show these projects as didactic demonstrations of how pedestrian-based urbanism and Modern architecture could be combined to counter an increasingly alienated and suburbanizing postwar world. Rogers, a postwar member of the CIAM Council, had been advocating similar ideas in Italy, evident in the Italian CIAM group's A.R. Plan for Milan of 1945.[13] After Rogers began teaching as a visitor at the National University of Tucumán in Argentina, he and Sert collaborated on a Pilot Plan for the City of Lima, Peru, in 1947 with the MIT-educated Peruvian architect Luis Dorich. This was followed by Sert and Wiener's project for Chimbote, a Peruvian industrial seaport, and then for several large urban design commissions in Colombia, where Sert established an active Colombian CIAM group. Eventually, Le Corbusier was brought in, along with Sert and Wiener, to produce a new Pilot Plan for Bogotá in 1949–1953.[14]

Sert announced this new CIAM direction, one focused on the pedestrian core of the city, at CIAM 7 in Bergamo, an event hosted by Rogers and the Italian group. There Sert connected this new focus on pedestrian urbanism to the Corbusian concept of the "synthesis of the arts," citing his own

[13] Bonfanti and Porta, *Città, Museo e Architettura,* A50–51.
[14] See María Cecilia O'Byrne Orozco, ed., *Le Corbusier en Bogotá: 1947–1951. Elaboración del Plan Regulador de Bogotá* (vol. 1) and *Le Corbusier en Bogotá: 1947–1951. Precisiones en torno al plan director,* vol. 2 (Bogotá: Ediciones Uniandes, 2010).

work with Picasso, Calder, and other artists at the Spanish Pavilion at the 1937 Paris Exposition as a model. But built work of this kind at an urban scale still eluded Sert himself, and ultimately his major contribution in this direction was developing the discipline of what he began to call "urban design" at Harvard after he became dean, a position that Rogers had turned down.

Sert and Rogers were not alone among Modernists in advocating this new urban-oriented Modernist path in the early 1950s. Eliel Saarinen had begun to use the term urban design in his Cranbrook Academy of Art town design program in the 1940s, and not only his son Eero but also another Cranbrook graduate, Edmund N. Bacon—who worked for a time, along with Louis Kahn, in replanning postwar Philadelphia—pursued closely related urban ideas in the 1940s and early 1950s. Sert, Bacon, and Kahn all advocated similar basic urban design concepts that involved dividing a city into walkable neighborhood units bounded by greenways, mixing different types of housing with community services, schools, and play areas, and creating sequences for pedestrian movement by combining existing historic landmarks with new interventions.[15] At the same time, like Rudolph in his more suburban Wellesley project, Eero Saarinen was proposing various campus design projects centered on public spaces that recalled European plazas. These mostly unbuilt projects also attempted to integrate works of modern art into continuous perceptual sequences of the kind that had been called for by Sert and Giedion. Saarinen's urban design projects for Brandeis University, the University of Michigan North Campus, and Yale University were not carried out as designed, with the exception of Morse and Stiles Colleges at Yale, but they demonstrate the parallels between the urbanistic approaches of Sert and CIAM and those of Saarinen at this pivotal time.[16]

In 1960, Saarinen would place Rudolph's Wellesley project in this new Modernist direction, saying in

2.5
Doge's Palace, Venice, Italy, 1340 and later

[15] Eric Mumford, *Defining Urban Design: CIAM Architects and the Formation of a Discipline, 1937–69* (New Haven: Yale University Press, 2009), 64–99.

[16] See Alan Plattus, "Campus Plans," in Eeva-Liisa Pelkonen and Donald Albrecht, eds., *Eero Saarinen: Shaping the Future* (New Haven: Yale University Press, 2006), 308–21. Saarinen's urban design associate Willo von Moltke worked with him on these projects from 1949–1952, notably at Brandeis University, before joining Edmund N. Bacon in Philadelphia from 1953–1961. Von Moltke then accepted Sert's offer to teach in the newly formed Harvard urban design program, which he directed from 1964–1977.

2.6
Ignazio Gardella, Olivetti canteen, Ivrea, Italy, 1953–1959

Architectural Record, "Paul Rudolph's Jewett Arts Center at Wellesley College stands out as one of the best examples of a building carefully designed to harmonize with a dominant existing pattern."[17] Rudolph, however, had gone farther than either Sert or Saarinen in his first scheme for Wellesley by literally copying the Doge's Palace **[Figure 2.5]**. This perhaps reflected his struggle to integrate Rogers's emphasis on existing historic context as a determinant of Modern design, which was exemplified in Italy by projects such as the decorative urban facade of the Bottega d'Erasmo in Turin (1953–1957) by the young firm of Gabetti and Isola, or the controversial work of Italian CIAM member Ignazio Gardella, whose Olivetti workers' cafeteria in Ivrea (1953) was widely published.[18] **[Figure 2.6]** Rudolph's second, more muted, scheme for Jewett demonstrated a much more successful relationship between the new building and its strong neo-Gothic campus (much of it designed by Charles Z. Klauder in the 1920s).

Despite its awkward synthesis of seemingly antithetical elements—the work of Wright, the

[17] Eero Saarinen, "Campus Planning: The Unique World of the University," *Architectural Record* (November 1960): 125.
[18] These projects and the reactions to them are discussed in Manfredo Tafuri, *History of Italian Architecture: 1944–1985,* trans. Jessica Levine (Cambridge: MIT Press, 1989), 53–56. The Gardella work for Olivetti is discussed in in the context of CIAM in Patrizia Bonifazio and Paolo Scrivano, *Olivetti Builds: Modern Architecture in Ivrea: Guide to the Open Air Museum* (Milan: Skira, 2001), 32–35.

Gropius-era Harvard box, the CIAM idea of the heart of the city, and even mannerist elements—Rudolph's Wellesley project represents a rare convergence of European and Late Modernist ideas about history and urbanism with his own characteristically American interests and influences. While Jewett differs substantially from Rudolph's subsequent work at Yale and elsewhere, it also marks the beginning of his effort to give architectural form to CIAM concepts about the importance of urban life to culture and democracy, efforts that would inform much of his later career.

The consultants on the Jewett project also show the impact of Rudolph's time at the GSD. They included Sasaki and Novak, a firm founded by Hideo Sasaki, who worked closely with Sert at the GSD and became the chair of landscape architecture there in 1957.[19] One of the engineers was William LeMessurier, who taught structures at the GSD at that time, and who went on to engineer many other major buildings in the following decades, including Kallmann and McKinnell's Boston City Hall (1961). The acoustical consultants were Bolt, Beranek and Newman, a firm founded by MIT professors in 1948, who were the acoustic designers for the United Nations Assembly building auditorium and for Saarinen's Kresge auditorium at MIT (1954), prior to their work at the Jewett.

In an article in the *Architectural Review* in 1960, the historian William Jordy grouped the Jewett project with other American examples of what he called "The Formal Image: USA."[20] This new direction included the work of Edward Durell Stone, Philip Johnson, and Minoru Yamasaki. Jordy saw affinities between the mannered complexity of the Jewett's partially screened glass facades and the facade of Palladio's Palazzo Valmarana in Vicenza. And like Rogers did at the Torre Velasca in Milan, Rudolph used exposed structural elements in a way that relates to an existing medieval or, at Wellesley, neo-medieval context: he saw the composite columns, screens, and pointed skylights at the Jewett as evoking Gothic architecture without literally imitating it. At the same time, while Jordy emphasized the temple-like basic organization of this and the other "new formalist" projects, the Jewett also has Wrightian aspects in its landscape-related horizontal forms and its decorative exterior metal screens, though these might also be mistaken for Italian neo-liberty ornamental elements, which Jordy did not mention. **[Figure 2.3]** One can see similar ideas in Fumihiko Maki's early work , where the former Sert student similarly explored both urbanistic and expressive decorative elements in a way parallel to both BBPR **[Figure 2.8]** and Sert's Baghdad Embassy (1954), in projects such as his unbuilt, prize-winning proposal for a new meditation chapel on the campus of Washington University in St. Louis (1958).[21]

Rudolph's successful effort at the Jewett to create an almost Italian hilltown-like series of public spaces, first by using the new building's picturesque silhouette to enclose the south and west sides of an existing campus green space and then by opening a monumental staircase beneath it that leads to the main vehicular drop-off area, shows him moving towards his mature ability to generate powerful urban forms by architectural means. The Jewett's site plan **[Figure 2.7]**, which transformed a typical Gropius GSD functional diagram for an arts center into a finely detailed and complex three-dimensional series of spaces related to pedestrian movement, sunlight, and topography, clearly demonstrated what Rudolph had called for in his 1954 speech to the AIA. It also demonstrates, like Sert's Fondation Maeght of 1958, how Modern architects began to engage with what still seem to be very contemporary issues of site planning, appropriate architectural vocabulary, and the integration and display of artwork within pedestrian sequences of movement.

While Rudolph himself did not find the Jewett project completely successful,[22] particularly in terms of its interior daylighting, as it had too many dark interior spaces, it remains an important artifact of the conflicted American architectural thinking of the 1950s. Like the Italian CIAM work

[19] On Sasaki, see Cammie McAtee, "From the Ground Up: Hideo Sasaki's Contribution to Urban Design," in Eric Mumford and Hashim Sarkis, eds., *Josep Lluís Sert: The Architect of Urban Design* (New Haven: Yale University Press, 2008), 166–97.
[20] William Jordy, "The Formal Image: USA," *Architectural Review* 127 (March 1960): 157–65.
[21] Eric Mumford, ed., *Modern Architecture in St. Louis* (St. Louis: Washington University, 2004), 97.
[22] "Paul Rudolph," in John W. Cook and Heinrich Klotz, *Conversations with Architects* (New York: Praeger, 1973), 94.

that it parallels, Rudolph's attempt to make contextual linkages and decorative effects evocative of that context now appears awkward and far less vigorous than the Brutalist efforts that soon followed, both in Rudolph's work and in the work of CIAM's Team 10 successors, including Alison and Peter Smithson, Jacob Bakema, and Aldo van Eyck. Yet, the Jewett reveals, more so than most of the now well-documented American architectural debates from this time, how Modern architecture gradually attempted to engage with historic urban contexts in ways that, ironically, would soon lead to Modernism's complete rejection, at a rhetorical level, by Post-Modernism.

2.7
Paul Rudolph, Jewett Arts Center, Wellesley College, site plan, 1955–1958

2.8 [next spread]
BBPR, Torre Velasca, Milan, view of entrance to lobby, 1956

Tropical Trysts: Paul Rudolph and the Bengal Delta

Kazi K. Ashraf

In 1965, Paul Rudolph was commissioned to make a campus plan for the East Pakistan Agricultural University outside the small town of Mymensingh in the northern part of Bangladesh. Over the next five years he produced a master plan and designs for key buildings on the campus, which in 1971 was renamed Bangladesh Agricultural University.[1] **[Figure 3.1]** The project is little known and little spoken about when considering Rudolph's work; even the architect himself had little to say about it—however, it is neither minor nor without significance in the narrative of a cultural encounter.[2]

First, the project in Mymensingh is significant for its scale and scope. It involved the master plan of a new agricultural university and designs for most of its key buildings, including academic buildings, dormitories, faculty housing, an auditorium, a gymnasium, and a stadium—that is, all of the critical facilities required for a full-fledged residential university. The scope and complexity of a university is like that of a microcity with all its institutions, groupings of buildings, and range of social constituencies and their interactions. Notably, the university at Mymensingh came on the heels of a project with similar prospects: Rudolph's plan for the University of Massachusetts at Dartmouth, formerly Southeastern Massachusetts Technological Institute (1963–1966).

The Mymensingh project also raised issues about the development of an educational institution in a country that was beginning to organize its national priorities, having achieved political independence after nearly two hundred years of British rule. Located in the eastern province of the new state of Pakistan, which was carved out of India following the British withdrawal from the Indian subcontinent in 1947, the university would continue to be critical after the formation of the independent nation of Bangladesh following the brutal liberation war from Pakistan in 1971.

The project is thus deeply imbricated in the developmental history of Pakistan and the United States' involvement in the political and economic life of that nation. The development initiatives included modernizing the sectors that were identified as part of the economic backbone of Pakistan, of which agriculture was the most significant in both provinces of the country. It became imperative to organize that sector into a modern and more productive institution, for which foreign—and especially American—aid was sought. The United States Agency for International Development (USAID), through Texas A&M University, sponsored the establishment of an agricultural university in each province of Pakistan: Mymensingh in East Pakistan (now Bangladesh), and Lyallpur in West Pakistan (now Pakistan).[3]

If the founding of an agricultural university provided a national narrative of modernization and Westernization, and, furthermore, an encounter between a new global power and an abiding Asian nation, the place of the project in Rudolph's own architectural itinerary provided another story of encounter. The university in Mymensingh represented Rudolph's first tropical adventure outside the United States (besides his unbuilt proposal for the United States Embassy in a less tropical Amman, Jordan, in 1955). From a climatic sense, Mymensingh was as remote as could be from New Haven, where Rudolph was living in 1965, but the climatic conditions and the architectural responses they elicited in Mymensingh were not alien to him. Designing Modernist buildings in Sarasota, Florida had already attuned Rudolph to the specific architectural demands of the tropics.

Is there an arc between Sarasota and Mymensingh—Sarasota as the site of Rudolph's brilliant articulation of a Modern tropical typology, and Mymensingh as a location of its exotic other? Or, is there a difference that Rudolph never reconciled, or perhaps even recognized? Rudolph's tropical trysts[4] distinguished him more than any other architect of his generation—the group that came out of the cold, so to speak, from the hallways in Cambridge or Chicago—to test the métier of

[1] Originally called the East Pakistan Agricultural University and established in 1961, it came to be known as the Bangladesh Agricultural University from 1971 on. The university started with a College of Animal Husbandry and Veterinary Science as the core; it has now six faculties or colleges, and 43 departments in various areas of agricultural education and research.

[2] One of the associates on the project, William Grindereng, has commented on Rudolph's strange ambivalence about the project, the commission for which may have coincided with a particularly busy professional time for Rudolph. Apparently, Rudolph visited the site only a few times, and never went to see it after its completion.

[3] The USAID support was carried out between 1961–1970. More support came from the World Bank, the Danish International Development Agency (DANIDA), the Ford Foundation, the Canadian International Development Agency (CIDA), and other organizations.

Modernism under the mesmerizing sun and furious rain of the tropics, and in the cultural politics of the "other." For Rudolph, Mymensingh was both familiar and different.

2

The 1960s represented a dynamic but volatile time in the emergence of Bangladesh, and a rather ebullient moment of American presence in Pakistan. Considered a critical geopolitical location in the theater of the Cold War, and an economically impoverished nation, Pakistan was seen as a strategic partner by the United States, and was propped up as a bulwark against the Soviet presence in Asia. This was carried out through huge supplies of aid, mostly in the form of defense, but also in social programs such as food, education, health, and institution-building for that developing nation. Many of the technical institutions that were vital to the development of a modern Pakistan were created by American financial and logistical support through the agencies of USAID, the Ford Foundation, and the World Bank. Part of the package involved establishing, and training people for a series of engineering and agricultural universities, which also included planning the universities and producing their facilities. The agricultural university at Mymensingh was one such venture.

That is how Rudolph found himself in the Bengal Delta at the height of a nation-building program under considerable U.S. patronage. He was not, however, the only traveling architect in the 1960s working in the mission of social and national development in then East Pakistan. The first foreigner to receive major commissions in East Pakistan (after 1971, Bangladesh) was the prolific Greek architect and planner Constantine Doxiadis, who by the late 1950s had already evolved an idiom suited to the tropics.[5] The Austrian-born, California-based architect Richard Neutra was invited to design a number of educational buildings throughout Pakistan beginning in 1963, which also included the first building for the agricultural university at Mymensingh.[6] When Rudolph arrived there, he made a master plan that ambivalently engaged the set of administrative and academic buildings that Neutra had designed. It appears that

3.1
Paul Rudolph, Bangladesh Agricultural University, Myemsingh, Bangladesh, view of academic building, 1965–1975

even in a remote corner of Asia, Rudolph found himself face to face with a European Modernist.

In the wake of the American development initiatives, three American architects were invited to Bangladesh through the intervention of the Bengali architect Muzharul Islam.[7] The lives of the three architects intersected both in the U.S. and in their independent itineraries in Bangladesh. Following Rudolph's 1965 commission, Stanley Tigerman teamed up with his Yale colleague Muzharul Islam in 1966 to design five polytechnic institutes.[8] Earlier, in 1962, Louis Kahn, once a visiting professor at Yale but by that time working and teaching in Philadelphia, had been invited to design the National Capital Complex, an epic venture and a narrative that is much better known.[9]

Through the work of these architects, Bangladesh became a rather fertile zone for architectural investigations. As Tigerman comments, "Bangladesh was loaded with poignancy for Kahn and Rudolph," meaning that the encounter is meant to bring a new alchemy or acuity to their own work rather than a progression of the same (which was far more actual as far as Tigerman's work was concerned).[10] In the rapid and even overwhelming presence of Western models of development then prevalent the world over, the work of these leading figures in culturally perceptive productions provides fresh insights into the encounter between architectural ideologies basically developed in the West, and conditions that are often totally different from their original milieu.

3

Muzharul Islam was the central figure in early Modern architecture in Bangladesh. He first trained at the University of Oregon in 1952, and did a course on tropical architecture at the Architectural Association School of Architecture in London. Before his Yale sojourn with Rudolph, Islam had already designed a number of buildings in Dhaka that showed an indebtedness to both Le Corbusier and Frank Lloyd Wright. His Art College (1953) remains a gem in Tropical Modernism. **[Figure 3.2]** Islam's work dominated the architectural scene in Pakistan in the late 1950s and 1960s, when he single-handedly established the Modern architectural idiom and a Modernist practice for the region.[11] His architectural activism, including educating architects outside the academic circle, establishing the norms of a profession where none existed, and attempting to bridge the new architectural manifesto with an emerging culture, had profound impact. He was an architect with a deep sense of the ethical dimension of architecture, especially in the

[4] I am using the word "tryst" in a double sense, referring first to the first Indian prime minister Jawaharlal Nehru's famous address after independence where he spoke of a "tryst with destiny," and, second, to Claude Lévi-Strauss's *Tristes Tropiques* (1955), written following the famous anthropologist's travels in the tropics, where the homophonic term suggests a kind of melancholia.

[5] Doxiadis was entrusted with the design of key educational buildings in a number of locations in Bangladesh, including the Teacher-Student Centre at the University of Dhaka, the Academy for Rural Development in Comilla, and the College of Home Economics in Dhaka. He was also responsible at the same time for a grander urban project, the master plan for the capital city of Pakistan, Islamabad (1959), and plans for Punjab University in Lahore (1959).

[6] Neutra was first commissioned for the U.S. Embassy in Karachi (1963), after which he embarked on designing various campus buildings in Pakistan. Neutra's relationship with the subcontinent is older. He was originally asked by the government of West Bengal in India in the early 1950s to be an adviser. Neutra, in turn, sent one of his younger colleagues, Joseph Stein, to West Bengal to head the Architecture and Planning Department at the Bengal Engineering College in Calcutta (now Kolkata) in 1952. Stein was to later set up a practice in Delhi and to become a key figure in the early Modern architecture of India. See "Joseph Allen Stein: A Tribute," by Ram Rahman (http://www.the-south-asian.com/Dec2001/Joseph_Stein_3.htm).

[7] It is important to note here Muzharul Islam's discerning leadership in bringing the American trio to Bangladesh. Islam had been a student of Rudolph in the Yale master's program in 1961. Tigerman was a classmate with whom he established a lifelong friendship and architectural camaraderie. As students, Tigerman and Islam resolved to work together someday, a vow that materialized in the polytechnic projects. While at Yale, Islam came to know Kahn's work and heard him speak on several occasions. His engagement of the American architects, as well as his own involvement, was triggered by a need to create both a principled practice and Modernist paradigms for what was then seen as a vacuous architectural landscape. Islam was seeking a better option than what was presented in the U.S. foreign aid package, which sometimes brought in expertise from lesser-known technical institutions in the U.S.

[8] Stanley Tigerman, *VERSUS: An American Architect's Alternatives* (New York: Rizzoli, 1982), 60. Through the USAID program, Texas A&M was contracted to plan and establish the academic programs for a number of institutions, including the agricultural university at Mymensingh.

[9] Muzharul Islam was originally asked to design the project, but he suggested inviting an internationally renowned architect. Three names were suggested: Le Corbusier, Alvar Aalto, and Kahn. See Kazi K. Ashraf, *Louis I. Kahn: National Capital Complex of Bangladesh* (Tokyo: GA Edita Publications, 1994).

[10] Tigerman, *VERSUS*. One of the results would be his work with inner-city projects for communities in Chicago, and another, perhaps, the inception of Archeworks.

[11] Kazi K. Ashraf and James Belluardo, *An Architecture of Independence: The Making of Modern South Asia* (New York: The Architectural League of New York, 1997).

3.2
Muzharul Islam, Faculty of Fine Arts, earlier known as the Art College, Dhaka, Bangladesh, 1953

evolving social and political scenario around him. His was neither a passing nor accidental tryst with the tropics; he was part of it, and committed to affecting its sociopolitical destiny.

Islam became increasingly conscious of the political status of Bangladesh within Pakistan, and soon enough became politically active as well. His response was not an isolated one; it was part of a heightened political and cultural consciousness among most Bengali intelligentsia since the 1950s of the social and economic inequity of Bangladesh in the emerging state of Pakistan.[12] His nationalist orientation dovetailed with a secular, socialist thinking, albeit not without some unresolved strands. But neither his nationalist nor socialist leanings impeded him from seeking an extranational architectural impetus, even if that meant inviting a group of Americans.

The political curve that Islam had brought to his architectural objectives also affected Stanley Tigerman whose encounters in the Delta were adventurous and educative in every sense. Working there, for the five polytechnics carried out by the Tigerman-Islam partnership for over a decade (1966–1978), was not only an opportunity to offer one's expertise, as Neutra and the Englishman Maxwell Fry would see it, but also a place to learn new ways of looking at things.[13] **[Figure 3.4]** What struck Tigerman immediately was the material and technical deficit in the region, where everything, from windows and their mechanisms to furniture, had to be designed from scratch. Tigerman admitted, and quite enthusiastically, that at the end of the day, the polytechnic projects affected his way of thinking about planning that bore the logic and rigor of "total design."[14] The polytechnic projects eventually

[12] See Rounaq Jahan, *Pakistan: Failure in National Integration* (New York: Columbia University Press, 1972).
[13] Tigerman, *VERSUS*, 59–67.
[14] The design and construction of the buildings was preceded by an extensive study of the tropics—site, materials, climate, techniques, and processes—with the study culminating in a remarkable but largely unpublished report that may be considered a tropical manifesto for architecture. Part of the study was published in the September 1968 issue of the *Architectural Record*, as an elaborate attempt to create rational, methodological, and creative principles for Modern building in Bangladesh and Pakistan.

3.3
"Bangala Ragini," 18th-century miniature painting from Rajasthan

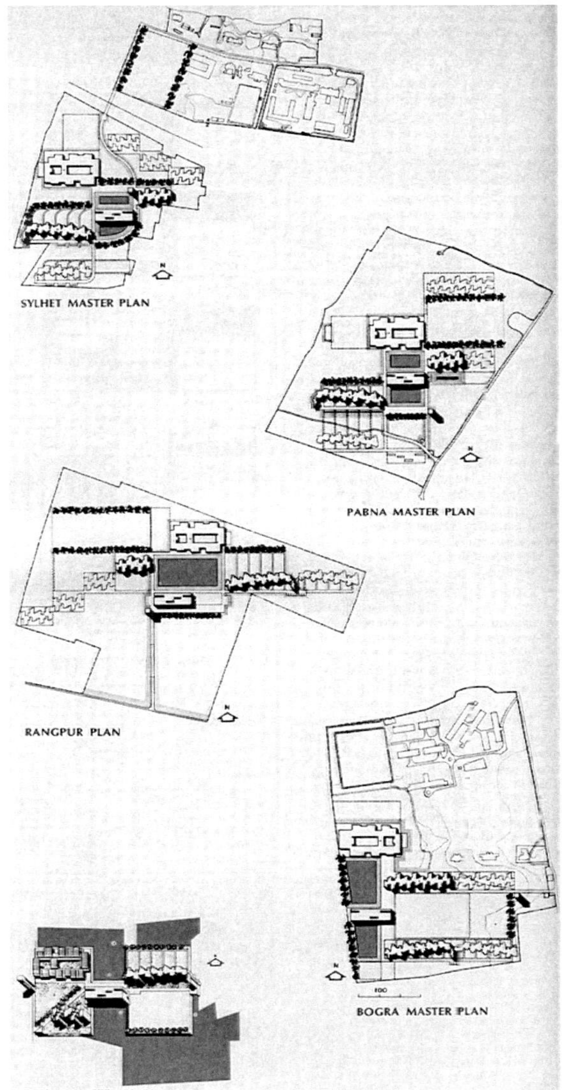

3.4
Muzharul Islam and Stanley Tigerman, plans of five Polytechnique Institutes, various sites in Bangladesh, 1966–1978

3.5
"Alexander's House," a Colonial-Period building now a library

কলেজ

took Tigerman into the depths of the political life of the place with which Islam was already deeply involved.[15] Tigerman admits that he returned to Chicago after all of those extraordinary episodes in Bangladesh with new insights into the "moral and responsible ways" of being an architect.[16]

4

The encounters of the universalizing architectural idiom of Modernism and the milieux of specific culture, climate, and place spurred the architectonic and spatial solutions for tackling specific climatic conditions, the intelligent arrangement of available materials and technology, and the subsequent sculptural rendering of the architectural organism in the brilliant tropical light. As narratives of diverse journeys to the "East," the encounters are also tinged with inescapable shades of orientalism and various forms of Kiplingesque quandaries. Tigerman remembers Rudolph swatting creepy crawlers with his shoes in the steamy darkness of a jungle town in Bangladesh, and Kahn surviving on a strict diet of boiled fish and rice while reading *Arabian Nights,* while Tigerman himself was searched at the airport by bayonet-flailing Pakistani soldiers during the Bangladesh War of Independence in 1971. While one could not fully escape a certain unease in these encounters, the tentative moment of the American meeting with the "other," what also registered was a new Asia emerging out of the orbits of the old British, or European, dominance, and the positing of an American optimism.

The critical, and eventually redemptive, factor in tropical topics was climate. If the native culture seemed impervious, or even invisible to the traveling architect, climate was the most viable and immediately accessible way through which an abstract Modernism could attempt to negotiate with the

3.6
Richard Neutra, Administrative Building, Bangladesh Agricultural University, Myemsingh, Bangladesh, c. 1963

[15] That included the turmoil in 1971 leading up to the Bangladesh War of Independence and its break from Pakistan, including scary experiences with Pakistani soldiers during Tigerman's visits.
[16] Tigerman admits to this as an opportunity that reflected on the concept of (social) responsibility, *VERSUS,* 60.
[17] Anthony D. King, *The Bungalow: The Production of a Global Culture* (New York: Oxford University Press, 1995).
[18] Otto Königsberger worked in India in the late 1930s and 1940s, then went back to London to establish the tropical architecture program at the Architectural Association school in 1954. He edited the July 1960 issue of the *Architectural Review,* which presented selected works of emerging Modern architects in nations of the former British Empire, including Muzharul Islam, Balkrishna Doshi, Geoffrey Bawa, and Charles Correa who would go on to become

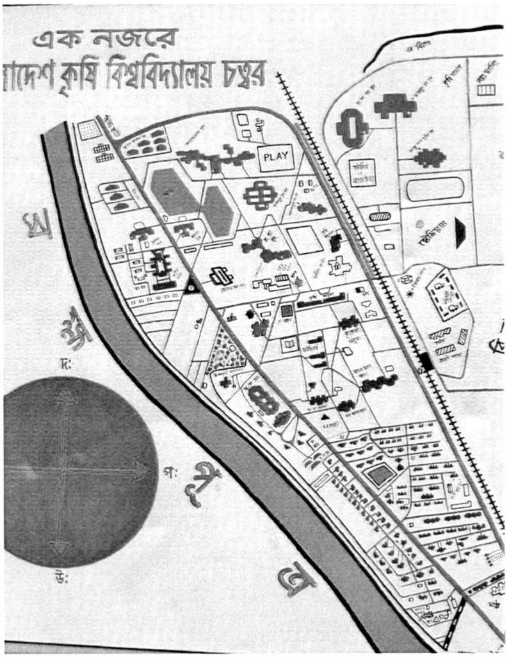

3.7
Map of the Bangladesh Agricultural University

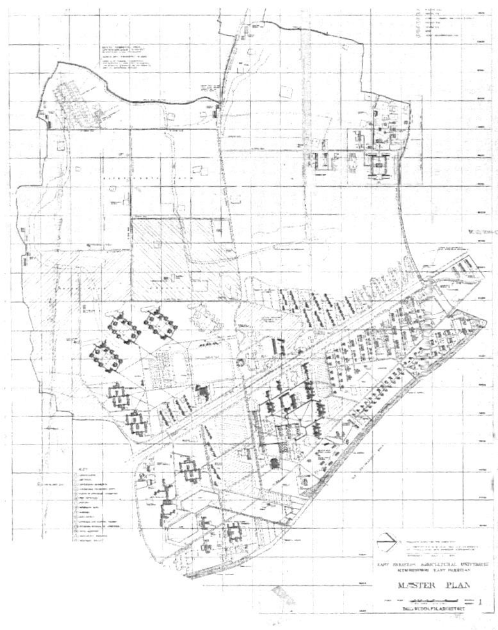

3.8
Paul Rudolph, Bangladesh Agricultural University, master plan, c. 1965

particularities of place. The genre of "tropical architecture," as a science of building, had established a climatic, material, and constructional rationale for planning and producing buildings in most Asian and African countries (many of them former colonies of one European nation or another). The work helped extend the tenure of British/European architects, who stayed on or returned to the old colonies—now independent—to help design and build schools, housing, and hospitals. The principles of a tropical architecture, based on the various climatic encounters and propositions, had been made by colonial architects and engineers who had toiled in the tropical sun. There was both a richness of environmental responses and colonialist-orientalist ideas in those encounters. The "bungalow," for example, which emerged from the continental confluence, was a typological reincarnation of a Bengali rural hut that later became a transcontinental emblem of an exclusivist, social space.[17] **[Figure 3.5]**

Otto Königsberger (1909–1999), the German-British architect, played a leading role in establishing a methodical approach to planning and design in warmer climates and to creating the principles of a tropical architecture.[18] A number of other architects participated in the larger discourse of tropical architecture—from the French architect Jean Prouvé[19] and Maxwell Fry to Edward Durell Stone and Richard Neutra. Neutra was one of the early Modernists who had worked on and written explicitly about site and climate as parameters in design, with a particular attention to warmer climates. His work in Puerto Rico in the 1940s, which was produced as the book, *Architecture of Social Concern: Regions of Mild Climate,*[20] evidences a keen understanding of the conditions of site, climate, and vegetation, with an anthropological and social slant. Neutra's predilection for a warmer clime is premised by more than a technocracy of "climate control"; he

leading figures in their respective countries. For Tropical Architecture, the grouping was analogous to the seminal Hitchcock, Johnson, and Mumford exhibition of the International Style in 1934.

[19] Prouvé's well-known Les Maisons Tropicales were built in the French colonies of West Africa between 1949 and 1951.

[20] Richard Neutra, *Architecture of Social Concern: Regions of Mild Climate* (São Paulo: Gerth Todtmann, 1948).

invoked a far more mythical quotient in his architectural mission by engaging what he described as a search for "southland."[21]

Whether deliberately contributing to the corpus of tropical architecture or not, the question of climate as a principal factor in an architectural response, if not a determinant in form-making, was clearly evident in Le Corbusier's work in India (1952 onwards). The *brise-soleil* and the roof canopy (that began from Algeria in the 1930s), and their various modulations, allowed Corbusier to create a new expressive language that seemed ideally oriented to address the conditions of warm climates.[22] The new building typology marked by a wide expressive range was demonstrated from public buildings to residences. The instruments of climatic modulation served more than techno-functional purposes; in most of his buildings they were adapted for a more symbolic or iconic significance: the roof canopy as an inverted dome for the unbuilt Governor's house, the mega-parasol over the high courts as a kind of Mughal chhatri, a miniature parasol in the governor's balcony in the Secretariat as an emblem of the office, and the porch as a theatrical entrance to the Assembly, not to mention its cryptic reference to bull's horns. Identifying the powerful presence of the sun as a spiritual substance in the life of warm places, Corbusier devised ideograms that spoke of solar movement as a cosmic image and rhythm of life, and as something to rely on when other references have dissipated.

This can be considered a turn from climatology to cosmology, in which protagonists in a late phase of Modernism seek something more substantive in the prosaic arrangement of buildings in light and sun. Kahn's Capital Complex in Dhaka (1962–1974) is marked by a whole new architectural vocabulary derived out of an initial reflection on climate, producing an architectural ensemble of double-wrap, deep terraces and shadow-works. Like Corbusier, Kahn also proceeded from the technicality of climate to creating a more symbolic and perceptual experience of form-space. Here, too, climate led to a cosmological construct. Kahn articulated a quasi-sacred connotation for his architecture in conjunction with an intimate relationship with the landscape.[23]

Until the 1960s, when climate was addressed primarily in a metrical sense—temperature gradient, heat loss, physical comfort zone, and all the precise categories of tropical architecture—climate and culture came to be seen as more intertwined. Charles Correa wrote on the phenomenology of warm climates; his declaration "form follows climate" imbricated climate in the discussion of architectural typology and collective spatial practices.[24] It slowly became evident that the persistence of an architectural typology in a particular geographical and cultural milieu indicates not just a technical redress but a synthesis of ecology, mythology, and sociology. Climatically derived paradigms would come to be reified through two architectural typologies of warm places: the courtyard and the pavilion. Valorizing the space of the interior courtyard in an arid region, Balkrishna Doshi has characterized it as a manifestation of the metaphysical Brahmand; this was echoed in a similar hoary language with the sky as a dome by the Egyptian architect Hassan Fathy. On the other hand, Geoffrey Bawa in Sri Lanka, in his notion of "the house as a garden," explored the open pavilion-structure in the landscape as a paradigm for dwelling in the hot, humid, and vegetal milieu. **[Figure 3.3]**

5

The emergence of a regionalist dialogue in South Asian architecture may be ascribed to this movement from climate to culture. There is, however, a difference between the strategies of tropical architecture and the discourse of regional architecture: the former is still an inflection of a Modernist monolith, while the latter aligns with a larger philosophical, cultural, and political discourse of identity. In that sense, tropical architecture was a safety net for the dispensation of Modern architecture. The principles of the Modern movement in architecture,

[21] "Man loves to immigrate to the south, or to conquer it," Neutra writes, "Like all Nordic barbarians we want to go to sunny Hellas . . ." From an unpublished autobiography, cited by Esther McCoy, *Richard Neutra* (New York: George Braziller, 1960), 8. Neutra's move from Vienna to California is a literal demonstration of what is perhaps an anthropological paradigm in his thinking, different than the mechanistic analysis of Königsberger and Fry.

[22] There was also no dearth of complaints about the malfunction of the climatic machines: how the concrete *brise-soleils* heated up under the merciless sun of Chandigarh, and how a puff of wind brought that unbearable heat into the interior if the windows were open. Aditya Prakash, an associate to Le Corbusier in Chandigarh remarks: ". . . I did a study of the sun in Chandigarh subsequently and found that sunbreakers cut out sun, but retained heat and dust. We found it was better to create deep verandas," in Barbara Crossette, "Le Corbusier's Chandigarh," *The New York Times,* April 25, 1982.

rather than being questioned, underwent "tropicalization," much like electronics and motor vehicles are tropicalized before they are imported to hot, humid regions, and this was carried through scientific measures of comfort, health, and efficiency.[25] Neutra, whose thoughts on climate and nature were also aligned with a "social concern," talked about a biotic environment for architecture using analogies from nature. He conceived of two geo-sociological polarities, the "metropolitan" and the "non-metropolitan," and how the former is obligated to rescue the latter.[26] He argued that architects must learn to give their services to broader areas of the world and urged governments "to use us in developing the human resources of the vast hinterlands." Neutra is both patronizing and solicitous in advancing the idea of this polarity, and he was sought out for helping the then non-metropolitan hinterlands of Puerto Rico, India, and Brazil.

Rudolph's point of departure was also climate, but not by creating a missionary pretense around a geographical imagination. Unlike Neutra, who went south, Rudolph was from the south. Florida was not a peculiarity for Rudolph, it was a particularity with which he identified. His climatic arguments were not so much about working out a tropical architecture as interceding in the Modernist discourse with a regionalist persuasion. He may have been one of the few among his Harvard classmates who would give the earliest consideration of situating Modernism when it was still overwhelmingly practiced as a universal principle. Rudolph would say that "regionalism is one way toward the richness of architecture which other movements have enjoyed and which is so lacking today."[27] While Rudolph acutely understood the particularities that make a region, as embodied in his Florida work, ambiguity and unevenness haunt the university project in Mymensingh.

6

Mymensingh is a place in the north of Bangladesh epitomizing all the features of a small town in the Bengal Delta. The Delta is a pure chemistry of land and water, an excruciatingly flat terrain formed by one of the most dynamic river systems of the world. This is where the tropical becomes the Delta, created by sedimentation of silt, and its constant reformation out of a powerful hydrology. Mymensingh is actually located by one of the indomitable rivers in that system, the old Brahmaputra, where the surrounding land is a patchwork of rice fields and homesteads on mounds, many of which vanish under water during the monsoon floods, and rise again magically afterwards. There is something about the liquid quality of the land that is characteristic of the Delta: it implies a special relationship with the cycles of nature, with the periodicity of the rivers, and the overwhelming presence of water with silt, clay, and vegetation.

It must have been the riotous vegetation in close proximity to Mymensingh that led Tigerman to describe the place as a "jungle town." That was in the monsoon of 1964, as Tigerman recalls, when Rudolph, Islam, and Tigerman arrived in that town driving a jeep. It must have been quite a sight: three fearsome characters—two gringos and the native honcho—riding into a lazy Bengali town. One wonders about the initial impression made on the most famous American architect of the time and the indomitable chairman from Yale's architecture school. There were insalubrious comments about poverty and poor hygiene, the unnerving presence of bugs and spiders, mold and fungus. Rudolph remained culturally aloof, expressing no particular anthropological or sociological interest in the place, and therefore his only recourse was to seek an autonomous architecture. While climate entered the equation, the hydrological and anthropological significance—the question of "life-world"—of the landscape lay far away.

As Tigerman describes, for Modern architecture in the 1960s, Rudolph's approach evolved as a product of pragmatism, as opposed to a kind of hermeticism associated with architecture with a

[23] Kazi K. Ashraf, "Taking Place: Landscape in the Architecture of Louis Kahn," in *Journal of Architectural Education* (November 1997).
[24] Charles Correa, "A Place in the Sun," *Places* (Fall 1983).
[25] Consider Maxwell Fry and Jane Drew's comments in Fry and Drew, *Tropical Architecture in the Humid Zone* (New York: Reinhold Publishing Corporation, 1956), 19: "Modern architecture is distinguished by nothing so much as its determination not to turn aside from science and the effects of science, but to enter into them and wring from them a solution of value to humanity."
[26] "We architects," Neutra wrote, "have been too much crowded into metropolises, mentally and physically crowded, and packed into a few restricted spots on earth and into the particular problems of a metropolitan minority." Neutra, *Architecture of Social Concern,* 37–38.
[27] Sibyl Moholy-Nagy, *Architecture of Paul Rudolph,* (New York: Praeger, 1970), 10.

3.9
Paul Rudolph, Bangladesh Agricultural University campus, model

capital A.[28] This is also consonant with a Modernist aversion to, and suspicion of, any kind of metaphysical or symbolic intonation in architecture, as perhaps was pursued by Kahn. Rudolph's layout of the agricultural university makes more sense from a functional and pragmatic point of view: an organizational schema derived from a general climatic condition. It does not ensure an ensemble that fosters, or is fostered from, an agricultural milieu, nor does it partake in the power of the immediate landscape of rivers and rice paddies (it was, after all, an agricultural university!). However, the project did not serve pragmatism from a purely functional point of view, it was, above all, a pragmatics of "visual delight." In a 1954 essay, Rudolph writes that the "architect's prime responsibility is to give visual delight." Concerned with the suppression of "visual design" in modern culture, and a lack of attention to the appearance of buildings, Rudolph intended to return functional architecture to pleasing the eye.[29] If this seems to be a gesture towards formalism, Rudolph privileges the phenomenology of appearance: "An architect should be concerned with a building's looks in the rain, or on a summer's day, its profile on a misty day, the different treatment required for that which is close at hand versus that which is twenty stories removed; with angles of vision, symbolism, and content."[30]

7

The agricultural university is actually located about 4 kilometers south of Mymensingh town. The site, about 1,200 acres in area, is a fairly linear one, bounded on the west by the Brahmaputra River and on the east by a railway line, which the campus

[28] Tigerman, *VERSUS*, 60.
[29] Rudolph's notions of "visual delight" appear in two essays: "Changing Philosophy of Architecture," *Architectural Forum* (July 1954), and "Six Determinants of Architectural Form," *Architectural Record* (October 1956). In the latter, Rudolph cites Nikolaus Pevsner in emphasizing that the qualities of the Modern movement were developed to please the eye, and that no functional architecture is possible without a visual acuity.
[30] Rudolph, "Changing Philosophy of Architecture."
[31] Rudolph's walkway, which came later, is a simple construction of exposed brick piers and concrete slab. In simply ending at that junction without making any explicit relation to Neutra's arcade, without making a contact, Rudolph's walkway posed an ambiguous, if not nonchalant, attitude towards the earlier

3.10
Paul Rudolph, Courtyard of an academic building, Bangladesh Agricultural University

spills over. **[Figure 3.7]** A few buildings, including an administrative building by Neutra, had been built without the guidance of a master plan before Rudolph's arrival. Neutra, who was devoted to environmental obligations, produced buildings that are forgettable boxes with interior spaces arrayed along a double-sided corridor that hardly engaged the site and were wrongly oriented. The redeeming element was a handsome arcade that ran independently of the building, seemingly in anticipation of the future campus. It may be of some esoteric interest that where Neutra's arcade ended, Rudolph's covered walkway system began.[31] **[Figure 3.6]**

Rudolph's reference for Mymensingh remains in his earlier essays on Florida regionalism, in which the work embodied and articulated the power of the climatic milieu. The tropical repertoire of Modern architecture that combined the canopy and porous walls (screens, lattices, and perforated planes) to create pavilion buildings was already in circulation by the late 1940s. The combination of these elements carried out in a crisp, modern way, with contemporary building materials and techniques inscribed in an open plan, would describe a number of brilliant pavilion houses by Rudolph in Florida, such as the Healy Guest House or the Cocoon House (1948), the Walker Guest House (1952), and the Hiss Residence (1953).[32] The language of roof canopies and permeable walls also describes larger institutional projects, such as his Riverview and Sarasota High Schools.

The final configuration of the university project came out of Rudolph's consideration of the technical aspects of climate, ventilation and light, and,

architect on that campus. Stanley Tigerman wonders whether Neutra's presence raised complex psychological apprehension in Rudolph. Despite having been commissioned the master plan of the university, Rudolph might have felt that he was doing merely an addition to Neutra—the thunder already stolen, so to speak. In conversation with the author, 2008.

[32]The Cocoon House and the Walker Guest House in Sarasota are featured in Fry and Drew's *Tropical Architecture in the Humid Zone,* 53–59.

of course, his own inimitable virtuosity in formal and spatial arrangements.[33] In establishing design parameters for Mymensingh, the master plan was first created as a matrix formed by a triangular grid system that is often implicit and very often clearly legible. **[Figure 3.8]** William Grindereng, associate architect for the project, describes how he found himself taking the initial decision of applying the triangular grid on which Rudolph worked and developing the subsequent ideas, although the latter had worked on a rectangular formation earlier.[34] The triangular grid may seem an amplification of Rudolph's application of the diagonal at the Jewett Arts Center at Wellesley College (1955) and the Creative Arts Center at Colgate University (1963), where the diagonal is introduced to inflect the orthogonal forms and create swaying spaces. **[Figure 3.9]** The triangular grid at Mymensingh extended from systematizing the grouping of buildings and network of movements to structural systems in the building and the articulation of the facade and openings.

Fractured and modulated facades in configuring the buildings through exposed red brick and concrete became a leitmotif for Mymensingh. The diagonal stagger of the walls, even with that ponderous brick mass, into an assemblage of smaller, scaled-down parts, and the angular openings, were carried out masterfully along Rudolph's notion of "visual delight." While the articulated openings created excessive geometricization, different-sized ones did some justification to flow of wind through the Venturi effect. **[Figure 3.10]**

In Mymensingh, architectural types were developed out of a climatic contingency, the principal one being the need to generate cross-ventilation. The basic type for most buildings was the free-standing pavilion, with its porous walls allowing unimpeded cross-ventilation. The ideal pavilion on the campus is the Sports Pavilion, a Laugerian structure with a sharply profiled roof canopy and no walls. **[Figure 3.11]** The teachers' residences are pavilions that face the direction of the prevailing breeze, but are also overly geometricized to conform to the order of the contrived walls. They have a sculpturesque quality, especially when the tropical sun hits the walls, but they also create quite odd spaces in the interior, when the geometric theme is carried down to the smallest details.

Rudolph used both the pavilion and the courtyard types for Mymensingh. The two tropical building typologies are already evident in Florida. A mix typology was far more successful with the academic buildings, with a greater openness and porosity for the courtyard and the staggered floor planes, creating miniature social spaces between separate structures. The form is perhaps predicted in the design for the City Hall in Syracuse (1964) where the enclosed volumes of a cold climate are arranged around an open court. Rudolph miniaturizes that plan-type for the academic building at Mymensingh to create a tropical ensemble out of a pavilion and courtyard where the open-ended court works fairly well in a humid climate. But in the dormitories for students, where the combination involves rooms arranged around a small, enclosed court, the spaces are dank and discomforting.

While Florida was a fertile ground for Rudolph for evolving a Modern idiom for the single building in the tropics, the trajectory of the larger complex seemed uncertain. The schools in Sarasota present an effective tropical formation with porous and near-pavilion buildings, slender and skeletal, framing a rather open courtyard. But, gradually, the orthogonal formations of the large complex literally start to receive some twists and turns, first organizationally when the orthogonality is linked with spiraling landshapes, and then attuned towards a baroque spatial unity (at the same time, the buildings start to become more mass-conscious). This is seen in the Chapel in Tuskegee (1960) and in the plaza for the Boston Government Service Center (1962–1971), with an influence perhaps from Wright's Florida Southern College (Lakeland, Florida, 1938–1959). This is a kind of medieval urbanism, of geometric buildings around irregular plazas and places, inflecting the rational plans of Modernism as an intimation

[33] Among his six determinants of architectural form, Rudolph cites the third as "the particular region, climate, landscape, and natural lighting conditions with which one is confronted." Rudolph, "Six Determinants of Architectural Form," *Architectural Record,* v. 120 (October 1956).
[34] Interview with William Grindereng.

of a picturesque urbanism, even when the site is not urban. The combination of the orthogonal and more capricious geometries began to appear in building forms too. Unlike the University of Massachusetts, Dartmouth campus, where there is a clear formation of a central space which is referred to by the various linear academic buildings around it, and clearly unlike Kahn's Capital Complex with its symbolically charged hierarchical set of buildings, the distribution at Mymensingh did not proffer any legible fabric of relationship other than what was suggested by the thin ribbons of covered walkways that crisscrossed the interval spaces and connected the buildings again without much to say about the spaces between the buildings.

While Rudolph may have been oriented towards regionalism and not just the metrical aspects of tropical architecture, the agricultural university at Mymensingh did not enter the discourse of regional architecture, despite the scope of the project. The measure of the project still lies within the parameters of tropicalism, for, at the end, the project remains delightful as an example of Tropical Modernism.

How then to locate Rudolph's university in the conversation of a Bengali modernity in the 1960s? Between Muzharul Islam's ethical Modernism, which proposed a reinvigoration of things regional, and Kahn's offering of a cryptically coded, sacred, and quasi-mythological landscape, Rudolph's work is a more pragmatic and picturesque proposition, neither provoking nor mystifying, but just doing its job.

3.11
Paul Rudolph, Sports Pavilion, Bangladesh Agricultural University

HOTEL

MATERIALS AND TECHNOLOGY

Paul Rudolph and "New Materials": From Plywood to Plexiglas and More

Pat Kirkham and Tom Tredway

4.1
Paul Rudolph, Ingram Hook Guest House, Siesta Key, Sarasota, Florida, 1953
© Ezra Stoller/Esto

Paul Rudolph is widely recognized for his innovative and imaginative embrace of new materials. This chapter maps out the broad contexts within which he approached and used plywood and plastics, while also suggesting new ways of thinking about these materials and, consequently, about Rudolph.[1]

Plywood is at the center of this analysis, which Rudolph first used in Florida in the early 1950s to make elegant vaulted roofs. **[Figure 4.1]** It had been a strong, durable, and cheap alternative to solid wood as well as a favored material of Modern movement architects and designers for more than a quarter of a century. The technology, however, was far from perfect. Plywood, a lamination of three or more layers or veneers of (often inexpensive) wood, laid with the wood grain in opposing directions for greater strength, was first successfully used for the commercial production of furniture in the mid-nineteenth century when John Henry Belter, a German immigrant to the United States, used heat to mold plywood in three dimensions. The Austrian firm of Thonet, better known for bentwood furniture, experimented with laminates, particularly in the 1880s, but did not pursue the project. Molded plywood chairs were patented in the United States in the 1860s and 1870s by Isaac Cole and the Gardner Company, the latter making large numbers of its "genuine American veneer seats" for both the domestic and export markets.[2] Cracking and splitting remained major problems, however, and, by the early twentieth century, plywood had become somewhat invisible, being used mainly as a substitute for solid wood, where it could not be seen in drawers, or for the back of cabinets and wardrobes.[3]

Before the 1920s, the strongest glues available were derived from animals and plants, but new

[1] For Rudolph's use of concrete see essay by Réjean Legault.
[2] For plywood in design see Christopher Wilk, *Plywood* (London: Thames & Hudson, 2017) and http://designmuseum.org/design/plywood (accessed September 2, 2010).
[3] The major U.S. producer in the interwar years, United States Plywood, was founded in 1921 by Lawrence Ottinger, who had supervised plywood production nationally during World War I, and was determined to raise the status of this lowly material. See "Corporations: Ply Again," *Time* (September 15, 1950): http://www.time.com/time/printout/0,8816,813382,00.html (accessed September 2, 2010).

4.2
Ralph Twitchell and Paul Rudolph, Knott Residence, Yankeetown, Florida, rendering, 1951

synthetic (and toxic) glues so greatly strengthened the product that it came to be thought of as a "new" material. The 1930s saw architects and designers across Europe creating furniture in bent, molded, and cut plywood, including Heinz Rasch in Germany, Gerrit Rietveld in Holland, Alvar Aalto in Finland, and Hungarian-born former Bauhausler Marcel Breuer for the British company Isokon.[4] In 1938, Aalto's furniture was exhibited at the Museum of Modern Art (MoMA), New York, and was available for sale in selected stores in the Unites States that featured Modern design, as was furniture by Summers.[5] Students were bending and cutting plywood in interesting ways at the New Bauhaus, Chicago, established by Bauhaus instructor László Moholy-Nagy in 1937, and elsewhere. Fascinated by all of these developments, in 1940, Charles Eames and Eero Saarinen submitted designs for plywood chairs to be molded in more than one direction to the *Organic Design in Home Furnishings* competition held at MoMA.[6] Unfortunately, the chairs proved impossible to mass produce by machine; Saarinen abandoned the project, but Eames continued in association with his wife, Ray Kaiser Eames.

In terms of larger structures, summer cabins and playhouses had been made from plywood since the 1880s, but the stronger plywoods of the 1930s led to a revival of interest in plywood homes, not least because of the great economic hardships during the Great Depression. The 1935 "stress-skin" plywood house, promoted by the Forest Products Laboratory of the U.S. Department of Agriculture, triggered a series of experiments aimed at mass-produced, well-insulated, low-cost homes. California-based Modernist architect Rudolph Schindler copyrighted a plywood panel system for use in house construction in 1936. His former

[4] http://designmuseum.org/design/plywood (accessed September 2, 2010); http://whyfiles.org/2010/old-new-glue-for-plywood-composites/ (accessed September 2, 2010); "Corporations: Ply Again," *Time* (September 15, 1950); Pat Kirkham, *Charles and Ray Eames: Designers of the Twentieth Century* (Cambridge, Massachusetts: MIT Press, 1995), 201–04.

[5] *Alvar Aalto: Architecture and Furniture,* MoMA, March 15–April 18, 1938; http://designmuseum.org/design/plywood (accessed September 2, 2010).

[6] Kirkham, *Charles and Ray Eames,* 203–04.

[7] For Schindler and Ain's use of plywood see Anthony Denzer, *Gregory Ain: The Modern Home as Social Commentary* (New York: Rizzoli, 2008).

[8] Denzer, *Gregory Ain,* 8, 101. Schindler, for example, used plywood ceilings in the Bubeshko Apartments, Silver Lake, California (1937–1938), and, in Ains's own home (1941), plywood panels were featured only on the inside.

[9] "While there are necessarily many parallels between the wood uses of World Wars I and II, there are also many products being employed in the present conflict, such as modified wood and plastics, which were unknown 25 years ago; other products, such as plywood and laminated wood, have been so improved as to be virtually new." George A. Garratt, *Wood in War and Peace* (Forest Products Laboratory–Forest

employee, Gregory Ain, followed suit in 1940, but neither system went into production.[7] A plywood house was exhibited at the 1939 New York World's Fair as part of a collective vision of "the future," but, before World War II, with the exception of sheathing and sidings, plywood was mainly used *inside* buildings: for walls, ceilings, and built-in storage and furniture.[8]

After Pearl Harbor and the U.S. entry into World War II in December, 1941, plywood was reserved for military use and the government poured huge amounts of money into improving molding techniques and developing glues with such greater durability and strength, and shorter setting-times, that they became known as "super-glues." Indeed, a government report, *Wood in War and Peace* (1944), argued that the wartime improvements in plywood were *so* transforming that it should be considered a new material.[9]

Plywood's many wartime uses included temporary housing (much of which continued to give plywood a bad name), barracks, aircraft hangars, assault boats, lifeboats, gliders, and parts for airplanes. Charles and Ray Eames and half a dozen employees, including Gregory Ain, working as the Molded Plywood Division of the Evans Products Company, made molded plywood items for the war effort, including leg splints for the U.S. Navy and parts for the Vultee BT-15 Valiant trainer for the aircraft industry.[10] Such work gave them access to classified information about glues and production techniques and, after the war, much wiser than when they began, they were able to successfully machine mass-produce the low-cost molded plywood chairs (1946), which greatly raised the profile of plywood as a material not only of strength and pliability but also of elegance and grace.[11]

In 1944, during his term of military service at the United States Navy Yard, New York (better known as the Brooklyn Navy Yard), Rudolph visited the *Design for Use* exhibition at MoMA, where he must surely have seen some of the Eames/Molded Plywood Division's large plywood parts for aircraft that were exhibited along with Ray Eames's plywood sculpture.[12] After the Eames group's plywood chairs were shown at MoMA in 1946, they were so lauded in the design press across the world that it is difficult to imagine Rudolph not being among those reminded yet again of the potential for bending plywood. In short, by the time Rudolph used plywood it was not only a "hot" material, but also a fairly familiar one: annual wartime output reached approximately one and a half billion square feet, and by 1954 it stood at nearly four billion.[13] This said, there were still many technical problems to be resolved in order for Rudolph to create large plywood vaults which were structurally sound.[14] Indeed, in 1951, the Eames Office's attempts to develop a low-cost prefabricated house with a curved plywood roof came to naught because of technical difficulties.[15]

It has become something of an orthodoxy to imply that Rudolph's plywood vaults were inspired by the hulls of the wartime Patrol Torpedo (PT) boats he would have seen when working at the Brooklyn Navy Yard.[16] There are two main problems with this assertion. Firstly, the form of the hulls, which transitioned from a deep V at the bow to a more flattened stern, were quite different from Rudolph's graceful, uniformly curved barrel vaults. Secondly, the hulls of those rather sizeable boats were not made of the thin-sheet plywood Rudolph experimented with—it would have smashed to smithereens—but rather from double-planked one-inch mahogany sandwiched together (sometimes with canvas) with the toughest waterproof superglues available and fixed together with a large number of screws and rivets. *Wood in War and Peace* separated comments on plywood from those on laminated units joined together with new saltwater-resistant superglues in order to construct large-span roof arches and noted that those large spans had a visual counterpart in the

Service, U. S. Department of Agriculture, October, 1944).

[10] John Neuhart, Marilyn Neuhart, and Ray Eames, *Eames Design: The Work of the Office of Charles and Ray Eames* (New York: Harry N. Abrams, 1989), 33–42.

[11] Neuhart, Neuhart, and Eames, *Eames Design,* 33-42 ; Kirkham, *Charles and Ray Eames,* 214–29.

[12] John Howey, *The Sarasota School of Architecture: 1941–1966* (Cambridge, Massachusetts: MIT Press, 1995), 38.

[13] In 1954, 101 mills produced 4 billion sq. ft. of plywood, and, by 1959, production stood at 7.8 billion sq. ft. See Milestones in the History of Plywood http://www.apawood.org/level_b.cfm?content=srv_med_new_bkgd_plycen (accessed September 2, 2010).

[14] Garratt, *Wood in War and Peace,* 4–5; the Eames's postwar ability to bring molded plywood furniture to viable low-cost mass production (1946) also involved bonding wood to metal, which, as stated in *Wood in War and Peace,* had seen a "recent advance."

[15] The house was developed for the Kwikset lock company, Anaheim, California. See Neuhart, Neuhart, and Eames, *Eames Design,* 155; and Kirkham, *Charles and Ray Eames,* 137–38.

[16] Howey, *The Sarasota School of Architecture,* 63. This point has also been made repeatedly during the last two years by friends of Rudolph and by people interested in his work.

curved keels of small naval craft.[17] Rudolph would have seen both the arches and the keels during his service in the Naval Reserve, but it bears repeating that in the early 1950s he focused on creating vaulted arches out of thin-sheet plywood. When, in 1952, Rudolph recalled his Naval Reserve service and its influence upon him, he noted many things about ships and their design, but not plywood or laminated arches. He recalled the heavy construction involved in shipbuilding, being fascinated by the elimination of unnecessary weight, the efficiency of the interior compartmentalization of ships, advances in fireproofing, and directing groups of workers repairing vessels. Indeed, he seemed much more interested in the architectural possibilities of steel suggested by ship construction—particularly bent plates, tension members, and continuous frames—than plywood.[18]

Rudolph first experimented with bent plywood vaults when designing the Knott Residence in Yankeetown, Florida, in 1951. **[Figure 4.2]** He used a series of modular curved plywood vaults as independent umbrellas over steel, glass, and concrete brick structures, and their repetition and separation from the rest of the structure allowed for maximum flexibility in the placement of partitions and other elements of the interior space. While the designs were widely published and well received, the project was never built, and thus the question of whether the vaults would have been structurally sound was not resolved.[19] Rudolph used bent plywood to span architecural space successfully at the Hook Guest House on Siesta Key, Florida, in 1952–1953. **[Figure 4.1]** He had boys jump on various thicknesses of bent plywood in his backyard in order to test their strength, and devised a system

4.3
Ralph Twitchell and Paul Rudolph, Healy Guest House, Siesta Key, Sarasota, Florida, 1951
© Ezra Stoller/Esto

[17] Garratt, *Wood in War and Peace,* 4–5.
[18] Paul Rudolph, "Three New Directions: Paul Rudolph, Philip Johnson, Buckminster Fuller," *Perspecta* 1 (1952): 21.
[19] Howey, *The Sarasota School of Architecture,* 63.

for forming the roof using two layers of standard one-quarter-inch-thick 4' x 8' sheets of plywood overlapped by two feet and glued and nailed together.[20] The resulting sheets of plywood were easier to bend than one-half-inch sheets and could be made to the exact dimensions of each vault. The vaults were formed by bending these sheets over a temporary frame erected under the high point of the vault, and bolting the ends to girders connected to buttresses to counteract the outward thrust.[21] *House and Home* estimated the cost of the plywood vaults at the Hook Guest House at only about three percent more than a comparable flat roof with plywood ceiling and sheathing, and Rudolph's subsequent plywood vaults reportedly cost less than comparable flat roofs.[22]

Rudolph used similar repeating plywood vaults for his first major non-residential project, the Sanderling Beach Club, also designed and built on Siesta Key, Florida, in 1952–1953. Here, similar sheets of double-layered plywood were formed into vaults using a different method from that employed at the Hook Guest House—the sheets were bound to form a shorter-than-needed radius while the glue set, then released to expand slightly to their final form and bolted to girders, eliminating the need for tie rods or buttresses due to decreased thrust.[23] Despite the success of the Hook Guest House and Sanderling vaults, however, Rudolph did not continue to use bent plywood vaults for small houses or other buildings, but their form did influence his work in other materials, particularly concrete. These designs also influenced a California Case Study House: Buff, Straub, and Hensman's Case Study House #20 (1957–1958, Altadena, CA) for designer Saul Bass, who collaborated with the architects on the design.

4.4
Paul Rudolph, *Good Design* exhibition of 1952, installation at the Merchandise Mart, Chicago

[20] Paul Rudolph, *The Architecture of Paul Rudolph* (London: Thames & Hudson, 1970), 36; "Rudolph and the Roof: How to Make a Revolution on a Small Budget," *House and Home* 3:6 (June 1953): 141.
[21] "Rudolph and the Roof: How to Make a Revolution on a Small Budget" *House and Home* 3:6 (June 1953): 144.
[22] Ibid., 141.
[23] Ibid.; "Sanderling Beach Club, Sarasota, Fla.," *Architectural Record* 114:4 (October 1953): 153.

Such vaults were so novel in California in 1957–1958 that building permits were refused in Altadena until a roof sample had undergone very extensive testing.[24]

Rudolph's early use of plastics related much more directly to his Naval Reserve service than his work with plywood. Beginning in 1943, the U.S. Navy began to plan Operation Mothball to weatherproof ships no longer in service by means of wrapping them in a "cocoon."[25] The cocoon—formed by spraying on a saran and vinyl plastic mixture, followed by a coat of clear vinyl, which could stretch over gaps up to four inches wide—was developed with part of the estimated $40 million the government invested in new spray-vinyl plastics during the war.[26] Rudolph later recalled: "I saw the mothballing of Navy destroyer escorts especially, and how that worked and that was fascinating to me because of its elasticity." [27] In 1948, Rudolph, then working in partnership with Ralph Twitchell, applied his observations of Operation Mothball when designing the roof of the Healy Guest House on Siesta Key, Florida. **[Figure 4.3]** Believing that "steel, when used in tension is more eloquent than when used in any other way, and sheet materials bent are more eloquent than when used flat,"[28] Rudolph developed a catenary curved form for the roof, with the center two inches shallower than the ends to facilitate drainage.[29] The roof was constructed using fiberboard and two-inch-thick flexible insulation resting on half-inch steel bars, then sprayed on both sides with cocoon for maximum flexibility.[30] Cocooning made the roof watertight, though susceptible to punctures and the resulting leaks. This interest in materials and technologies developed for the war effort won him the American Institute of Architects Award of Merit; his later work with plastics would bring no such accolades.[31]

Rudolph continued to develop the cocoon roof, using it at the Coward House and Wheelan Cottages, both commissioned in 1951, and both also in Florida.[32] In both, he altered the shape of the roof to create more tent-like spaces, as he felt the curve of the Healy Guest House roof resulted in an unsatisfactory and uninviting interior, but the basic materials and construction process remained similar. He used large sheets of half-inch-thick insulating building board beneath a one-inch-thick layer of fiberglass insulation, all covered on both sides with a one-sixteenth-inch-thick layer of spray-vinyl cocoon and resting on one-eighth-inch-by-one-and-a-half-inch steel straps in tension. The resulting roof was only one and five-eighths inches thick and weighed about four pounds per square foot.[33] Cocooning was a brilliantly clever idea but was estimated to cost approximately fifteen percent more than a conventional five-ply tar-and-gravel equivalent and to last only eight to ten years.[34] Thus, when Rudolph proposed cocooning the plywood-vaulted roofs of the Sanderling Beach Club, it was ruled out as too expensive.[35] These Florida projects show Rudolph, like so many other idealistic postwar Modernist architects, trying to use new materials and techniques to bring "good design" to the small family home and holiday chalet.

In the early 1950s, Rudolph also began to experiment with other types of plastics, including Plexiglas and Lucite—the names given by two different companies, Dupont and Röhm & Haas, respectively, to the same acrylic resin (polymethyl methacrylate). First marketed in 1938, this substitute for glass was tougher, lighter, and transmitted slightly more light than the material it was designed to replace. Despite all the hallmarks of a good Modernist material, and despite its promotion by industrial designers such as Gilbert Rohde, Modernist designers and architects

[24] Built of factory-produced stressed-skin plywood panels; see Elizabeth A.T. Smith, et. al., *Blueprints for Modern Living: History and Legacy of the Case Study Houses* (Los Angeles: Museum of Contemporary Art; Cambridge, Massachusetts: MIT Press, 1998), 67–69; "Case Study House #20 By Buff, Straub, and Hensman in association with Saul Bass," *Arts & Architecture* 75:9 (September 1958): 20–21, and "Case Study House #20 by Buff, Straub and Hensman in association with Saul Bass," *Arts & Architecture* 75:11 (November 1958): 11–17.

[25] Guy Moon, "Revitalizing the Mothball Fleet," *Army Information Digest 6,* no. 7 (July, 1951): 53–57.

[26] "Cocoon House Uses the Navy's Moth-Balling Material to Weatherproof its Catenary Curved Roof," *Architectural Forum* 94:6 (June 1951): 157; Guy G. Rothenstein, "Sprayed-on Vinyl-Plastic Sheeting," *Progressive Architecture* 33:7 (July 1952, 99–102): 99.

[27] For the quotation, see Christopher Domin and Joseph King, *Paul Rudolph: The Florida Houses* (New York: Princeton Architectural Press, 2005), 30.

[28] "Rudolph and the Roof," *House and Home* 3:6: 141.

[29] "Cocoon House Uses the Navy's Moth-Balling Material to Weatherproof its Catenary Curved Roof," *Architectural Forum* 94:6 (June 1951): 158.

[30] Ibid.

[31] Tony Monk, *The Art and Architecture of Paul Rudolph* (Chichester, West Sussex: Wiley-Academy, 1999), 125.

[32] "Guest Houses with Plastic Roofs," *Progressive Architecture* 33:7 (July 1952): 104.

largely ignored Lucite, partly because in the interwar years "decorators" mainly used it in ways that Modernists abhorred.[36] Those who appreciated the material's plasticity included Elsie de Wolfe, the internationally known American-born interior decorator who featured Lucite chairs in several interiors and whose eclecticism and modern versions of "period" designs stood for everything that Modernists hated; Cora Scovil, a New York mannequin sculptor who designed Lucite furniture in "Regency," "Empire," and other classical revival styles; and French interior decorator and art and antiques dealer Serge Roche, whose furniture in stucco and mirror glass had a strong Neo-Baroque flavor. Perhaps more important in embedding Lucite and other transparent materials in the popular imagination of the period—and remember Rudolph was a teenager and young man in the 1930s—were Hollywood set designers who used it alongside cellophane, mirror glass, high-gloss linoleum, lamé, and other silvery materials in the movies that brought "Art Deco" glamour to millions of cinemagoers.[37] It was the continued use and promotion of Lucite as suitable for "modern" objects, including automobile and airplane windshields and automobile taillights, and the wartime use of all sorts of plastics, including Lucite for airplane cockpits and shields for motorboats, however, that led to its reassessment by certain Modernists after the war.

Rudolph used several new plastics, including Lucite, plastic string, translucent Synskin Polyplastex, and semitransparent wire mesh sprayed with vinyl cocoon, together with varying intensities of light, for the *Good Design* exhibition that opened in Chicago in January, 1952, and later moved to MoMA.[38] *The New York Times* called Rudolph's installation "breathtakingly spectacular" and, according to *Architectural Record,* he "stole the show."[39] Two inverted half-circles made with plastic string lines opened the exhibition—"an entry gate though which you could look," as Rudolph called it—a structure that suggests he was conversant with the exhibition strategies employed by European Modern movement designers of the interwar period, most notably Ludwig Mies van der Rohe and Lilly Reich.[40] **[Figure 4.4]** When discussing his concept for the installation, Rudolph emphasized the centrality of transparency in relation to the experience of the viewer moving through the exhibition: "There is a prescribed route to follow, although there are many bypasses. Opaque and translucent screen walls made of plastic cords, cocoon (a plastic spray developed by the Armed Forces to preserve their material), woven cane, are so arranged that one can compare visually an item seen earlier with one just coming into view."[41] For the New York installation, Rudolph designed drop ceilings in which tubes of light were shielded behind panels of Synskin Polyplastex in a wood grid frame, and some of the windows

4.5
Paul Rudolph, 23 Beekman Place Residence, New York City, living room, 1967
© Ezra Stoller/Esto

33 "Rudolph and the Roof," *House and Home* 3:6: 141.
34 "Cocoon House Uses the Navy's Moth-Balling Material to Weatherproof its Catenary Curved Roof," *Architectural Forum* 94:6: 157; Rothenstein, "Sprayed-on Vinyl-Plastic Sheeting," *Progressive Architecture* 33:7 (July 1952): 99; Navy tests, however, indicated that Cocoon would last 30 years.
35 "Sanderling Beach Club, Sarasota, Fla.," *Architectural Record* 114:4 (October, 1953): 153.
36 Rohde used it to considerable effect in exhibition design, but on the downside, it showed fingerprints and scratched very easily (indeed, its recent revival is due in part to a new wonder cream that removes scratches). For more on Rohde and Plexiglas/Lucite see Phyllis Ross, *Gilbert Rohde: Modern Design for Modern Living* (New Haven: Yale University Press, 2009).
37 See Donald Albrecht, *Designing Dreams: Modern Architecture in the Movies* (London: Thames and Hudson, 1987), and Howard Mandelbaum and Eric Myers, *Screen Deco* (New York: St. Martin's Press, 1985)
38 Mary Anne Staniszewski, *The Power of Display: A History of Installations at the Museum of Modern Art* (Cambridge, Massachusetts: MIT Press, 1998), 184.
39 "Good Design 1952: Paul Rudolph's Installation Gets Raves," *Architectural Record* 111:3 (March 1952): 26.
40 For the quotation, see Staniszewski, *The Power of Display,* 184; for Rohe and Reich, see Matilda McQuaid, *Lilly Reich: Designer and Architect* (New York: Museum of Modern Art, 1996).
41 "Good Design Exhibition: Installation by Paul Rudolph," *Arts and Architecture* 69:5 (May 1952): 19.

4.6
Paul Rudolph, 23 Beekman Place Residence, New York City, bedroom, 1967
© Ezra Stoller/Esto

4.7
Paul Rudolph, Hirsch Residence, New York City, lucite tube handrails, 1969
© Ezra Stoller/Esto

in the gallery space were given a similar treatment, resulting in a space described by *Interiors* magazine as "in effect a white interior ranging from pearly to dazzling luminescence."[42] Rudolph would later revisit his exploration of the interplay between plastics and light, particularly in his own apartment's combination of mirrors, plastic, and white light, which he described as "like living in a milk bottle."[43] Many of the objects on view in the *Good Design* exhibition incorporated plastics of some sort, from furniture such as the Italian Gio Ponti's Leggera Side Chair (1951) with a cellophane rush seat and GRP (Glass-Reinforced Plastic) fiberglass chairs from the Eames Office (1949–1950), to rugs made from plastic-impregnated paper and other floor coverings made from cotton and a new plastic called Fibre E. The display of these objects at MoMA indicates a far greater acceptance of plastics as a "serious" material for serious designers than in the prewar period.[44]

Rudolph's second period of preoccupation with transparent materials came in the 1960s during a huge revival of interest in Lucite, especially for furniture. Erwine and Estelle Laverne, who both studied painting with artist Hans Hofmann at the Art Student's League and went on to design textiles, wall coverings, and furniture, produced some of the most notable examples, including the molded acrylic "Invisible Group" introduced in 1957. Available at department stores like B. Altman, New York, as well as at the Lavernes' own showroom and through their company catalog, this furniture was very popular and often used as a marker of modernity in advertisements and fashion photography.[45] One design in the group, the "Light" chair, a Lucite

[42] "The New York Version," *Interiors* 112:3 (Nov. 1952, 130–31): 130.
[43] "A Spectacular Apartment by Paul Rudolph," *House and Garden* 148:10 (October 1976): 116.
[44] "Good Design Exhibition," *Arts and Architecture* 69:5 (May 1952): 18.
[45] Michael Krzyzanowski, *Laverne: Furniture, Textiles & Wallcoverings* (Atglen, Pennsylvania: Schiffer Books, 2007), 111–26.

4.8
Paul Rudolph, Halston Residence, New York City, furniture, 1978
© Harry Benson

porter's chair that lit up by means of an electrical source beneath the seat, mirrored Rudolph's own experimentation with light and plastics, as did Joe Colombo's *Acrilica* lamp (1962). Morris Lapidus, an architect-designer who combined Modernism and glamour in postwar Miami, used plastics in his later work, including Lucite dining chairs in his own dining room in the 1970s. These examples, taken together with the many Lucite objects currently circulating via flea markets and eBay, indicate something of the broad appeal of the material at that time, and provide a context for Rudolph's designs for Lucite and chromed metal furniture that, from the 1960s, he used for private commissions and in his own apartments.

Among the many factors leading to a resurgence of interest in Lucite and other plastics was the general revival of interest in "Art Deco" (a term coined in the 1960s), including the so-called "all-white" rooms of interior decorators such as Syrie Maugham, which featured chromium, mirror glass, cellophanes and other shiny surfaces. Another was the spate of "futuristic" design that coincided with the so-called "Space Race" between the U.S. and the USSR (ca.1957–1969), best epitomized by the designs of Joe Colombo, and those for the film, *2001: A Space Odyssey* (1968, directed by Stanley Kubrick). Tranparency was perhaps most famously achieved in the inflatable Blow chair designed by De Pas, D'Urbino, Lomazzi, and Scolari for Zanotta in 1967; Embargo's clear, tube-like Inflatable chairs, also from 1967; and Quasar and Emmanuelle Khanh's inflatable house and furniture, part of the *Structures Gonflables* exhibition at the Musée des Arts Decoratifs in 1968, the latter sold through the Khanhs' Paris shop. Along with see-through chairs came see-through clothing, notably the organza blouses and dresses by Yves Saint Laurent beginning in 1968.

It was within this context that Rudolph employed a number of different types of plastics in his residential work from the 1960s through the end of his life. Rudolph used his New York apartment on Beekman Place, beginning in 1965, as a laboratory for exploring the relationship between plastics and light. In the late 1960s, Rudolph's apartment included several decorative elements that fused light and plastic, mostly using readily available or found items. In the virtually all-white living room, Rudolph built low platforms out of white translucent plastic, which supported vinyl patent leather seating units; incandescent lights on dimmers beneath the platforms created glowing planes that surrounded the room. **[Figure 4.5]** A simple Lucite table, similar in design to the dining-room table used at the Hirsch Residence (see below), sat in a corner near the fireplace, and on the white kid floor he placed and lit from underneath a hollow translucent plastic cylinder—a "found" object. A white sculpture composed of layered plastic by Will Ryman hung in front of the hundreds of small round mirrors glued to clear nylon fishing wire on tracks that formed the curtains. The resulting effect was not unlike that achieved by disco lights reflecting off of a plastic-and-metal Paco Rabanne dress. Rudolph later composed a large light mural over the fireplace using pieces of foil, colored plastic, and small photographs placed into plastic photo-transparency holders and epoxied together, with a series of red night-lights rigged up behind.[46] The bedroom walls were covered with mirrors, and curtains of plastic amber beads on fishing wire hid the closets and an air conditioner.[47] **[Figure 4.6]** Other, more overt, markers of male sexuality and Queerness, including a Roman torso and a large section of a billboard for men's deodorant featuring a handsome shirtless man with bedroom eyes, dominated the room, the most private part of the apartment—an idea that Rudolph would repeat later in the Beekman Place penthouse.[48]

In 1966 Rudolph transformed an 1870s coach house on the Upper East Side of Manhattan into a glass-and-steel residence for Alexander Hirsch, a real estate developer and lawyer, and Hirsch's partner, Lewis Turner.[49] Rudolph designed a floating main staircase, but instead of a conventional stair rail used Lucite tubes for handrails that virtually disappeared into the wall. **[Figure 4.7]** The walls of the master bathroom were covered in silver Mylar and small, randomly placed circular mirrors of various sizes (Andy Warhol's collaborator and Factory photographer Billy Name had covered the Factory with aluminum foil and silver paint three years before, and Rudolph also used silver Mylar and mirrors for a bathroom in Mrs. Gardner Cowles' Fifth Avenue apartment, completed in 1970).[50] The small mirrors echoed the many mirrored surfaces throughout the house—from the coffee table in the living room to the three mirrored walls of the "greenhouse" that reflected back into the living room via a 27-foot-tall glass wall.[51] The master bedroom featured a mirrored headboard with a large, white nylon-rope macramé wall hanging by artist Molly Chalfant placed behind.[52] The Hirsch Residence also contained perhaps the earliest use of Rudolph's Lucite furniture outside of his own apartment; a large, thick slab of Lucite rested on two thin, rectangular Lucite supports to form the dining room table, and several small Lucite side tables were placed throughout the space.[53] The interior was a meditation on transparency and reflection, themes Rudolph would continue to explore for the rest of his life.

Rudolph renovated the space after the fashion designer Halston purchased it in 1974. Photographs of the apartment during this period, when Halston hosted his famous caviar-cocaine-and-baked-potato dinner parties, show a profusion of Lucite furniture, including small side tables, night tables, nesting tables, and the large dining table from Hirsch and Turner's tenure.[54] **[Figure 4.8]** Halston was particularly fond of the living room: "Except to sleep or look at TV, I rarely use any room but this,

[46] Jean W. Progner, "The Kinetic Electric Environment," *Progressive Architecture* 49 (October 1968): 201.

[47] Robert A. M. Stern, Thomas Mellins, and David Fishman, *New York 1960: Architecture and Urbanism Between the Second World War and the Bicentennial* (New York: The Monacelli Press, 1995), 548–50; C. Ray Smith, "The Designers: Floating Platforms," *Progressive Architecture* 48 (May 1967): 152; Barbara Plumb, "Paul's Pacesetter," *The New York Times,* July 23, 1967.

[48] Plumb, "Paul's Pacesetter," *The New York Times;* for the role of sexuality in Rudolph's Beekman Place interiors, see Timothy M. Rohan, "Paul Rudolph: Casa Rudolph, New York 1977–1997: Spettacoli Pubblici E Privati/Public and Private Spectacles," *Casabella* 63:673–74 (December/January 1999): 138–49, 171–73.

[49] David Hay, "Halston's Old House," *New York* 38:35 (October 10, 2005): 74–76, 78–79.

[50] For more on Warhol's interiors, see Stern, Mellins, and Fishman, *New York 1960,* 545.

[51] "The Total Townhouse," *House and Garden* 136:5 (November 1969): 126.

[52] Ibid.: 124–27.

4.9
Paul Rudolph, 23 Beekman Place Residence, New York City, furniture, 1977–1997
© Peter Aaron/OTTO

its proportions are so interesting to me . . . And it's here that I've discovered that modern is the only way to live. I like the simplification of living with only a few things."[55] Indeed, there is a clear relationship between Halston's townhouse and the luxe minimalism of his clothing designs from the 1970s, particularly those that emphasize transparency or utilize metallic elements and reflective sequins. Halston's parties also exposed other design professionals to the possibilities of the distillation of form that he found there. Tom Ford, the fashion designer whose remarkable revitalization of Gucci in the mid-1990s owed much to Halston's influence, remarked on the impact of the space on his design aesthetic when he saw it in the early 1980s: "I remember being stunned by the beauty of it. Clean, simple, streamlined . . . It really had an effect on me. In many ways I have integrated this design philosophy into my life."[56]

When redesigning his Beekman Place apartment in 1975, Rudolph, like many interior designers of the period, used carpet in interesting ways and largely eschewed conventional furniture. Like many designers before and after, Rudolph could not find any furniture to his liking or pocket and, in addition to the simple carpeted plywood platforms used instead of seating furniture, he designed a white Plexiglas dining table that swiveled on the found plastic cylinder and chairs made from balls of stretch fabric pulled through square Plexiglas panels in the bedroom.[57] Following the gendered conventions still common in interior design, the entrance hall was darker than other spaces, but Rudolph gave it a twist by featuring dark green Plexiglas panels that marked the room as both original and "Modern."[58] Like Charles Rennie Mackintosh and Margaret Macdonald Mackintosh in the early 1900s, Rudolph pushed gendered conventions to the limits in spaces coded as

[53] Rudolph also occasionally collaborated with his clients when designing his Lucite furniture, adding tiny lights, for example, to a low coffee table designed by Joanna Steichen when they redesigned her New York apartment in 1973–1974; see "Space Design: For Joanna Steichen, a Living-Working Apartment That's Part Fly-Away Space, Part 'Cave,' Designed by the Architect Paul Rudolph," *Vogue* 165 (September 1975): 294–97.
[54] Hay, "Halston's Old House," *New York,* 38:35.
[55] For the quotation, see Elaine Gross and Fred Rottman, *Halston: An American Original* (New York: HarperCollins, 1999), 17.
[56] For the quotation, see Steven Bluttal, ed., *Halston* (London: Phaidon, 2001), 530.
[57] "A Spectacular Apartment by Paul Rudolph," *House and Garden* 148:10 (October 1976):116–17.
[58] For more on gendered conventions in interior design see Juliet Kinchen, "Interiors: Nineteenth-Century Essays on the 'Masculine' and the 'Feminine' Room," in *The Gendered Object,* ed. Pat Kirkham (Manchester, UK: Manchester University Press,1996), 12–29.
[59] Ibid.

"feminine"—namely living rooms and bedrooms—to create rooms that were hyper-feminized according to interior design conventions.[59] Following the concept of floor-level lighting established in the apartment's previous incarnation (where, in addition to the floor-level lighting beneath the platforms of the living room, lines of densely grouped incandescent bulbs hung close to the floor on long, exposed cables next to the walls of his bedroom), Rudolph embedded lines of miniature light bulbs set in translucent plastic on the floor between strips of carpet in the dining and living areas.[60] In the bedroom he hung curtains made up of strings of lights in translucent plastic tubes against mirrored walls, creating shimmering sensual effects; in the dining room he wrapped a glittering curved curtain of thin mirrored plastic strips around the walls.[61] After buying the Beekman Place building in 1975, he began to plan a spatially complex penthouse in Plexiglas, chrome, and silver Mylar-covered steel (1977–1979) that he continued to modify until his death in 1997.[62]

White, or white-and-silver, interiors full of bright shining chrome, glass, mirror glass, Lucite and other plastics were part and parcel of glamorous, "hip" circles in the late 1960s and what has been called "the decadent 1970s": one thinks of the white Deco-influenced interiors of Paris fashion designer Karl Lagerfeld and Halston's parties in his Rudolph-designed apartment.[63] If we had not already heard from people who knew Rudolph of the "hip," "happening," gay (in all senses of the word) gatherings in his apartments in the 1960s and 1970s—complete with designer drugs and Jacuzzi parties—then the interior and its materials offer clues.[64] Much like Saint-Laurent's see-through clothing, there is an eroticized purity about Rudolph's use of transparent plastic for furniture and interiors; indeed, in the pristine Beekman Place penthouse one could play a "Peeping Tom" game through the transparent bottom of part of the master bath into the guest suite below—and vice versa.[65]

The Lucite used for the so-called "Rolling Chair" is thin—at first glance it can be mistaken for glass—whereas the thick Lucite tabletop boldly proclaims that it is plastic. **[Figure 4.9]** When Rudolph realized that he did not like the way you could see clothing, legs, napkins, and other messy things through the tabletop, he covered it with thin sheets of opaque Plexiglas, like a milky-white tablecloth. **[Figure 4.10]** A simple, elegant solution. As a centerpiece, Rudolph created a grouping of Roman terracotta heads perched on thin Lucite stems set into a Lucite base, a blend of antiquity and modernity that mirrored the Modernist fascination with the classical.

The Modernist concern with function is also evident in Rudolph's adaptation of a Danish chromed metal modular shelving and display system to construct the elaborate frame holding the Lucite panels of the chair, which allowed the back to adjust to the sitter.[66] This chair gets bad press, but, functionally, it holds the back well. Unfortunately, however, the joint pieces are not sufficiently robust for heavy wear and mass production.[67] In formal terms, this slightly anthropomorphic chair pays homage to interwar European Modern movement designers who made chairs seem to disappear. It is often likened to Breuer's "Wassily Chair" (1925–1927), but the seating materials used by Breuer—canvas and, later, leather—have a certain give that Lucite does not. The stiff, angular forms refer back to Rietveld's work, especially the High Back chair (1919) and Zig-Zag chair (1932), both now regarded as "classic" Modernist designs. The structure of Rudolph's Rolling Chair as well as the legs and casters suggest both supermarket carts and the hospital beds to which Bauhaus furniture was so often compared by critics. Like many other Modernists, Rudolph found a mass of legs on tables and chairs to be visually distracting, but this chair has multiple legs and large casters. At first consideration, the casters seem an overly self-conscious show of "functionalism," but the chairs are surprisingly heavy and awkward to move without them.

Rudolph's interior designs, particularly for his own spaces at Beekman Place in the late 1960s and 1970s,

[60] Progner, "The Kinetic Electric Environment," *Progressive Architecture* 49, 202; "A Spectacular Apartment by Paul Rudolph," *House and Garden* 148:10: 116–17.

[61] Rudolph used similar mirrored plastic strips at the Cowles and Edersheim Apartments, both completed in New York in 1970.

[62] For the penthouse, see Rohan, "Paul Rudolph: Casa Rudolph, New York 1977–1997," *Casabella* 63:673–74.

[63] For more, see Alicia Drake, *The Beautiful Fall: Fashion, Genius and Glorious Excess in 1970s Paris* (New York: Back Bay Books, 2006).

[64] Ernst Wagner, in conversation with the authors, New York, New York, December 2008.

[65] Though the tub was rarely used, Gene Leedy, an architect and friend of Rudolph's, recalled one party where he looked up and

take one away from mainstream Modernism and Post-Modernism and towards less orthodox aesthetic expressions and an interest in decoration. His interiors were also often theatrical and experiential, evidencing a range of materials and effects, including green Plexiglas panels suggestive of a forest, silver Mylar glued to exposed steel columns, Lucite stalactites hanging from a ceiling, large plastic tubing inset into walls used to display objects, small plastic tubing holding tiny lights against walls and ceilings of mirror glass, and dental mirrors adorning melamine kitchen cupboards. Transparency, twinkling lights, and reflective surfaces were elements in Rudolph's magical *Gesamtkunstwerk* interiors. He used a variety of materials to create, amongst other things, spaces for the display and contemplation of objects from other cultures—what the Eames and the Smithsons called "functioning decoration" and "cross cultural surprise"—and spaces for living out very particular and very personal lifestyles. Rudolph's use of Mylar, melamine, and mirror glass both within and beyond the category of "new materials" and the parameters of orthodox Modernism are deserving of further study.

4.10
Paul Rudolph, 23 Beekman Place Residence, New York City, furniture, 1977–1997
© Peter Aaron/OTTO

4.11 [next spread]
Paul Rudolph, Yale Art and Architecture Building, Yale University, New Haven, Connecticut, view of concrete facade, 1958–1963

quite clearly saw a fellow party-goer using the bathroom; see Fred Bernstein, "Let In the Light. Show Off the Tub. Who Needs Privacy?," *The New York Times,* March 23, 2006; Kay Kipling, "Portrait of an Architect: To the World, Paul Rudolph Was a Genius of Modern Architecture; to His Friends in Sarasota and Beyond, He Was Affectionate, Loyal and Vividly Alive," *Sarasota Magazine,* December 1, 2004, available at http://www.paulrudolph.org/writings/Portrait.pdf (accessed September 2, 2010).

[66] A smaller version, without the adjustable back, served as a desk chair in Rudolph's New York City apartment.

[67] The system was the Abstracta System; Ernst Wagner, in conversation with the authors, New York, New York, December 2008.

Paul Rudolph and the Shifting Semantics of Exposed Concrete

Réjean Legault

5.1
Paul Rudolph, Yale Art and Architecture Building, Yale University, New Haven, Connecticut, exterior view, 1958–1963 © Ezra Stoller/Esto

One of the most provocative, but also most memorable, aspects of the Yale Art and Architecture Building (1958–1963, known in abbreviated form as the A&A, and, after 2008, called Paul Rudolph Hall) is the rough, corrugated concrete surface that envelops the building inside and out.[1] **[Figure 5.1]** Its designer, the architect Paul Rudolph (1918–1997), was then an enthusiastic advocate for the material. "Concrete is mud," he said in 1966, "I work with concrete, not against it. I like mud."[2]

[1] This essay is based on a paper delivered in the symposium on Paul Rudoph held at the Yale School of Architecture on January 23–24, 2009. It has not been updated to reflect publications after 2009. I thank Timothy M. Rohan for inviting me to participate. I also thank Cammie McAtee for discussing this text during its many phases and for her constant support. My appreciation also goes to Gregory E. Marcangelo at the Library of Congress for his help with original materials, and to Elizabeth Cropper, Dean of the Center for Advanced Study in the Visual Arts, for hosting me at the National Gallery while conducting research on this paper. Part of the research for this text was supported by a research grant from the Fonds Québécois de Recherche sur la Société et la Culture (FQRSC).

[2] In "Concrete. Where do we go from here?" *Progressive Architecture,* October 1966, cover page.

The A&A's rugged finish soon became emblematic of the building as a whole. By the end of the 1960s, it had also become emblematic of so-called Brutalism in American architecture. As Marcus Whiffen writes in his 1969 book, *American Architecture since 1780: A Guide to the Styles:* "In America exposed concrete left in its rough state—or sometimes, as in Paul Rudolph's Art and Architecture Building at Yale, artificially roughened—is common to a great many, if not most, of the buildings by which the adjective Brutalist comes to be applied."[3] The reasons why Brutalism as a design approach came to be so closely associated with textured concrete remain to this day a historiographical enigma. But they certainly point to the need to look again at Rudolph's contribution to the culture of materials in the postwar period.

In a compelling essay published in 2000, Timothy M. Rohan showed how the striated concrete of the A&A derived from Rudolph's unique technique of architectural rendering.[4] He has also convincingly argued that the surface of the Yale building can be interpreted as a form of ornament that has been literally pressed—or repressed—into the concrete. In the following essay I shift focus to another facet of the design process, what I have called the materialization of materials, examining Rudolph's unique architectural gesture at the A&A in light of his long-term interest in exposed concrete. My goal is to reveal other sources for Rudolph's corrugated concrete and to assess its troubled legacy.

To study the origins of the A&A's rugged surface, it is helpful first to place it within the context of Rudolph's own trajectory. Early on, he insisted on the importance of materials in architecture, arguing that one of the shortcomings of the International Style was its "lack of feeling for materials."[5] Seeking an alternative to glass curtain wall buildings, which he derisively called "goldfish bowls," Rudolph turned to concrete as a means of producing works that were more expressive, more responsive to light and shadow, and more attuned to their environments.[6] Three projects, all commissioned in the year before the A&A, are revealing of this new approach.

The first is Sarasota Senior High School in Florida (1957–1959), a project where Rudolph employed prefabricated concrete panels that were suspended from the concrete frame. Used as fixed sunshades, the smooth white stuccoed precast panels helped accentuate the box-like, modular organization of the facade. The second project is the Blue Cross/ Blue Shield Building in Boston (1957–1960). Here again, Rudolph employed precast concrete panels, this time using them to cover the building's columns and spandrels. The surface of these panels was not perfectly smooth, however, but was made of a white quartz aggregate that resembled a mosaic of small stones. Known by the trade name Mo-Sai, these veneer panels enabled Rudolph to emulate the lithic character of the surrounding buildings.

The third project is Yale University's Greeley Memorial Laboratory (1957–1959). Combining smooth precast columns and ceiling sections, and mosaic-like precast wall panels, the building was aptly described by a critic as a "glorification of precast concrete."[7] Most striking were the monumental columns, with their Y-shaped capitals that are evocative of the sinuous forms of Art Nouveau. **[Figure 5.2]** Given the sophisticated form and load-bearing function of the columns, their fabrication required all the control and precision factory production could provide. And, despite the organic shapes, the concrete was still conceived as an exact material, not unlike steel.

In his 1956 article on the "Determinants of Architectural Form," Rudolph postulated that "Each material has its own potential, and one

[3] Marcus Whiffen, *American Architecture Since 1780: A Guide to the Styles* (Cambridge: MIT Press, 1969), 279.

[4] Timothy M. Rohan, "Rendering the Surface: Paul Rudolph's Art and Architecture Building at Yale," *Grey Room,* vol. 1, no. 1, 2000: 85–107. See also Timothy M. Rohan, "Architecture in the Age of Alienation: Paul Rudolph's Postwar Academic Buildings," PhD dissertation, Harvard University, 2001.

[5] In a letter to Peter Blake, Rudolph writes: "In addition there is a lack of feeling for materials which seems to me to be highly questionable in the International Style." Letter from Paul Rudolph to Peter Blake, September 14, 1954, Peter Blake Archive, Avery Library, Columbia University.

[6] In a 1959 interview with John Peter, Rudolph surmised: "If one were to make a prognostication again, one would say that the aesthetics of pre-cast reinforced concrete will lead us to an architecture which depends on the play of light and shadow, as opposed to the architecture which depends basically, for its aesthetic values, on the reflections which come from the curtain wall." Interview with Paul Rudolph, March 27, 1959. John Peter Collection. Library of Congress, Box 7, Folder 73. On Rudolph's critique of the curtain wall, see Timothy M. Rohan, "Challenging the Curtain Wall: Paul Rudolph's Blue Cross and Blue Shield Building," *JSAH,* vol. 66, no. 1, March 2007: 88–89.

[7] "The Concrete Orchard," *Architectural Forum,* October 1959: 138–141.

5.2
Paul Rudolph, Greeley Memorial Laboratory, Yale University, New Haven, Connecticut, interior view, 1957–1959

5.3
Le Corbusier, High Court Building, Chandigarh, India, exterior view, 1952–1955
© Scott Norsworthy

5.4
Paul Rudolph, Temple Street Parking Garage, New Haven, Connecticut, exterior view, 1959–1962
© Ezra Stoller/Esto

[8] Paul Rudolph, "The Six Determinants of Architectural Form," *Architectural Record,* October 1956: 183–90 (184).
[9] He reiterated this idea in his 1959 article on the "Creative use of materials," writing: "(...) since the war Le Corbusier and his school of thought have turned increasingly to a more direct use of materials of all kinds." He added that the architect "must search for the innermost potentiality of every material and use it to make a meaningful whole." Paul Rudolph, "Creative use of materials," *Progressive Architecture,* April 1959: 92–94.
[10] Rudolph took part in the World Design Conference that was held in Tokyo May 11–16, 1960.
[11] Rudolph recounted his visit to Le Corbusier's Chandigarh in "The contribution of Le Corbusier," *Architectural Forum,* April

seeks the most eloquent expression possible."[8] As these three projects make clear, his conception of concrete at the time was primarily that of a seamless, industrial material. Yet, by the first years of the 1960s, precast concrete proved not to be eloquent enough for Rudolph. In a sudden change of heart, he turned to cast-in-place *béton brut* as a more appropriate expression of the material.[9] A trip to Japan in May 1960, followed by an excursion to India, seem to have had a significant impact on his approach.[10] Kenzo Tange's newly completed City Hall at Kurashiki and his Kagawa Prefecture Building in Takamatsu were stunning examples of the expressive potential of plastic forms made in rough concrete. The same is true of Le Corbusier's High Court and Secretariat Buildings in Chandigarh, which Rudolph experienced firsthand.[11] **[Figure 5.3]**

Rudolph's first significant use of raw concrete was in the Temple Street Garage in New Haven (1959–1963), a project that reflected the architect's new belief that concrete was best expressed in continuous, monolithic forms. Like Le Corbusier's *béton brut,* Rudolph's raw concrete exploited the marks left after the removal of the formwork, treating the thin striations left by the boards as an integral part of the design. **[Figure 5.4]** Of course, by 1960 Rudolph was not the only American architect eager to fully exploit the plastic possibilities offered by the material. Others architects like Eero Saarinen, Marcel Breuer, and I.M. Pei were engaged in the same search, as the editors of *Progressive Architecture's* special 1960 issue on concrete made clear.[12] Yet, if the garage was a bold statement of Rudolph's conversion to the virtues of rough concrete, the surface he achieved proved not to be rough enough for him, as he regretfully admitted that Chandigarh was "rougher still."[13] It was his next commission, the Art and Architecture Building, that would provide the ideal testing ground for his newfound fascination with roughness.

In his early project dated December 1959, the A&A Building was depicted with smooth concrete walls.[14] But six months later, Rudolph had opted

1961: 100.

[12] "This freedom to mold a material to suit one's idiosyncrasy has considerable appeal to the more imaginative and ambitious architects." In "Concrete. Where do we go from here?," *Progressive Architecture,* October 1960: 142.

[13] "Paul Rudolph Designs a Place to Park in Downtown New Haven," *Architectural Record,* February 1963: 148.

[14] Richard Pommer, "The Art and Architecture Building at Yale, once again," *The Burlington Magazine,* vol. CXIV, no. 837, December 1972: 858 and fig. 87.

for a more textured surface. As drawings show, the crafting of the A&A's striated surface was a two-step process. First the molding, then the hammering. The formworks were made of plywood panels on which triangular-shaped wood strips were nailed in a vertical pattern.[15] **[Figure 5.5]** The forms were then filled with a concrete mix made of stone aggregates chosen for their warm yellow and gold tones. After the concrete was cured and the forms removed, the fins were hammered by hand to expose the aggregates.[16] **[Figure 5.6]** The crafting process was at once controlled and haphazard, enabling the serial pattern to accommodate intentional incidents—like the encrusted seashell in the basement—and unexpected accidents.

In his discussion of the building, Rudolph was eager to refer to his experience of Le Corbusier's work: "One of the most humanizing elements in Corbu's concrete is the oozing, dripping, and slipping of concrete between poorly placed forms."[17] Yet, the concrete he achieved at the A&A was anything but "oozing, dripping, and slipping."[18] In fact, the creation of this unique texture required extensive experimentation that took five months and three dozen prototypes.[19] One such experiment involved placing vertical steel wires at the surface of the formwork, and ripping them off to form the ribs.[20] But, most importantly, this experimental phase would not have been possible without the dedication and financial support provided by the George B.H. Macomber Company, the building's general contractor.

The treatment ultimately devised for the A&A was nothing less than a rejection of industrial methods in favor of handmade, on-site production. Rudolph hinted as much when he wrote that the successful use of concrete "calls for a craftsman-like care hard to find in the age of mass production."[21] Four workers worked nearly full time at a special pay rate to hammer the freshly made fins.[22] For Rudolph, the search for expression now seemed to go hand in hand with time-consuming craftsmanship.[23] Paradoxically, this attention to manual production put the very Modernist tenet he sought to achieve to the test: that of "truth to materials." His effort to reveal the aggregate can no doubt be read as a desire to emphasize the internal "truth" of the material. But the excessive working of the surface, both in its molding and its subsequent hammering, could not help but generate the opposite effect: that of a material artifice.

One of the most striking features of the design is that the textured concrete can be found both inside and out, a practice that calls to mind the "allover" technique of Abstract Expressionism.[24] To be more precise, there is more than one surface treatment: most horizontal elements, like beams and slabs, are treated as smooth concrete; staircases are made of *béton brut* with diagonal forms.[25] In fact, construction drawings refer to as many as five types of finishes. Despite this variety, the overwhelming impression is of a building made of a single material and texture. This "allover" treatment was both expensive and obsessive—textured concrete can be found everywhere, even in some mechanical rooms in the basement—enticing some contemporary critics to talk about the A&A in terms of exhibitionism and excess.[26] An excess it would be tempting to read in light of Georges Bataille's notion of *dépense* (expenditure).[27] If we accept the definition of expenditure as "a squandering of force that has no other end but the process itself," Rudolph's artificially roughened surface may appear as a true architectural embodiment of Bataille's idea of the spectacular discharge of surplus energy.[28]

[15] "Concrete. A special report," *Architectural Forum,* September 1962: 89.
[16] This technique has often been referred to as "bush-hammering." This is not completely accurate. The bush hammer is a kind of hammer with spikes, and bush hammering is a technique used to "scorch" the surface of the concrete to expose the aggregates. At A&A, workers likely used normal hammers to break the ribs.
[17] According to Richard Pommer, Rudolph wrote this on the proofs of Vincent Scully's article, "Art and Architecture Building, Yale University," for *Architectural Review* published in February 1964. Pommer, op. cit.: 860.
[18] On this issue, Rudolph's good friend, Sybil Moholy-Nagy, wrote: "The concrete surface has been widely criticized as being arty in an age of technology. However, the visual relief from the *béton brut* cliché of random formwork in the wake of Le Corbusier's revolution is so pleasing, and the purpose of the building so non-technological, that the artifice seems wholly justified." S. Moholy-Nagy, "Yale School of Art and Architecture. 2. The Measure," *Architectural Forum,* vol. 120, no. 2, February 1964: 77.
[19] Marshall Burchard, "Yale's School of Art and Architecture. 3. The Builder," *Architectural Forum,* vol. 120, no. 2, February 1964: 81. According to Pommer, the experimental phase took place in Fall 1961.
[20] I would like to thank Gregory E. Marcangelo for sharing this information with me. Another unsuccessful experiment involved backing the trapezoidal elements with cross slats in order to achieve the rough surface, without the necessity of hammering. In "Paul Rudolph's Fluted Concrete Buildings," Aberdeen Group, 1965, n.p.

5.5
Paul Rudolph, Art and Architecture Building, Yale University, New Haven, Connecticut, detail of formworks and reinforcement, 1958–1963

5.6
Paul Rudolph, Art and Architecture Building, Yale University, New Haven, Connecticut, view of hammering operation, 1958–1963

[21] In "Concrete. A special report," *Architectural Forum,* September 1962: 81. Rudolph further expanded after the building was completed: "One of the reasons why American architecture has had difficulty using this medium is that our contractors take great pride with the precision of their work, which helps to give so much of it the thin, metallic-like quality." Cited in Pommer, op. cit.: 860.
[22] "Paul Rudolph's Fluted Concrete Buildings," Aberdeen Group, 1965.
[23] Rudolph recognized that there was a paradox in the A&A Building, writing: "It is relatively carefully built, but the handling of the surface renders it purposefully mud." Statement by Rudolph, 1963/64; cited in Pommer, *The Burlington Magazine,* op. cit.: 860.
[24] The connection between Rudolph's work and Abstract Expressionism is well examined in Timothy M. Rohan's 2001 dissertation.
[25] According to Scully, "the original intention . . . was to surface all the beams and slabs in the same way." But "the visual illogicality of the system for horizontal elements was soon apparent." V. Scully, "Art and Architecture Building, Yale University," 332.
[26] See Jürgen Joedicke, "New Brutalism – Brutalism in Architecture," *Bauen+Wohnen,* no. 11, November 1964, summary, n.p. More recently, Thomas Fisher underlined the Nietzschean quality of the A&A's surface, seeing in it "a love of excess, a fascination with the outrageous." T. Fisher, "Nietzsche in New Haven: How One Philosophizes with a Hammer," *Perspecta* no. 29, 1998: 50–59.
[27] See Georges Bataille, *La part maudite précédé de La notion de dépense,* Paris, Editions de Minuit, 1949.
[28] Simon Blackburn, *The Oxford Dictionary of Philosophy* (Oxford: Oxford University Press, 1994), 47.

5.7
Paul Rudolph, Endo Laboratories, Long Island, New York, exterior view, 1960–1963

The use of corrugated concrete throughout helped blur the distinction between interior and exterior. Following in the footsteps of Eero Saarinen, who had employed the same concrete "masonry" for inside and out at another Yale building down the road—the Morse and Ezra Stiles Colleges (1958–1962)—Rudolph sought to achieve unity by means of poured-in-place textured concrete. Within a few years it became "the dream of many architects to build with concrete consistently, throughout the interior as well as the exterior," as the editors of *Progressive Architecture* remarked in 1966 in a special issue on the material.[29] Rudolph himself would later affirm that most works of architectural merit, whether modern or historic, were, like sculpture, formed from a single material.[30] But there were high costs to this ideal. The search for material unity at A&A was partially satisfied at the expense of technical logic, generating problems such as thermal bridges and condensation.[31] The looming problems were so great that the editors of *Progressive Architecture* did not hesitate to predict that the use of concrete throughout "may in time prove to be one of the major aesthetic rationalizations, if not aberrations, of this century."[32]

For some observers, the A&A's textured surface was well suited to the character of the Yale campus, going so far as to compare it to "tweed" or to the fuzziness of a "collegiate Shetland sweater."[33] At the moment of the building's inauguration, Rudolph also hinted that its concrete surface bore a relationship to the weathered masonry of Yale's traditional buildings.[34] At the same time, Rudolph also explained that "the ridges break down scale and perform the same function that flutes do in a classical column," insisting on the perceptual qualities of this unique surface.[35] A few years later, he

[29] "Concrete Interiors," *Progressive Architecture*, vol. 47, October 1966: 215.
[30] See Tony Monk, *The Art and Architecture of Paul Rudolph* (John Wiley & Sons, 1999), 12.
[31] Rudolph stated: "My argument always is that it is a lot better than glass. I don't build double walls because of the expense. It is easier offset by conditioning the air." In "Concrete Interiors," *Progressive Architecture*, op. cit.: 215.
[32] "Concrete Interiors," 215.
[33] "Yale School of Art and Architecture," *Progressive Architecture*, vol. 45, February 1964: 111.
[34] See "Yale Art and Architecture Building. Notes by Paul Rudolph," *Architectural Design*, April 1964: 161. Timothy M. Rohan has suggested that Rudolph "intended the building's textured concrete surface to be the Modern equivalent to the weathered masonry of Yale's traditional buildings." Timothy M. Rohan, *Model City: Buildings & Projects by Paul Rudolph for Yale and New Haven*, exhibition catalog no. 29, Yale School of Architecture, 2008, n.p.
[35] Statement by Rudolph, 1963/64; cited in Pommer, op. cit.: 860. Some years later, Rudolph added that the concrete surface "caught the light in many different ways because of its heavy texture. Light was fractured in a thousand ways and the sense of depth was increased. As the light changed, the walls seemingly quivered, dematerialized, took on additional solidity." Paul Rudolph, "Enigmas of Architecture," *A+U*, no. 80: 1977.
[36] See especially Paul Rudolph, "Enigmas of Architecture," op. cit.
[37] See Michael J. Crosbie, "Paul Rudolph on Yale's A&A," *Architecture* (November 1988): 104.
[38] As Raymond Epstein pointed out: "a rough texture looks different in a small interior space than it would in an exterior applica-

added that textured concrete, with its deep ridges that take the brunt of the staining, weathered much better than smooth concrete.[36] From then on, Rudolph consistently returned to scale and weathering as the two main arguments to explain his creation and use of textured concrete.[37]

Though compelling, these explanations have serious shortcomings. For if the analogy with the fluting of classical columns worked well for the concrete on the exterior, it did not work for the surfaces inside the building. Likewise, the striated concrete could indeed weather better when exposed to the elements, but this argument held little explanatory value for the concrete that was inside the building. In a word, the interior use of corrugated concrete was at odds with the weathering and scaling function it served on the outside.[38]

That Rudolph would insist on weathering and scale, rather than the context of the Yale campus, may be explained by later events. If the architecture of the A&A was unique, its materiality was not, and many of Rudolph's projects of the mid-1960s would wear this unusual brand of ribbed concrete. We now know that Rudolph also planned to use this finish for the Temple Street Garage Manager's Office, designed in 1961.[39] It was followed by the Endo Laboratories on Long Island (1960–1963), a project developed alongside the A&A.[40] It was then employed in a number of commissions he received around 1962, including the Boston Government Service Center (1962–1971), the IBM Building in East Fishkill, New York (1962–1966), and the Christian Science Student Center, University of Illinois in Urbana (1962–1967). In all of these buildings, the concrete finishes were described by reviewers as being "similar to those at Yale."[41] Such was the extent of Rudolph's use of this type of exposed concrete that the trade journal, *Concrete Product,* remarked in 1964 that "his corduroy-like, textured surfaces have become something of a trademark."[42] Seemingly oblivious to context, Rudolph appeared to have finally found for concrete "the most eloquent expression possible."[43]

It seems, however, that the textured surface could convey different meanings in different locations. Endo Laboratories is revealing in this regard.[44] **[Figure 5.7]** In this project, Rudolph used the same type of concrete finishes that were codified at Yale. Yet contrary to the A&A Building, the concrete frame is here concealed within the mass of the building, stressing the volumetric character of the design. A drawing of the conference room even shows the concrete mass treated as *poché,* in the tradition of 18th-century masonry construction.[45] Here, the image that comes to mind is not the weathered masonry of the Yale campus but that of a modern castle. At Endo, the concrete surfaces became a synecdoche of the fortress-like structure, complete with turrets and defensive walls.[46]

Rudolph's exploration of the expressive, but also narrative, potential of exposed concrete did not stop with his Yale project. Soon after the completion of the A&A, he was involved in a new phase of experimentation: this time with prefabricated concrete blocks. Working with concrete blocks was in no way new for him: he had made an extensive use of them in some recent projects, like the Frederick A. Deering House (1958–1959) and the Arthur W. Milam Residence (1959–1961), both built in Florida. But, by 1964, he began developing two new types of precast blocks: a rough-textured ribbed block, and a smooth fluted block.

The rough-textured ribbed block was first used at the Charles A. Dana Creative Arts Center for

tion, when seen at some distance." In "Concrete. Where do we go from here?," *Progressive Architecture* (October 1966): 215.

[39] See *Model City,* op. cit.

[40] The execution drawings showing the textured concrete are dated May 1962, only four months after the ones produced for the A&A.

[41] *Architectural Forum* (February 1964): 88. The reviewer underlines that the reasons for using textured concrete were the same: "[The IBM project], like the Yale building, also demonstrates Rudolph's interest in the potential of concrete surfaces for scale and texture": 86.

[42] "Paul Rudolph: artist in concrete," *Concrete Products* (October 1964): 31.

[43] Discussing the Urbana building in his 1986 interview with Rudolph, Robert Bruegmann surmised that the corrugated concrete had nothing to do with Urbana but was something that Rudolph was interested in at the time. Rudolph's answer was "yes." Robert Bruegmann, Interview with Paul Rudolph, February 28, 1986, Chicago Architects Oral History Project, The Art Institute of Chicago, 1993–2000, 49.

[44] A contemporary review states that the laboratories, like the A&A Building, feature "concrete walls with a texture resembling narrow-wale corduroy, created by specially ribbed wood forms and hand bush hammering." In "Buildings in the News," *Architectural Forum* (September 1963): 16.

[45] The lithic analogy was also picked up in an ad that said, "the concrete surface has the appearance of line-drilled stone." In "Paul Rudolph: artist in concrete," *Concrete Products,* (October 1964): 35.

[46] This image was quickly seized upon by the press. See "Turreted, Castle-Like Structure to Be a Laboratory on Long Island," *The New York Times,* November 4, 1962, Section: Real Estate, R11.

PAUL RUDOLPH UTILIZES CORDUROY BLOCK AT COLGATE U.

Specially patterned precast masonry units give a ribbed-like appearance to Charles A. Dana Creative Arts Center

Charles A. Dana Creative Arts Center at Colgate University, Hamilton, N.Y.

5.9
First page of article on Crawford Manor, New Haven, by Paul Rudolph in *Journal of Concrete Products*, 1962–1966

Architect Paul Rudolph, left, examines fluted block with Plasticrete President Philip Paolella

Paul Rudolph and Plasticrete team up on tallest all-block building in U. S.

5.8
First page of article on Charles A. Dana Creative Arts Center, Colgate University, by Paul Rudolph in *Journal of Concrete Products,* 1964–1967

5.10
Advertisement of the Plasticrete Corporation in the *Journal of Bay State Architecture*

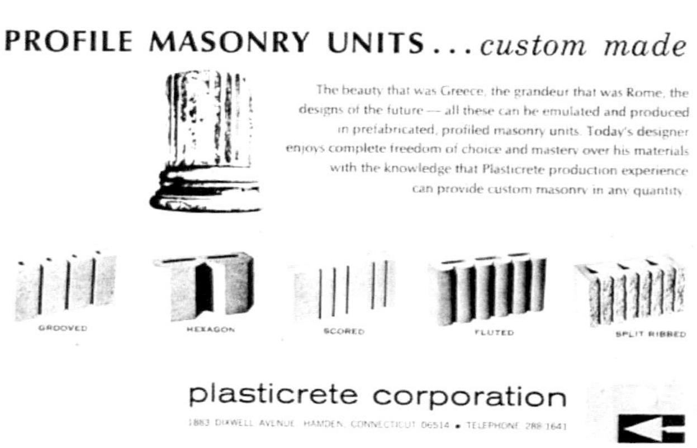

Colgate University in upstate New York, a project initiated in 1963 and inaugurated three years later. **[Figure 5.8]** This masonry unit was a specially patterned precast concrete block which, when laid up in a stacked bond pattern, gave a ribbed-like appearance.[47] The result was a type of "fluting" that resembled the striated surface at the A&A.[48] However, the idea to use rough-textured ribbed blocks for the Arts Center came only later in the design. As the May 1964 issue of *Progressive Architecture* noted, the construction of the Center was to be "of exposed aggregate concrete similar to that used by Rudolph at Yale."[49] It was confirmed by the project specifications, dated May 1964, which indicated poured-in-place concrete and a procedure for the breaking of the fins.[50] The use of this distinctive treatment was again justified with a contextual rationale that argued, "the texture as well as the color of the new building represents a modern interpretation of the stone that has become prohibitively expensive."[51] But, in the end, the cost of even cast-in-place corrugated concrete proved prohibitive. In a letter to the university's representative sent in June 1964, Rudolph offered an alternative:

"We have determined that we can make a considerable saving by pre-casting the interior and exterior walls rather than casting them in place as originally contemplated. This will still have the same light and shadow and color effect as before, but it will not show the individual aggregate as the Art & Architecture Building. We must do this in order to stay within our budget and still not decrease the facilities to be provided. The basic effect will be the same."[52]

The revised specifications, issued in September 1964, are more explicit about the alternative method proposed: "Exterior walls shall be faced with fluted pre-cast concrete units (FPCU) manufactured for exterior work."[53] The construction documents also specify that all joints will be 3/8 inches thick, that vertical joints shall line up plumb and shall be raked, that horizontal joints shall be flush, and, most importantly, that mortar color match that of the block. In addition, only full-size units shall be used except for internal corners and at ends of wall panels. These specifications also bring to light another consequence of Rudolph's alternative, namely, a fundamental change in the building trades involved. Cast-in-place concrete required the skills for the fabrication of wooden coffers, the placement of steel reinforcement, and the pouring of concrete. With the adoption of precast blocks, the work was now brought back to the realm of masonry construction.

Used as an infill unit both inside and out, the rough-textured ribbed block contrasted with the *béton brut* of the cast-in-place concrete frame.[54] Textured block was not in itself new, and various types had been in use for some time.[55] The key innovation had to do with Rudolph's semantics of exposed concrete—that is, the development of a block that was specifically designed to *imitate* the rugged, striated texture created for the A&A. The imitation was so compelling that observers did not hesitate to call it "corduroy block."[56] Rudolph's design intention was clearly spelled out: to produce a more economical version of his handmade corrugated concrete while achieving the same weathering and scaling function.[57] The rough-textured block was materially different from its model in that the surface was not as abrasive, and the stone aggregates were not as conspicuous. But the idea of corrugated concrete was preserved.

[47] See "Paul Rudolph utilizes corduroy block at Colgate U," *Concrete Products* (April 1967): 57.
[48] Rohan, 2001, op. cit., 226–227.
[49] "Another Art Center by Rudolph Unveiled," *Progressive Architecture* (May 1964).
[50] Specifications for Creative Arts Center, Colgate University, May 4, 1964. Library of Congress, PMR-3107-4, folder 3.
[51] The text of the April 1964 university brochure reads: "The angular roof repeats the contours of other rooftops on the hill, the location of the building effectively extends the lines of the quadrangle, and the texture as well as the color of the new building represents a modern interpretation of the stone that has become prohibitively expensive." Creative Arts Center, Colgate University, April 1964. Library of Congress, PMR-3052-1, folder 7.
[52] Letter from Paul Rudolph to Dr. Herman Brautigam, Colgate University, June 18, 1964. Library of Congress, PMR-3126-2, folder 12.
[53] Specifications for Creative Arts Center, Colgate University, September 1, 1964. Library of Congress, PMR-3107-4, folder 3.
[54] "Three varieties of the precast block were used on the job: 4 inches one-side fluted; 6 inches one-side fluted; and 6 inches both sides fluted." In "Paul Rudolph utilizes corduroy block at Colgate U," op. cit., 57.
[55] The various types of precast blocks then available are presented in the article "The many faces of concrete," *Concrete Products*, vol. 65 (February 1962): 45.
[56] "The units used at Colgate… have a rough textured fluted surface resembling split block. For that reason, the units are called corduroy block." In "Paul Rudolph utilizes corduroy block at Colgate U," op. cit., 57.
[57] "Paul Rudolph's latest block job," *Concrete Products* (September 1966): 55.

Rudolph's other contemporary venture was with smooth fluted blocks. Begun in January 1964, this experiment was done with the technical and financial support of the Plasticrete Corporation.[58] The design phase took seven months and the result was a series of forty different models of blocks, all featuring regularly spaced, rounded fluted sections. This set of fluted blocks could accommodate a broad variety of wall configurations both inside and out.[59] What began as a simple design idea had turned into a complex building system.

These rounded fluted blocks were first used in Crawford Manor in New Haven (1962–1966). **[Figure 5.9]** The walls of the building were laid in a stacked bond pattern, and observers were quick to see that "their straight vertical grooves resemble to some degree the corduroy-like textured surfaces of cast-in-place concrete for which Rudolph has become known."[60] Unlike Colgate, however, the fluted blocks covered the concrete frame, creating an uninterrupted wall surface. Smooth fluted blocks were also employed in other contemporary projects, like in the first group of buildings at the Southeastern Massachusetts Technological Institute in Dartmouth (1964–1966).[61] But here, as at Colgate, the block was treated as an infill, with the concrete framework vividly expressed.

Rudolph's use of prefabricated blocks was, once again, a radical break from his previous approach to exposed concrete. It marked a shift from the monolithic concrete wall to the light masonry partition, from the process of casting to that of bonding, from the building site to the factory. If the surface of the A&A stood as a critique of a mass-production society, the walls made of precast blocks seemed to signal a renewed embrace of it.[62] But this shift was not only technical. It was also conceptual, revealing Rudolph's changing vision of the material. Relinquishing the idea of concrete as a continuous plastic mass, he seemed to focus instead on the surface patterns made possible by the material. At Colgate, he abandoned the continuous wall surface, but kept the rough texture and the ridges. At Crawford Manor, he abandoned the rough texture, but kept the ridges. In both cases, the primary focus of interest was now the striated pattern, not the sculpted mass.

With the precast block, the texture and ridges of Rudolph's original design at the A&A were now machine-made. Self-expression had been replaced by anonymous reproduction. If Rudolph's concrete treatment at the A&A could be equated with the creation of a unique "allover" à la Jackson Pollock, it is enticing to interpret the architect's turn to the serial employment of textured precast block as a shift towards a Warholian practice of mechanical reproduction. The different types of textured blocks that were soon made available by the Plasticrete Corporation—grooved, hexagonal, scored, fluted, split-ribbed—only confirmed the open-endedness of the process.[63] **[Figure 5.10]** Severed from the context of their invention, stripped of their original connotation, the textured blocks have now become mere products, readily available as part of an interchangeable syntax of exposed concrete finishes. Thanks to the possibilities offered by mass production, Rudolph's aesthetics of striated concrete could finally trickle down from "high art" architecture to everyday construction.

The treatment invented for the A&A Building revolutionized the aesthetic of exposed concrete, and Rudolph's corrugated concrete was to be an inspiration to many architects. Place Bonaventure in Montreal, a project by Raymond Affleck and his associates completed in 1968, is the consummate example of this process of architectural emulation. Though the A&A's special surfacing was not often reproduced *à l'identique,* its characteristic ridges reappeared in countless buildings across North

[58] Rudolph was involved throughout the seven-month-long design phase. In "Paul Rudolph and Plasticrete team up on tallest all-block building in U.S.," *Concrete Products* (January 1966): 55.
[59] The block "featured six raised 'flutes' on its surfaces that were convex rather than concave so that the rain and snow dripped off them more easily." Rohan, 2001, op. cit., 298.
[60] In "Paul Rudolph and Plasticrete team up on tallest all-block building in U.S.," *Concrete Products* (January 1966): 55.
[61] "For flexibility, as well as for economy, all walls, including interior partitions, are made of concrete block . . . The blocks are fluted to produce a weathering effect as they stain between the flutes, and also destroy the ungainly scale of the block." In "Paul Rudolph's latest block job," *Concrete Products* (September 1966): 55. This institution is now called University of Massachusetts Dartmouth.
[62] This idea was echoed in his declared interest for the large-scale prefabrication of housing. See especially Paul Rudolph, "The Mobile Home Is the 20th-century Brick," *Architectural Record,* vol. 143, no. 4 (April 1968): 137–146.
[63] See Plasticrete advertisement in *Bay State Architecture,* vol. 2, no. 1 (January 1970): 2.

America. The same is true of the A&A's ersatz: the rough-textured precast block first used at Colgate University's Creative Arts Center. After the example was set by Rudolph in a series of notable buildings, including the Orange County Government Center in Goshen, New York (1963–1971), the ridged blocks were employed by architects and builders alike, finding their way into both professionally designed buildings and the architecture of Main Street.[64]

This broad dissemination had radical consequences. The A&A's corrugated concrete was quickly singled out as the most tangible sign of American Brutalism as a whole.[65] But with the negative connotation that was soon to be attached to Brutalism, striated concrete—rough or otherwise—became the most egregious trait of this newly vilified style. Rudolph was not impervious to this. In the 1960s, he could state confidently that, though he would like the public to appreciate his concrete buildings, he was not primarily concerned with pleasing them.[66] Yet, by the 1970s, he was well aware that the tide had turned. He recognized that for most people, materials have connotations "which are not necessarily intended," to which he resignedly added, "concrete suggests a bunker."[67]

Rudolph's invention of the A&A's rugged surface was first motivated by his critique of the International Style, a critique that highlighted the expressive limitations of the curtain wall. Yet by the mid-70s onwards, it was Rudolph's own corrugated concrete—whether cast-in-place or prefabricated—that had become the symbol of the new dominant style, and, from then on, a favorite target of critics.[68] While the diffusion of his concrete surfacing was no doubt much more limited than that of the industrialized curtain wall, its image had become no less iconic. This was an ironic turn of events. As many have claimed, Rudolph's invention of textured concrete at the A&A was at once a radical critique of architectural conformity and a powerful act of self-expression. Born out of excess, this unique architectural gesture appeared to be immune to imitation. But it wasn't. And the primary culprit may have been its own creator.

5.11 [next spread]
Paul Rudolph, Yale Art and Architecture Building, Yale University, New Haven, Connecticut, concrete detail, 1958–1963

[64] A notable example is Eva Vescei's La Cité in Montreal (1973–1977), an urban complex comprising a 500-room hotel and three residential towers characterized by its conspicuous use of Rudolph's typical rough-textured split block.

[65] In 1969, Jürgen Joedicke wrote: "Today for many the idea of Brutalism has faded into nothing more than a rugged exterior." Joedicke, *Architecture Since 1945, Sources and Directions* (London: Pall Mall Press, 1969), 126. See also Whiffen, note 3.

[66] Rudolph added: "The public usually waits for the critics to tell them what they like." In "Concrete. Where do we go from here?" *Progressive Architecture,* op. cit.,185.

[67] Paul Rudolph, "Enigmas of Architecture," op. cit.

[68] Jürgen Joedicke wrote: "For its fellow-travellers uncouthness has taken the place of the elegant industrialized form, the curtain wall: one architectural fashion has superseded another." Joedicke, *Architecture Since 1945,* op. cit., 126. For a critique of corrugated concrete, see especially Brent C. Brolin, *The Failure of Modern Architecture* (New York: Van Nostrand Reinhold Company 1976); and Marvin Trachtenberg, *Architecture From Prehistory to Post-Modernism* (New York: Abrams, 1986), 548.

Rudolph and the Construction of Urban Building Blocks

Ken Tadashi Oshima

For Paul Rudolph, prefabrication was the means to realize a twentieth-century brick that was "an important material in creating a truly human city."[1] Like actual bricks which offer the advantage of speed and economy of assembly over stone construction, Rudolph proposed the assembly of prefabricated oversized "bricks" that could actually be inhabited, and thus address the economic constraints of public housing. Motivated by a quest to develop a "consistent theory for relating one building to another and to the environment,"[2] Rudolph realized this vision most vividly in New Haven with his 148-unit housing complex, Oriental Masonic Gardens, designed and built between 1968–1971, and then demolished a decade later in 1981. This project was featured in the Museum of Modern Art's 2008 exhibition, *Home Delivery: Fabricating the Modern Dwelling,* which highlighted the broader historical trajectory of architects' exploration of prefab today.[3] Arguably, Rudolph's work with prefabrication, as envisioned within Oriental Masonic Gardens and other projects, as a means to connect the design of the individual room with the urban fabric, illuminates primary aspects of his modus operandi.

Rudolph's interest in prefabrication, both as an assembly of mass-produced parts and the construction of entire units, likely originated when he was studying under Walter Gropius at the Harvard Graduate School of Design (GSD) and encountered Gropius's work with Konrad Wachsmann, seen in their "Packaged House/General Panel System" that sought to construct entire units using factory-cut panels. In an interview with *A+U* in 1977, Rudolph explained that from this experience he inherited principles emphasizing "strict adherence to

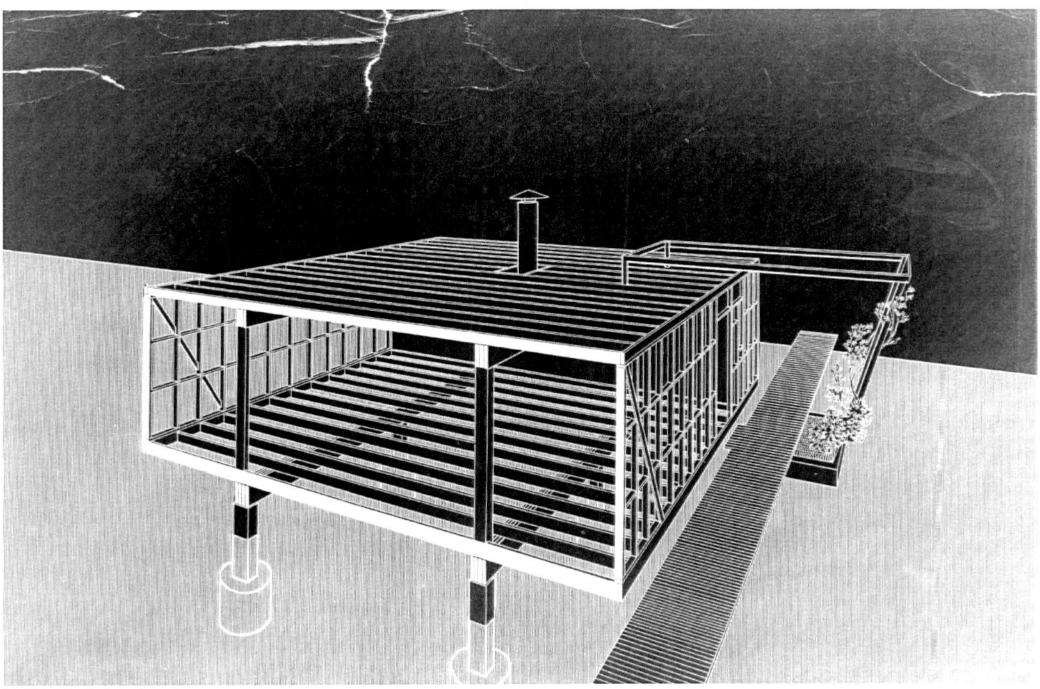

6.1
Paul Rudolph, Miller Guest House, Casey Key, Florida, drawing, 1949

[1] Paul Rudolph, "The Nature of Prefabricated System Design," *Japan Architect,* January–February 1971, p. 20.
[2] Rudolph, Paul Marvin, 1918–1997. "The Form of the City," *Canadian Architect* 4 (March 1959): 49–67.
[3] The exhibition featured a wooden model of Oriental Masonic Gardens, Barry Bergdoll and Peter Christianson eds., *Home Delivery: Fabricating the Modern Dwelling* (New York: Museum of Modern Art, 2008): 154–57.

function, clarity, and articulation of individual parts" and employing "regular structural wood systems with infilling walls of wood or concrete block."[4] Concrete, literally the "twentieth-century brick," was seen as an economical means to reduce the cost of poured-in-place concrete, and was used in Rudolph's early work, such as the Deering Residence (1956–1958) in Casey Key, Florida, and in his later work, such as the campus buildings of the University of Massachusetts at Dartmouth (1963–1972).

When the United States entered World War II shortly after Rudolph's first semester at Harvard, he enlisted in the Navy, was briefly trained as a naval architect, and then was stationed at the Brooklyn Naval Yard. As Rudolph scholar Joseph King writes, "[Rudolph's] wartime experience, from 1942 to 1946, proved to be an internship in industrialized construction on a vast scale, an opportunity that would have hardly been possible in the civilian world. His Florida work after the war possesses a characteristic lightness and efficiency of space and structure that can be thought of as being derived from the characteristics of modern ship construction."[5]

In his 1949 Miller Guest House in Casey Key, Florida **[Figure 6.1]**, for example, Rudolph literally created a floating box. Here he employed the simple post-and-beam structural system akin to traditional Japanese house construction that Gropius had found perfect for modern prefabrication. As Rudolph later wrote in *A+U:*

"I had observed that in traditional housing, especially in Japan and Europe, the humanness and scale of towns and cities were achieved by revealing the interior dimensions of individual rooms on the exterior. A hierarchy of building types was established by juxtaposing small-scale residential and commercial quarters to larger scaled and more monumental buildings. Modular, or "Twentieth-Century Brick" construction is an outcome of the Industrial Revolution. It has not yet been developed to its fullest possibilities."[6]

[4] Paul Rudolph, "Enigmas of Architecture," *A+U* special issue "Paul Rudolph" (July 1977), 317

[5] Joseph King, "Twitchell and Rudolph," in *Paul Rudolph The Florida Houses* (New York: Princeton Architectural Press, 2002): 30.

[6] Paul Rudolph, "Enigmas of Architecture," *A+U* special issue: "Paul Rudolph" (July 1977), 319.

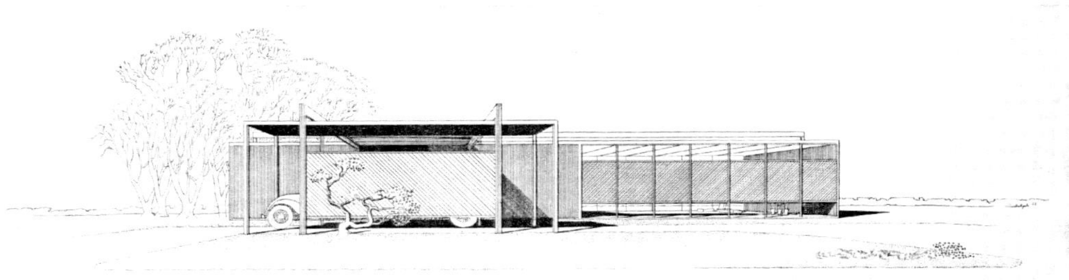

6.3
Paul Rudolph, Wilson Residence, Sarasota, Florida, elevation, 1953–1954

6.2 [opposite page]
Paul Rudolph, Hook Guest House, Siesta Key, Sarasota, Florida, aerial perspective, 1952–1953

In his continuing preoccupation with rational modular construction techniques, Rudolph experimented with a plywood vault in his 1951 unbuilt Knott Residence in Yankeetown, Florida, designing rhythmical roofs that exploited the bending characteristics of modern plywood in a manner akin to the curved planar hull of a ship. He first realized the plywood vault in the Hook Guest Residence (1952–1953) in Siesta Key, Florida **[Figure 6.2]**, which brought light and spatial expanse to the trabeated frame structure infilled with board siding panels and with fixed windows and operable jalousies.

Through the course of designing a number of simple post-and-beam houses in Florida, Rudolph followed modular proportions to facilitate the use of standardized infill windows and door panels. He explicitly embraced prefabricated structural honeycomb paper panels in the 1953–1954 Wilson Residence in Sarasota, Florida **[Figure 6.3]**. These low-cost four-foot-wide panels for doors and interior partitions, originally developed by the airline industry for use as lightweight bulkheads, were delivered to the site and assembled in one day. Promoted for their "amazing strength and durability," these panels, impregnated with a phenol resin, could withstand bugs, moisture, and rot, and resist the equivalent load of thirteen feet of snow.

For Rudolph, prefabrication would also facilitate the construction of entire residential units, which could be multiplied and then hung in clusters from high-rise structural frames. As early as 1953, he began sketching schemes composed of mobile home units plugged into a structural circulation and utility core.[7] As Sarasota School architect John Howey argues, ideas based on Rudolph's 1954 unbuilt tower scheme of a central core with office or residential units hung by cables in Sarasota would be realized in the majority of his late work including the Colonnade Condominiums, Singapore, 1980–1987.[8]

When Rudolph returned to the GSD to teach in 1954, one of his students was Fumihiko Maki. In his introduction to a 1968 Japanese monograph

[7] John Howey, *The Sarasota School of Architecture 1941–1966* (Cambridge, MA: MIT Press, 1995), 136–37.
[8] Ibid, p.137.

of Rudolph's work, Maki noted the resonance of Rudolph's early Florida houses with Japanese traditional residential design with its frame and prefabricated infill.[9] Maki had earlier served as Rudolph's guide around Japan during the 1960 World Design Conference in Tokyo. Maki and his classmates from Tokyo University, studying under Kenzo Tange, had launched the Metabolist Movement in 1960 as a kind of biomorphic interpretation of Archigram's Plug-In architecture.

The Metabolists' idea of a structure that would accommodate changeable, prefabricated units could be seen perhaps most explicitly in Kiyonori Kikutake's Sky House (1958) in Tokyo, which featured prefabricated "Movenetts" in the form of kitchen units, baths, and bedrooms hung from a concrete-frame structure. Rudolph would find resonance in both the Metabolists' work and the vernacular elements of simple greenhouses in Japan, which echoed the basic forms of his early houses.

In the years following his chairmanship at Yale, Rudolph also worked on prefabricated megastructural pursuits in parallel with Archigram and the Metabolists. In 1967, *Perspecta* 11 featured Rudolph's "Proposed Trailer Tower" **[Figure 6.6]** alongside projects and articles by "Amazing Archigram," commentary on Buckminster Fuller, Moshe Safdie's Habitat '67 under construction, Component Housing by Noriaki ("Kisho") Kurokawa, Le Corbusier's "Plug-in" Housing System Proposal from 1948, Tange's Yamanashi Broadcasting System, and a prefabricated ski cabin unit from G. Komatsu Industrial Design Associates.[10] The Trailer Tower was Rudolph's megastructural plug-in scheme, rising from the American context. In contrast to the heavy concrete slabs of the Art and Architecture Building

6.4
Paul Rudolph, Graphic Arts Center, model perspective
© Ezra Stoller/Esto

[9] Fumihiko Maki, "Poohru rudorufu ni tsuite," *Paul Rudolph,* Tokyo: Bijutsu shuppansha, 1968, p. 6.
[10] *Perspecta* 11 (1967) reflected interests in future urbanism by co-editors Peter de Bretteville and Arthur Golding through a portfolio of 29 projects.

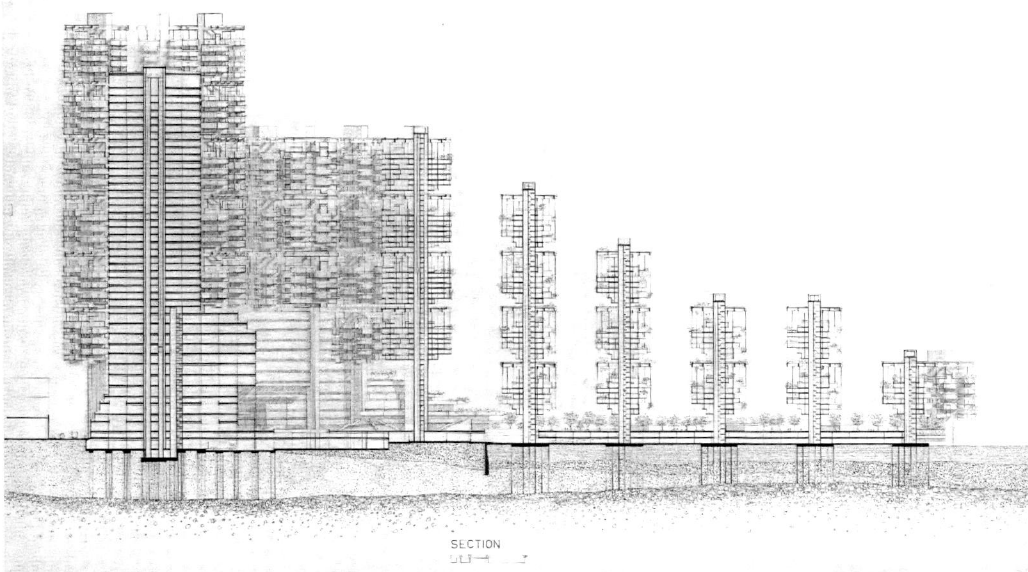

6.5
Paul Rudolph, Graphic Arts Center, section

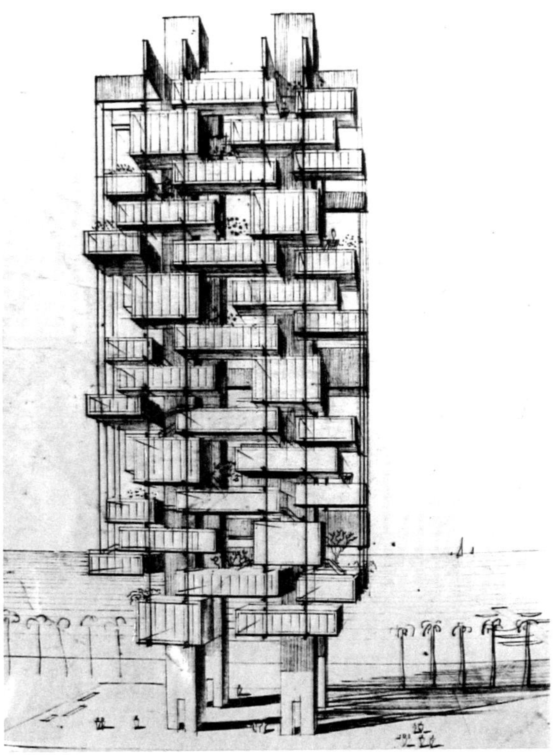

6.6
Paul Rudolph, Proposed Trailer Tower, perspective

at Yale, Rudolph turned to lightweight manufactured trailer units to be suspended from a megastructural tower. Writing in *Perspecta,* he said:

"For a number of years now I have felt that one way around the housing impasse would be to utilize either mobile houses or truck vans placed in such a way that the roof of one unit provides the terrace for the one above. Of course the essence of this is to utilize existing three-dimensional prefabricated units of light construction originally intended as moving units but adapted to fixed situations and transformed into architecturally acceptable living units. One approach would be to utilize vertical hollow tubes, probably rectangular in section, 40 or 50 stories in height to accommodate stairs, elevators, and mechanical services, and to form a support for cantilever trusses at the top. These cantilever trusses would give a "sky hook" from which the three-dimensional unit could be hoisted into place and plugged into its vertical mechanical core."[11]

Rudolph's Trailer Tower sought to transform the mobile home industry in the United States at this time in the late 1960s. *Architectural Record* concurred, featuring Rudolph's work under the title, "The Mobile Home is the 20th Century Brick,"

"The mobile home industry leads the low-cost housing field. The Mobile Homes Manufacturers Association now claims approximately one out of every four single-family housing starts. Rudolph believes that, given the opportunity to properly design, upgrade and test its product as the basic unit for a project of the magnitude of the Graphic Arts Center **[Figure 6.4, 6.5]**, the mobile home industry could become the leader in lightweight steel box frame technology, meeting this nation's and the world's great need for handsome, well-engineered low-cost dwelling units."[12]

Architectural Record continued, underscoring the primary imperatives of mobile home construction for speed, economy, and urban impact:

"The industry therefore realizes it must redesign for higher densities, while upgrading quality for wider public acceptance. Only 15 percent of mobile homes are ever moved once they reach their initial site. Their interest to Rudolph is not mobility—his, of course, are designed without the standard chassis, wheels, and brakes. The single unit's appeal is as a mass-produced, fully furnished, ready-to-occupy dwelling hauled from factory to site as a ready-to-position unit. The advantage is in quantity buying of components and quick erection, thus lower cost."[13]

For Rudolph, this trailer measuring between 12 and 14 feet wide and 59 feet long was the new "brick," with dimensions that he noted were legally established, but also a familiar measuring device,[14]

"I am very interested in these twentieth-century bricks . . . because I believe that urban design basically needs environmental building elements with distinctive scale. Certainly it is possible to express the housing scale by means of these prefabricated units—twentieth-century bricks. But instead of thinking of them as a new method, we must consider them materials that make possible the expression of humanity through variety. Moshe Safdie's Habitat ('67) was based on this idea, but unfortunately it was not related to ordinary cost standards, as is clear from the fact that it was seven or eight times as expensive as general building projects."[15]

For Rudolph, "Architecturally, the vertical dimension is the most important, and this has the possibility of turning a scale-less high-rise apartment building into a vertical village."[16] In essence, he multiplied the Trailer Tower to fill up an entire district of Lower Manhattan off of the West Side Highway for the Graphic Arts Center (1967–1968). This multipurpose megastructure called for the construction of 4,050 dwelling units above seven floors of 200,000 square feet each for legal and financial printers. Rather than being caged like the units of his Archigram

[11] "Proposed Trailer Tower, " *Perspecta* 11, 1967, p. 191.
[12] "The Mobile Home is the 20th Century Brick," *Architectural Record,* April 1968, p. 137.
[13] Ibid, p. 137.
[14] Rudolph wrote, "After I found out how expensive prefabrication can be, I turned my attention to the trailer industry. At present 30 percent of American residences are trailers. And it is noteworthy that architects and structural designers have had absolutely nothing to do with this development. The very volume of the individual trailer is not determined by an architect but by highway technicians who say that the trailer body must not exceed the dimension 12 feet wide, 59 feet long, and 9 feet high." Paul Rudolph, "The Nature of Prefabricated System Design," *Japan Architect,* January–February 1971, p. 20.
[15] Paul Rudolph, "The Nature of Prefabricated System Design," *Japan Architect,* January–February 1971, p. 20.
[16] Paul Rudolph, "Conversation at 23 Beekman Place [with Peter Blake, ca. 1996]," in Roberto de Alba, *Paul Rudolph The Late Work* (New York: Princeton Architectural Press, 2003), 207.
[17] Tony Monk, *The Art and Architecture of Paul Rudolph* (West Sussex: Wiley & Sons, 1999), 69.
[18] The Mobile Home is the 20th Century Brick," *Architectural Record,* April 1968, p. 145.
[19] Rudolph, Paul Marvin, 1918–1997. "Revere House Grouping," *Architectural Forum* 89 (December 1948): 28.

and Metabolist colleagues, Rudolph's capsules were hung.

From the proposed 26 service cores, cantilevered steel trusses carried 10 stories each by steel cables encased in concrete. Once hoisted by hydraulic lifts, the mobile units were attached to the main truss and then joined to adjacent sections and to the central core tower. The units formed a pinwheel, the dynamic design strategy in Frank Lloyd Wright's Cloverleaf Quadruple Housing Project (1942) planned for Pittsfield, Massachusetts, which created a sculptural effect and reduced the scale of its high-rise incarnation. With the main pedestrian concourse on the third level, the visionary megastructure featured pierlike decks with traffic-free streets, an elementary school, community center, swimming pool, marina, and a series of restaurants and shops. However, as Rudolph noted, "because of the changes in NYC's government this proposal remained a splendid and imaginative concept that was never implemented."[17]

While Rudolph literally used brick in his 1960 Married Student Housing at Yale, which both added scale and continuity to the housing units and the courtyards they defined, he sought to engage the mobile home industry to produce Married Student Housing at the University of Virginia in 1967 **[Figure 6.7]** with "tip-outs," or "roll-outs," which allowed the living units to be expanded to accommodate additional functions. Perhaps not surprisingly, however, city officials vetoed the proposal, deeming the progressive scheme inappropriate for the Jeffersonian character of Charlottesville.[18]

Back in New Haven around 1968, however, Rudolph gained the support of Mayor Richard Lee, noted for his efforts to halt urban decline and turn New Haven into a "model city," to realize Rudolph's trailer-based urbanism as HUD-financed housing. Sponsored by the black fraternal organization Oriental Lodge No. 6, Prince Hall Masons, Rudolph's Oriental Masonic Gardens **[Figures 6.8–6.12]** was composed of 333 modules forming 148 townhouse units of low- to moderate-income housing on fifteen acres of land on Wilmot Road in northwest New Haven. Built for approximately 3.5 million dollars, the housing complex recalled Italian hilltowns that Rudolph had admired during his European travels on Harvard's Wheelwright Fellowship in the late 1940s, as well as Wright's Cloverleaf Housing Project. Oriental Masonic Gardens also continued ideas from Rudolph's 1948 Revere Development in Siesta Key, Florida, where he had proposed an urban grouping of prototypical houses to connect the ideals of his single-family detached Florida houses on an urban scale "to relieve the monotony of too much repetition and still keep within economic bounds . . . [as an exciting] real and urgent architectural problem."[19] Rudolph's Oriental Masonic Gardens project almost immediately followed Habitat '67, Moshe Safdie's

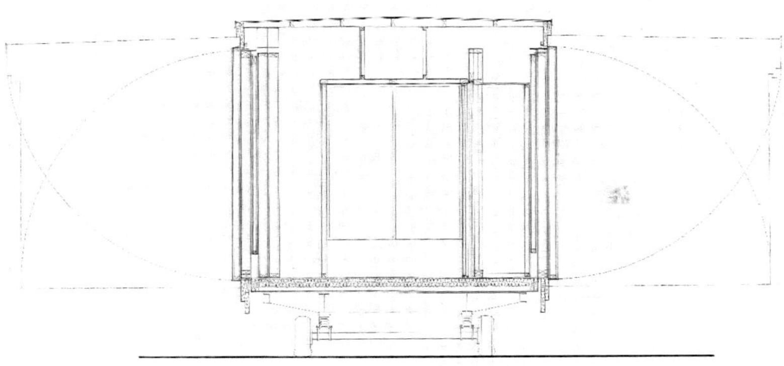

6.7
Paul Rudolph, Married Student Housing, University of Virginia, Charlottesville, Virginia, 1967

6.8 [next spread]
Paul Rudolph, Oriental Masonic Gardens, New Haven, Connecticut, aerial perspective, 1968–1971

16A

interlocking precast concrete housing scheme, and Safdie and Rudolph had each presented different types of prefabricated schemes during this period for the unbuilt Fort Lincoln Housing project in Washington, D.C. (1968).

Continuing his affinity for the sculptural aesthetic of suspended pinwheel schemes affording maximum light and views, the metal-framed wood construction residences were grouped in fours around a utility core. The modules, each 12 feet wide by 27, 39, or 51 feet long, were factory-assembled with plumbing, wiring and finishes outside of Baltimore and then trucked to New Haven. The lower module of each townhouse unit contained living spaces and the second module set above had two or three bedrooms. While half of the units contained three bedrooms, four- and five-bedroom units were made possible through the addition of a third module parallel to the lower one. For Rudolph, the three-dimensional pinwheel composition of the modules formed outdoor rooms, facilitating the roofs to be used as terraces and the spaces underneath as sheltered outdoor space for each family.

In 1972, *The New York Times* highlighted the apparent success of Rudolph's scheme in an article titled, "Thanks to Prefabs, Out of the Slums and Into Their Own Co-ops."[20] This was indeed a rosy picture, illustrated by the unit of resident Abraham Flynn, who, as noted in the caption, "painted his living room five shades of red and hung fishnet from the vaulted ceiling." Reporter Rita Reif explained that the resident population, which was 75 percent black, 15 percent white, and 10 percent Puerto Rican, with 40 percent of the residents on welfare, "had a pride of ownership and sense of community involvement . . . evident [in it being] meticulously maintained." She continued, "The vaulted roofs, picture and clerestory windows, fenced yards, and staggered stacking in T-shape arrangements of the modules make the development look far less like a railroad yard than so many communities of factory-built, trailer-type housing do." She added, "In all the houses, the noise level is surprisingly low." The rents ranged from $118 to $263 a month, and 20 percent of the residents received a federal rent supplement.

The article concluded, however, with the subtitle, "Some Questions Still Remain." Namely, residents complained about high electricity bills, about 50 percent more than for comparably sized apartments. In the end, the final cost for the units was between $21,000 and $23,000, close to the cost of a conventionally constructed house. In reality, the ideal of factory-produced housing reduced on-site labor costs, but this savings was offset by high transportation costs of nearly $500,000.[21] While the modules were trucked 250 miles from Maryland, the plywood vaults made in Connecticut had to be shipped to and from Maryland.[22] Moreover, modular plants serving a wide geographic area had to be modified for local code variations, which also added to the cost. In this case, the need to address regional conditions was less about the climate and more about navigating regional bureaucracy of rules and regulations. Rudolph admitted that the greatest problems arose on the construction site to address non-conforming situations and "a great deal more simplification is needed in the use of trailer units."[23]

Rudolph's experience highlights the general major factors preventing the acceptance of so-called mobile homes: negative cultural perceptions as lower-class dwellings by the general population and confusion as to whether they are "personal property" or "real estate." According to a 1968 survey, taxes on mobile homes based on different methods of assessment ranged from $20 to more than $200.[24] In general, the lower cost of mobile homes resulted in lower assessments than those on equally desirable conventional housing, with tax revenues not necessarily correlating to actual tax expenditures on civic services provided.

Problems at Oriental Masonic Gardens escalated. In 1979, the *New Haven Journal-Courier* reported, "Persistent Leaks Just One Problem at Oriental Gardens."[25] As the editor noted, "It began as a co-op, but stapled walls, no foundations, leaky roofs and electrically caused fires spelled trouble for the 'boxcar' settlement called Oriental Gardens." It had become a co-op shortly after construction in 1971, but "ceased being such when it could no longer

[20] Rita Reif, "Thanks to Prefabs, Out of the Slums and Into Their Own Co-ops," *The New York Times,* February 11, 1972.
[21] Peter Bilodeau, "Persistent Leaks Just One Problem at Oriental Gardens," *New Haven Journal Courier,* March 9, 1979.
[22] "Twentieth- Century Bricks," *The Architectural Forum,* June 1972, p. 50.
[23] Paul Rudolph, "The Nature of Prefabricated System Design," *Japan Architect,* January–February 1971, p. 20.
[24] "Facelift for Mobile Homes?" *Design and Environment* 3 (1972), pp. 42–46.
[25] Peter Bilodeau, "Persistent Leaks Just One Problem at Oriental Gardens," *New Haven Journal Courier,* March 9, 1979.
[26] Rudolph's remarks on the Oriental Masonic Gardens included in the posthumous article "Rethinking Designs in the 60s," *Perspecta*

pay its mortgage." "Roof leaks, roaches, and mice" were the three problems most cited by residents. In addition, the concrete posts, rather than full foundations, reportedly resulted in soaked floors when it rained, and many exposed pipes froze in winter. A former board president of the Oriental Gardens co-op noted the lack of fire escapes and that leaks caused electrical fires in the walls. Moreover, the project suffered from rampant vandalism, from animals and residents themselves who reportedly "were mainly single women with children who became difficult to supervise."

Rudolph himself noted late in his life that:

"The whole notion of making a project for about 150 people using trailers was difficult to persuade anybody to do. I suppose it was a mistake; it was eventually demolished. People hated it. First of all it leaked, which is a very good reason to hate something, but I think it was much more complicated than that. Psychologically, the good folk who inhabited these dwellings thought that they were beneath them. In other words, the deviation of the dwelling was not something to their liking. I thought, and I suppose the mayor thought, that trailers were perfectly good enough for them. . . . I am very tenacious about certain things, and in the long run it seems to me that with the correcting of mistakes one can make something much more successful."[26]

Following his early interest in the open and closed systems of prefabrication in traditional Japanese dwellings, Rudolph returned to Japan in 1970 to lecture on "the twentieth-century brick" while also judging the 1970 Misawa Homes Prefabricated House International Design Competition. Through connections with former Yale student Tsukasa Yamashita, Rudolph received his first important commission in East Asia to design the Daiei House & Company Office Building (1971) in Nagoya, an exhibition space for home-buying customers and offices for many of the company's staff.

In 1980, Rudolph received a commission to design 100 condominiums in Singapore in which he realized the formal composition of his Graphic Arts Center scheme for New York. Although the 24-story tower employs a conventional in-situ reinforced-concrete frame, the cantilevered beams carry the large terraces and projecting bedrooms much like the Graphic Arts Center scheme. In contrast to Rudolph's earlier, low-income housing, this was for an exclusive clientele who could afford to have eight units per floor, high ceilings, double-story balconies, and mezzanine galleries.

Rudolph lectured on the prefabrication of "twentieth-century brick" as the basis for his design pursuits up to the end of his career, and this aspiration did not go unnoticed by some of his Yale students, including Stanley Tigerman, as seen in his 1960 thesis project for housing incorporating precast concrete, and Richard Rogers and Norman Foster. As Foster has noted,

"In 1961 Paul Rudolph was the main reason that I chose to go to Yale University for the masters course in architecture. . . . Many of (his) drawings, especially the perspective sections, would encapsulate in a single image the range of Rudolph's concerns as an architect. . . . his explorations into modularity and the potential of prefabrication—a later interest in high-density urban mega-structures."[27]

The resurgence of interest in prefabrication today underscores the importance of Rudolph's pioneering work.[28] Techniques of digital fabrication have indeed opened new possibilities for prefabrication as a method of construction as common as brick. The biggest impediments to realizing prefabrication as the twenty-first-century brick are not technical, but rather perceptual and procedural—such as the stronghold of construction unions, the mandates of local building codes, and a complicated system of subcontractors. Nonetheless, as realized in Rudolph's work and that of his students and his contemporaries around the world, prefabrication is technically possible. As Rudolph himself noted,

"The history of architecture has often been written when the techniques intended for one phase of human activity have been adapted for another."[29]

29, 1998, pp. 1–97.

[27] Tony Monk, *The Art and Architecture of Paul Rudolph* (West Sussex: Wiley & Sons, 1999), p. 4.

[28] In 1997, Oriental Masonic Gardens was a critical case study for the manufactured housing studio taught by Carol Burns at the GSD where students sought to redesign the mobile home. The 2006 exhibition "Out of the Box: Design Innovations in Manufactured Housing" at the Field Museum in Chicago also highlighted the specific redesign of the mobile home "brick" and included studio-SUMO's "Minimax," David Khouri's "Packed House," and Parallel Design's "house nine." Even Herzog and de Meuron's housing tower at 56 Leonard Street for Manhattan could be seen to recall Rudolph's Graphic Arts Center in its composition of units attached to a superstructure.

6.9 [above]
Paul Rudolph, Oriental Masonic Gardens, New Haven, Connecticut, 1968–1971
© Massachusetts Institute of Technology, photograph by G. E. Kidder Smith

6.10 [below]
Paul Rudolph, Oriental Masonic Gardens, New Haven, Connecticut, 1968–1971

6.11–6.12
Paul Rudolph, Oriental Masonic Gardens, New Haven, Connecticut, 1968–1971

THE INTERIOR

Unhabituated Architecture

Sylvia Lavin

7.1
Paul Rudolph, Edersheim Residence, New York City, library, 1970
© Oberto Gili

Paul Rudolph once described his work as ranging from Christmas lights to megastructures.[1] He was presumably referring, on the one hand, to a small series of theatrical decors done mostly for New York City residential interiors that are virtually unknown, despite an increase in Rudolph studies, and in which he often used miscellaneous and as-found materials, from subway grating to holiday decorations. **[Figure 7.1]** The term megastructure, on the other, explicitly points to the very large buildings that Rudolph constructed throughout the world, mostly in concrete and for which he is very well known.[2] While the antipodes of this range are extreme in comparison to the house-to-tower range that typified the portfolio of successful mid-century professional architects, Rudolph's claim of mastery over such vastly dissimilar tasks belongs comfortably within the paradigm of the modern architect who can, in theory, design anything from the spoon to the city. In fact, the exaggerated contrast between a Christmas tree light and a megastructure underscores Rudolph's attachment to the modern mythology of the architect as total designer. The statement, made by Rudolph in an effort to shape his legacy, was clearly intended as a gauntlet challenging the historian to bridge the gap Rudolph himself staked out and to make of this prodigious diversity a single oeuvre expressing the masterful voice of one author.

Describing these extremes as belonging to a single continuum, however, does not make them so. In fact, megastructures and Christmas lights can just as easily be described as wholly incomparable phenomena sitting across an impassable divide made not only by size but also by the systems of command and control through which they are produced and assigned cultural value. Both are made of industrially produced materials, for example, but those used in the apartments to which Rudolph was referring were determined not by large economies of scale but by haphazard discoveries in a flea market, the incongruous misuse of stationery supplies as ornament, and imitation assembly-line fabrication. **[Figure 7.2]** And if Christmas-light architecture and megastructures therefore belong to fundamentally different orders of things, Rudolph's oeuvre, if such a term of false coherence has any remaining legitimacy, is in fact more important to history if understood as made of inconsistent parts. To write a history of the domain defined by the weightless ephemerality of lights hung about as if for a holiday is, through its very discontinuity with canonical narratives of Modern architecture, to write a history of forms of design and experience that disregard the architectural values of standardization and efficiency established as universal by the dominant discourses of Modernism.[3] Regardless of what Rudolph himself said, the procedures through which odds and ends picked up on the street are procured and deployed as architecture are anathema to the regimes of centralized control and predictable outcomes intrinsic to the construction of large Modern buildings. The minor architecture of Christmas lights is therefore an anomaly—its own tiny territory of disruptive speculation and experimentation – and, by virtue of its exceptional status, a provocation to resist the urge to construct historical narratives by imposing coherence on everything.[4]

In scientific terms, an experiment that does not produce hypotheses which can be maintained in different contexts and which cannot be repeated is a failure. Rudolph's Christmas-light projects are few and yielded virtually no material suited for other projects. The Edersheim Residence, the early phases of his own Beekman Place apartment and the Elman Residence—all in New York and done between 1967 and 1971—are, literally, spectacular failures, unwitting masterpieces of a minor architectural typology. These anomalies are characterized by monolithic material palettes: allover shag carpet and extensive mirrors; extreme plays of luminous grisaille; crowded agglomerations of surfaces and furnishings; and mass-produced materials used in an artisanal fashion that mimics assembly-line production **[Figure 7.3]**: tape cut and stuck repeatedly on windows, mirrors applied one at a time, again and again, and projectors intended for the board room redeployed as décor for the living room. The bricolage of new materials used in cross-purposed ways produced dense, distracting and highly variable optical effects, the kind of

[1] The comment was made in "Nineteen Questions to Paul Rudolph," *A+U* 75, no. 1 (January 1975): 140.

[2] There is a growing contemporary literature on the history of the megastructure, but in the 1970s, the term would have been most strongly associated with Reyner Banham's book, *Megastructure – Urban Futures of the Recent Past* (London: Thames and Hudson, 1976).

[3] For a discussion of the importance of discontinuities in the construction of historical narratives, see Carlos Ginzburg, "Microhistory – Two or Three Things That I Know About It," *Threads and Traces* (Los Angeles: University of California Press, 2012), 193–227.

[4] My use of the term "minor architecture" refers to Deleuze and Guattari's notion of minor literature. Their idea that a minor literature deterritorializes the major language is useful for understanding the historical situation of these projects by Rudolph. Rudolph, for the most part, deployed architecture in support of the dominant

7.2
Paul Rudolph, 23 Beekman Place Residence, New York City, seating detail, c. 1970
© Oberto Gili

effect Rudolph explicitly deemed psychological rather than architectural, appropriate to a painting by Van Gogh and not to an architectural design.[5] Further evidence of the fact that these projects fall outside what Rudolph himself considered architecture is that he neither drew them in the style of his fame-making renderings, nor organized them around building materials such as concrete or dry wall or through spatial disposition and structural expression. They lack what he, and most other architects of the period, understood as the constituent elements of architecture.

Rudolph explained these deficiencies by arguing that only large-scale buildings allow architects to deal with structure, whereas the small scale of interiors requires designers to focus on physiological and psychological issues.[6] But Rudolph's explanation, which relies on oppositions between public and private, between interior and exterior, is not entirely satisfactory, since other interiors he designed of the same period—the Steichen apartment (1973–1974) or the Dean Residence (1969)—are structurally expressive and depend on complex spatial planning for their effects, characteristics that earned high praise in the architectural press. The "Christmas-light" misfires, on the other hand, depended largely on optical effects and were described in the press as trifles, as but a decorator's new interest in "White on White," for example.[7] Some of these frivolities proved surprisingly durable despite their flimsy materials. As buildings like the Orange County Government Center intended to be permanent face demolition, interiors like the Edersheim apartment remain unscathed, their unexpected longevity perhaps due to the fact that they were never "built" in the first place. Rudolph himself said that "architecture does not exist unless it is built" so according to his own logic, these interiors that were held together with tape, Christmas lights and Mylar, can barely be said to have existed, certainly not as architecture proper. To the contrary, they exemplify everything that Rudolph thought was wrong with experimental architecture, which he described as "too subject to fashion, whims, and the media, and

culture, but these projects worked against that majority. On the concept of minority, see Gilles Deleuze, Félix Guattari, and Robert Brinkley: What Is a Minor Literature?" *Mississippi Review,* Vol. 11, No. 3, Essays Literary Criticism (Winter/Spring, 1983),pp. 13–33.

5 Rudolph explicitly contrasts his drawings, which seek to empirically represent architectural reality, to Van Gogh's interiors, which use the representation of architecture to evoke psychological conditions, in his introduction to *Paul Rudolph, Drawings* (London: Lund Humphries, 1974).

6 Interview with Peter Blake in Roberto de Alba's *Paul Rudolph: The Late Work,* (New York City: Princeton Architectural Press: 2003), 202.

7 "Foreshadowing a future of white-on-white, its optical surprises" is the caption given to three photographs by Ezra Stoller of Rudolph's Beekman Place apartment in *House Beautiful* (September 1967):148–49.

7.3
Paul Rudolph, Elman Residence, New York City, industrial lighting detail, 1971
© Oberto Gili

too concerned with substituting peripheral fields . . . for the real study of architecture and its limitation."[8]

There were apparently two different architects named Paul Rudolph, one concerned with upholding Modern architectural proprieties and the other operating in a contradictory realm located outside the limits of architecture, a realm filled with fashion sense and whimsicality. Not only were the architectural concerns associated with each zone contradictory, but they produced and relied on contradictory understandings of the architect and of the user/inhabitant—in other words, on contradictory understandings of the way in which architecture turned individuals into subjects. One relied on a space determined by an architect who operated according to the predictable and calculable logic of structure, and the other on a space determined by an architect who experimented with the unpredictable logic of desire. Given that his own apartment ultimately contained both zones, Rudolph might be said to have experimented on himself, dividing his person into two kinds of subjects. This division has been understood in relation to Rudolph's hidden homosexuality but it is not just the closet that is at stake here.[9] Christmas-light architecture more broadly, calls into question what Reyner Banham called the profession's "Black Box," the habits of mind that establish architecture's sense of itself. However unintentionally, these whimsical "surface jobs," projects that *Domus* described as covering up architecture rather than constituting architecture, untethered Rudolph from the overwhelmingly comprehensive and hence alienating systems the idea of a megastructure relied on.[10]

Christmas trees differ from megastructures in abundant and obvious ways, but two important to note in this context are that they use the intermittent nature of illumination to intrude upon and momentarily transform preexisting and often familiar spaces and they tend to be produced in ways determined by the quixotic pathways of sentiment rather than systematic habits of mind. A Christmas tree, in other words, provokes a media happening to unfold in an existing architectural setting. Happenings are largely defined by the fact that they do not follow a script, making their unplanned character precisely the kind of thing that belonged outside Banham's black box of the mental habits of architecture, planning being chief among them. In fact, Rudolph may have been led to pursue this form of experiment not by a gay client but by the Ford Foundation which, in 1962, decided to encourage architects to explore the way new forms of performance had changed theater.[11] Rudolph was one of eight architects selected by the foundation to produce an ideal theater, and his scheme stands out from the rest for being the only one to focus on combining live action with film and projected images. **[Figure 7.4]** Indeed, it went much farther than merely accommodating film by imagining that projection technology would dominate the architecture: the exterior silhouette reveals these new pieces of equipment pushing up and out to create a complex skyline, and the interior auditorium was to have been covered by projections to the degree that what would normally be considered walls, ceilings, and floors would have lost these architectural identities. Instead, they would have become generators of an intermittently visible mise-en-scène wherein the elements of architectural reality—its limitations—would be transformed into virtual images mingling with live actors and audience, generating what the theater and architecture critic C. Ray Smith called a confounding synthesis of media.[12]

Rudolph pursued the incorporation of projection technology even when there was no theater program to use as an excuse and even when there were no actual projection devices. In the Elman Residence, for example, the conventional clock over the mantle was replaced by images of numerals that kept time when the projector on the opposite side of the room changed slides. Less analog and more virtual projection effects were achieved by making the interiors operate as projection devices rather than as merely containers for the mechanical equipment itself. Wide-screen crosscurrents of light and color were

[8] "Nineteen Questions to Paul Rudolph," *A+U* 75, no. 1 (January 1975): 140.

[9] On this topic, see Timothy Rohan's excellent essay, 'Rendering the Surface: Paul Rudolph's Art and Architecture Building at Yale', *Grey Room* 1 (Autumn 2000), 84–107.

[10] See Banham's essay, "The Black Box: The Secret Profession of Architecture" in Mary Banham (ed), *A Critic Writes: Essays by Reyner Banham* (Berkeley, CA: University of California Press, 1996), 292–300. See also *Domus,* 502 September 1971, 30–32.

[11] In 1962, the Ford Foundation sponsored a competition on the ideal contemporary theater. The projects were ultimately circulated by the American Federation of Arts in an exhibition called "The Ideal Theater: Eight Concepts," which was designed by Peter Larkin.

[12] The Ford Foundation competition was the principal subject of the February 1962 issue of *Progressive Architecture.* For C. Ray Smith's comments and the description of Rudolph's project, see both "Rehousing the Drama," *Progressive Architecture* 43 (February 1962): 96–100, 110–11. See also, *Progressive Architecture* (December 1961, vol. 42): p. 49, 51–53.

created by setting Plexiglas sheets at angles like stage wings that projected colored light into adjacent spaces. These forms of luminosity appeared both to be independent of any architectural apparatus and to catch the human figure within their midst. And, like an electric projector, these interiors have the dramatic ephemerality of phenomena that turn on and off with the flick of a switch. The surfaces are covered in self-evident, superficial appliqués of ephemeral material—visitors to the Edersheim apartment were surprised that the tape Rudolph used didn't immediately peel off the windows. The shag carpet that covered virtually everything guaranteed, as Walter Benjamin said of Victorian plush, that human traffic would always leave behind a temporary trace. Cinematic special effects abounded, with furniture floating around like flying saucers and the perception of depth interrupted by reflections or curves or continuous materials that inhibit any fading away of intensity towards the viewer's peripheral vision—one's eye never escaped the constantly shifting scene. Unlike architecture proper, which operates with ontological durability, here an ambient interior is conjured like a magic trick with unknown causes.

The delicate interior became a strong idea during the 1960s when its capacity to be held loosely together by non-architectural means permitted it to serve as a venue for the convergence of architecture and a whole series of other media, from interior decoration and installation art to environments and film, as well as a place to explore the new ranges of time, from the merely durable to the instantly obsolete, that the post-war world had invented. No longer simply the residual effect of architecture, the interior gained autonomy from architecture's various master narratives and total design dictates. Indeed, the Christmas-light projects are more profitably compared to the work of product designers or installation artists than to the work of other architects because they expose the impact of what Rudolph may have dismissively called peripheral fields, but what today we can better describe as fields not compelled to adhere to architecture's protocols. For example, despite much commonality in the emphasis on lighting or the repurposing of found objects, Rudolph was more interested in the continuity of visual and optical effects than was the Italian industrial designer Joe Colombo, who remained focused on the design of products and their arrangement.

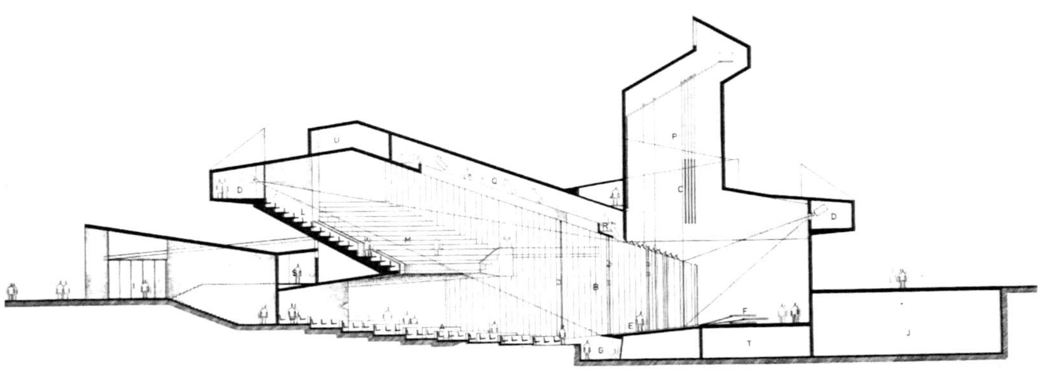

7.4
Paul Rudolph, Ford Foundation Theater, section, 1960

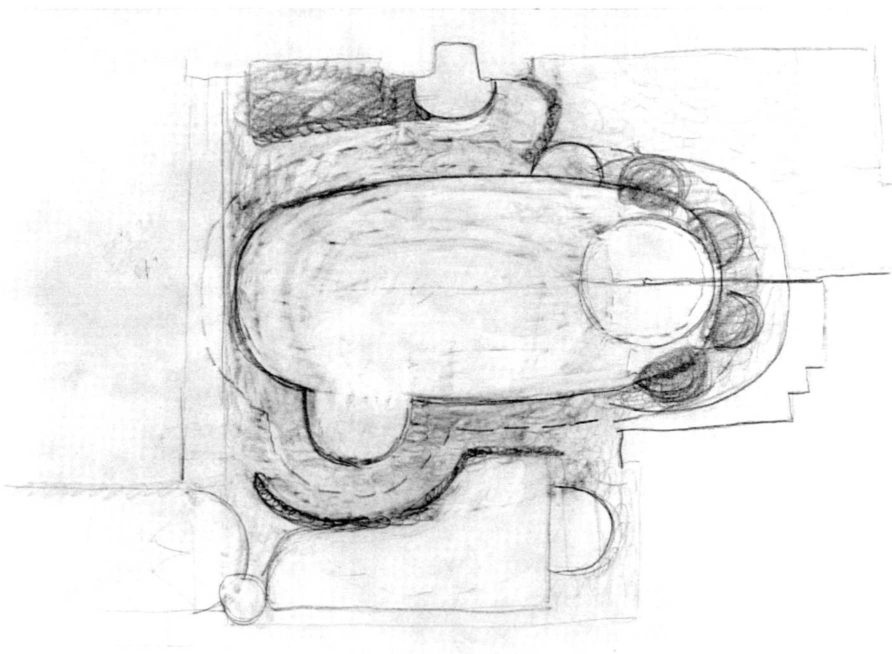

7.5
Paul Rudolph, 23 Beekman Place Residence, New York City, sketch, c. 1965

Colombo's interiors had blank spots, so to speak, whereas Rudolph's liquid mercury poured into every crevice, filling them up with exaggerated luminosity. Perhaps Rudolph's work most closely paralleled that of the Danish furniture and interior designer Verner Panton, who used pattern and color rather than shades of brightness to produce consistently dense arrays of visual effects over continuously sculpted surfaces, or the photographer and lighting designer Billy Name who used nothing but silver to fill the complete volume of the Warhol Factory's inside with "interiorness."[13]

Panton, although an architecture student, did not become an architect, and Name opted to follow no proper profession at all, so their neglect of architecture's sense of propriety, while perhaps naïve, is not transgressive in disciplinary terms. Rudolph, however, had to knowingly abandon architectural verities in order to unleash the interior, because it is not that interiors have no structure, as Rudolph argued, but that they can weaken the heroic epistemological certainty of structure itself. Key evidence for this lies in the ways Rudolph drew, the activity that everyone from Leon Battista Alberti to Banham has defined as the primary way architects identify as architects and identify their work as architecture. First, no drawings appear to have been made for the Christmas-light projects even though Rudolph was more than adept at drawing interiors, as his markedly detailed renderings demonstrate. Second, Rudolph always—and only—produced these renderings when he understood the project at hand as properly architectural. Not drawing and not considering the Christmas-light projects as architecture are conceptually parallel. Finally, the few times Rudolph drew when he was not designing/constructing/conceiving *ab ovo* but when he was encountering a ready-made container or architectural objet trouvé, as was the case in the New York interiors, he drew in a decidedly anomalous way **[Figure 7.5]**.

[13] For a more detailed comparison of these interiors, see my *Flash in the Pan* (London: Architectural Association Publications, 2014).

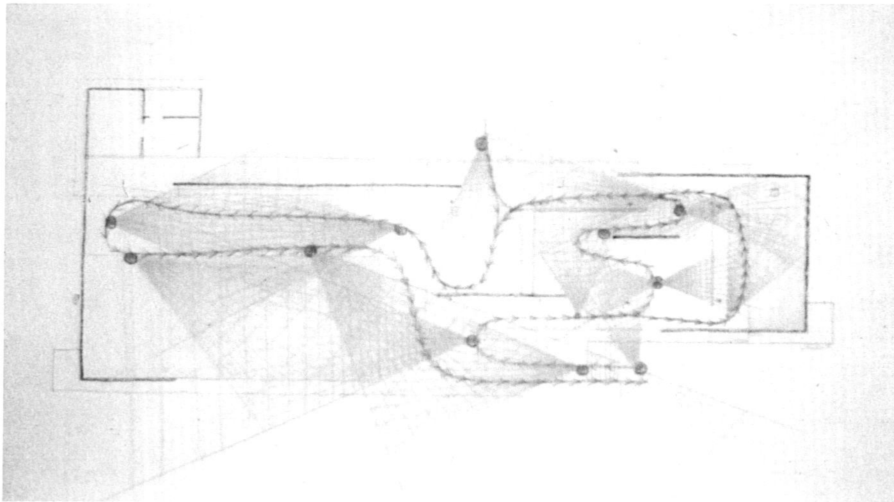

7.6
Paul Rudolph, Sketch of Barcelona Pavilion (Mies van der Rohe, Barcelona, Spain, 1929, reconstructed, 1986)

7.7
Paul Rudolph, Tuskegee Chapel, Tuskegee Institute, Tuskegee, Alabama, sketch, 1960–1969

7.8 [next spread]
Paul Rudolph, Tuskegee Chapel, Tuskegee Institute, Tuskegee, Alabama, plan, 1960–1969

Although much later than the Christmas-light projects, Rudolph made a series of drawings of what he called the reconstructed Barcelona Pavilion's "architectural magic."[14] Rudolph never actually drew the pavilion, although he expressed excitement and trepidation at finally seeing the "real building," and was enormously attentive to the veining and color of the marble. Rather, to a badly Xeroxed plan, he added a series of imaginary moving lights, reflections, lines of vision, and flows of space, as if these immaterial and mobile elements had literally filled up a pavilion that Mies van der Rohe had worked so hard to give an inside without an interior. **[Figure 7.6]** In the drawings, restless lines concoct not a building but a magic show of light, animation, and color that inhabit the pavilion without centrality or dominance. He said the interior was green, as if without color there would be no interior at all.

In his later work, Rudolph produced colored drawings of exteriors that also use what theorists of the Art Nouveau would have called "agitated lines" to express or give emotional poignancy to the perturbations of the atmosphere.[15] **[Figure 7.7]** But he is best known for the colorless if intricate renderings that, while crowded with quasi-photographic detail and often of sectional perspectives, which intrinsically emphasize interiority, implacably reveal nothing at all about the interior represented. The renderings make no effort to approximate the actual conditions anticipated in the structure, either in terms of spatial experience or visual character, and are instead, as Rudolph said, "fixed . . . ideal and completely unlike the building."[16] The drawings deploy a wide range of grays but deliberately exclude chiaroscuro or sfumato, the graphic equivalent to those "reflections" and "climatic conditions" that overwhelmingly establish the atmosphere of the decor. Indeed, Rudolph made a clear distinction between the inside of architecture, which he constructed through buildings and renderings, and the varying moods he associated with interiority, which he sketched and colored in an explicitly painterly manner, even when the moods and their sense of interior ambiences were outside.

The twinkly Christmas-light interiors are indeed painterly atmospheres that cannot be contained by the linear striations of Rudolph's dominant architectural manner but are arguably at their best in photographs. Veritable flashes in the pan, they turned the interior on, making it a place of significant, if ephemeral, architectural performance captured poorly by the techniques of traditional architectural drawing but well by lights-camera-action.[17] It is no wonder that the mark of their importance is not to be found in histories of architecture but rather in the parties that attracted Andy Warhol and writers for *The New Yorker's* "Talk of the Town."[18] This is no doubt not where Rudolph hoped his legacy would be made—Studio 54 was not Rudolph's hangout, even though Halston, Warhol, and his Superstars ultimately came to inhabit an apartment designed by him—but it is where an alternate, even anomalous, historical reality was shaped around unpredictable behaviors of architects, craftspeople, and inhabitants. Rudolph's Christmas-light architecture exemplifies all that he said was not architecture: whims, fashion, media, and even the periphery itself. While the zone outside the black box was intermittent, apparently trifling, and without historical duration, it was precisely these qualities that enable it to contain the traces of less subjectified habits of mind.

[14] These comments are on page 2 of the 16-page typewritten manuscript titled, "The Barcelona Pavilion, March 14, 1988 En route to Hong Kong," contained in the Rudolph Archive, Prints and Photographs Division, The Library of Congress.
[15] See, for example, his a so-called "energy study," for the Tuskegee Chapel, Tuskegee Institute, 1967–1969. These lines recall the linear agitation discussed by Wilhelm Worringer in his *Abstraction and Empathy: A Contribution to the Psychology of Style,* written as his doctoral thesis and first published in Germany in 1907.
[16] For Rudolph on his own approach to drawing, see his comments in *Paul Rudolph: Drawings,* Yukio Futagawa, ed., (Tokyo: ADA Edita, 1972). [Edition for 1974 published under title: *Paul Rudolph, architectural drawings.* See http://trove.nla.gov.au/work/21556427?q&versionId=25842673]
[17] On the idea of turned-on architecture, see "Instant Interiors," *Progressive Architecture* 48:6 (June 1967), 176–181 and "Projection: The New Turned-On Décor," *House Beautiful* 109:9 (1967), 130–32.
[18] Warhol's visit to a Rudolph interior is mentioned in George W. S. Trow, "Three Gatherings," The Talk of the Town, *The New Yorker* (30 January 1971): 22.

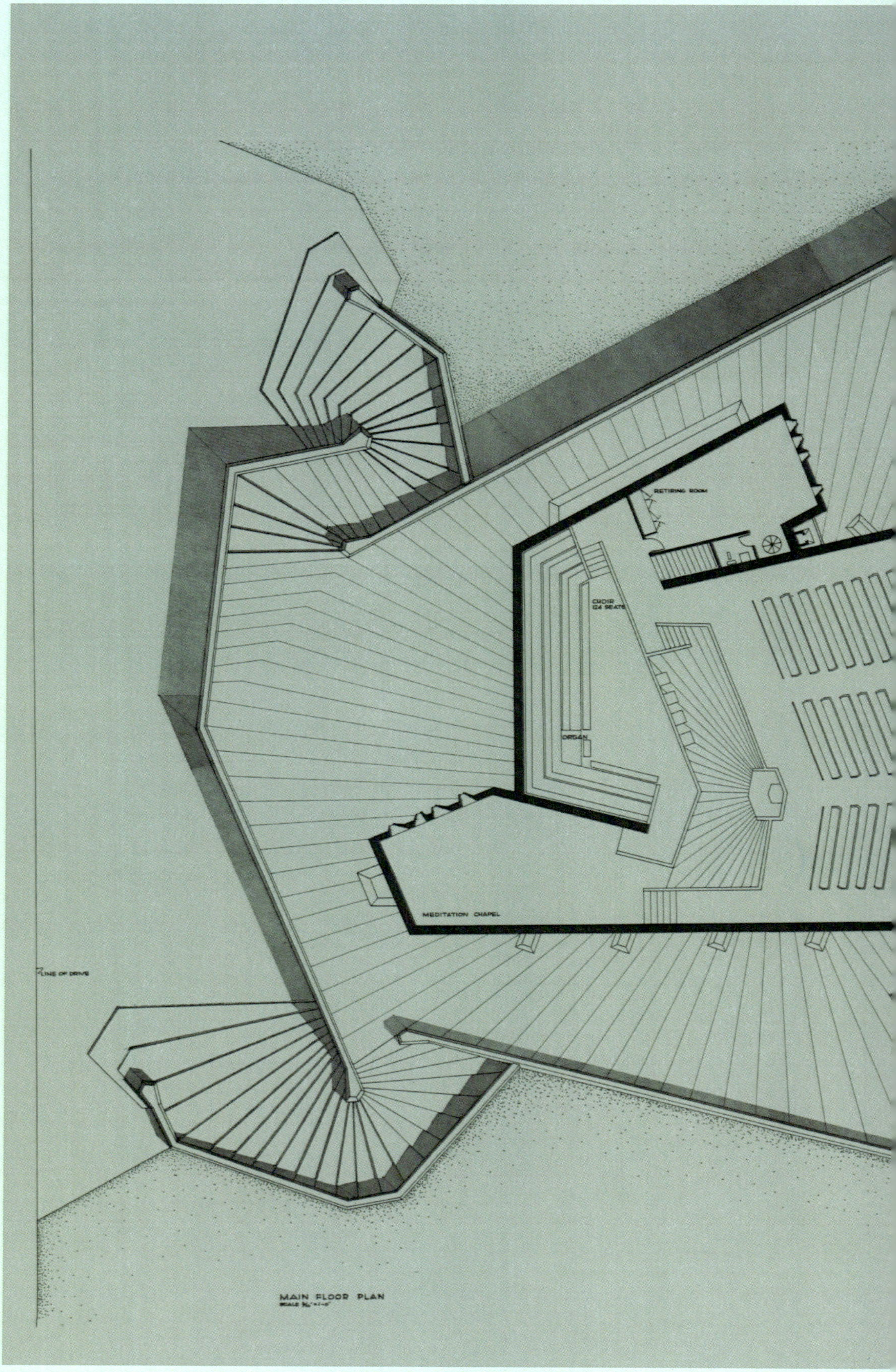
RETIRING ROOM
CHOIR
124 SEATS
ORGAN
MEDITATION CHAPEL
LINE OF DRIVE
MAIN FLOOR PLAN

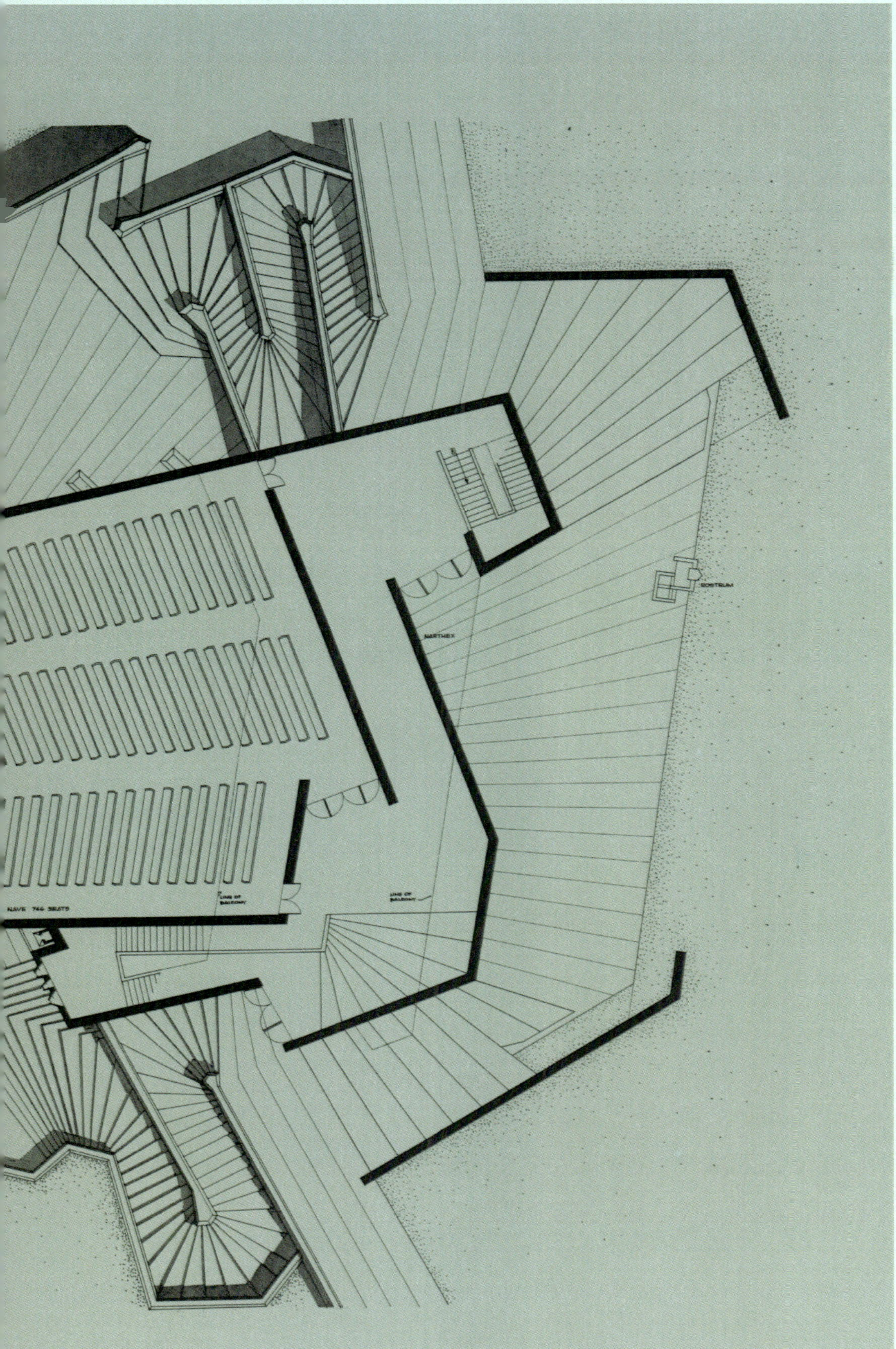
ROSTRUM
NARTHEX
NAVE 744 SEATS
LINE OF BALCONY
LINE OF BALCONY

Drawing as Signature: Paul Rudolph and the Perspective Section

Timothy M. Rohan

The perspective section is one of the most compelling types of architectural representation because it simultaneously reveals the structure of a building and its interior spaces. Though he certainly did not invent the perspective section, Paul Rudolph was its great popularizer during the 1960s; it is nearly impossible to open an American, European, or Japanese architectural journal from that decade and well into the next without finding a section by Rudolph or one of his admirers. The perspective section of Rudolph's most famed work, the Yale Art & Architecture Building (1958–1963), known as the A&A and renamed Rudolph Hall in 2008, is a striking depiction of spatial complexity executed in a labor-intensive manner, especially impressive today when rendering in ink is a thing of the past **[Figure 8.1]**.

Such drawings showcased Rudolph's draftsmanship, a skill he cultivated to make his reputation and for which he was much admired. Rudolph was regarded as a virtuoso for his design and drawing skills early in his career. Without blindly accepting such a characterization, identifying the attributes of Rudolph's virtuosity helps in understanding that it was also something he consciously constructed or designed. The distinctive signature note of Rudolph's draftsmanship was its many closely spaced parallel lines drawn by Rapidograph pen. They extend across almost every surface of the A&A Building rendering, signifying Rudolph's complete mastery and control of his structure. The technique related to Rudolph's other widely emulated architectural signature, the raised parallel ridges of the corrugated concrete walls he first developed for the A&A Building. Employed by him to the point where it became synonymous with him, the corrugated concrete treatment was his unique rendition of the *béton brut,* signifying Rudolph's originality.

The perspective section is still another of Rudolph's architectural signatures, the traits that his colleagues instantly associated with him, that gave him and his work a distinctive identity, and therefore helped advance his career, at least for awhile. Rudolph often signed his drawings with a cursive signature, but it is nowhere nearly as distinctive as the perspective section, his Rapidograph linework, or his corrugated concrete. These signatures should be taken into account when reconsidering Rudolph's architecture because they help in understanding him, his buildings, and their relationship to postwar architecture and society.

Rudolph explained the section's significance for him in a 1986 interview: "The section is as important, or more important, for me than the plan. That is because it does depict the space, it does depict the light in ways in which the plan alone does not do. I don't mean to say not to have a plan, but I do mean to say you must have a section."[1] Architects have recently recognized how the section enriches the design process and have acknowledged Rudolph's skillful employment of this drawing type.[2]

In contrast to the quickly dashed-off sketch often regarded as the origin of a building, Rudolph's highly finished perspective sections are midterm statements usually made near the end of the design process, but before completion of the building. They had many functions. Produced for publication to bring attention to Rudolph's architecture, enhance his reputation, and garner more commissions, they were compelling drawings legible to both architects and a broader public unfamiliar with architectural representation. At the same time, they helped Rudolph understand his complex spaces and how they might affect users. Ideological as well, the perspective section also registered Rudolph's partisan views about Modern architecture. Shading, the careful depiction of shadows, and use of perspective attest to Rudolph's desire to control space and light in order to produce a subjective, expressive, and emotional architecture that would be an alternative to the seemingly objective and rational functionalism of the 1940s in which he was trained, and the International Style, which he frequently criticized in the 1950s.

While certainly egotistical, Rudolph's stress upon subjectivity was not his alone, but part of a broader tendency in postwar architecture that sought to "humanize" Modernism by focusing it upon the

[1] Paul Rudolph, "Excerpts from a Conversation," *Perspecta,* 22 (1986): 103.
[2] Paul Lewis, Marc Tsurumaki, David J. Lewis, *Manual of Section* (New York: Princeton Architectural Press, 2016).

8.1 [next spread]
Paul Rudolph, Yale Art and Architecture Building, Yale University, New Haven, Connecticut, perspective section, 1958–1963

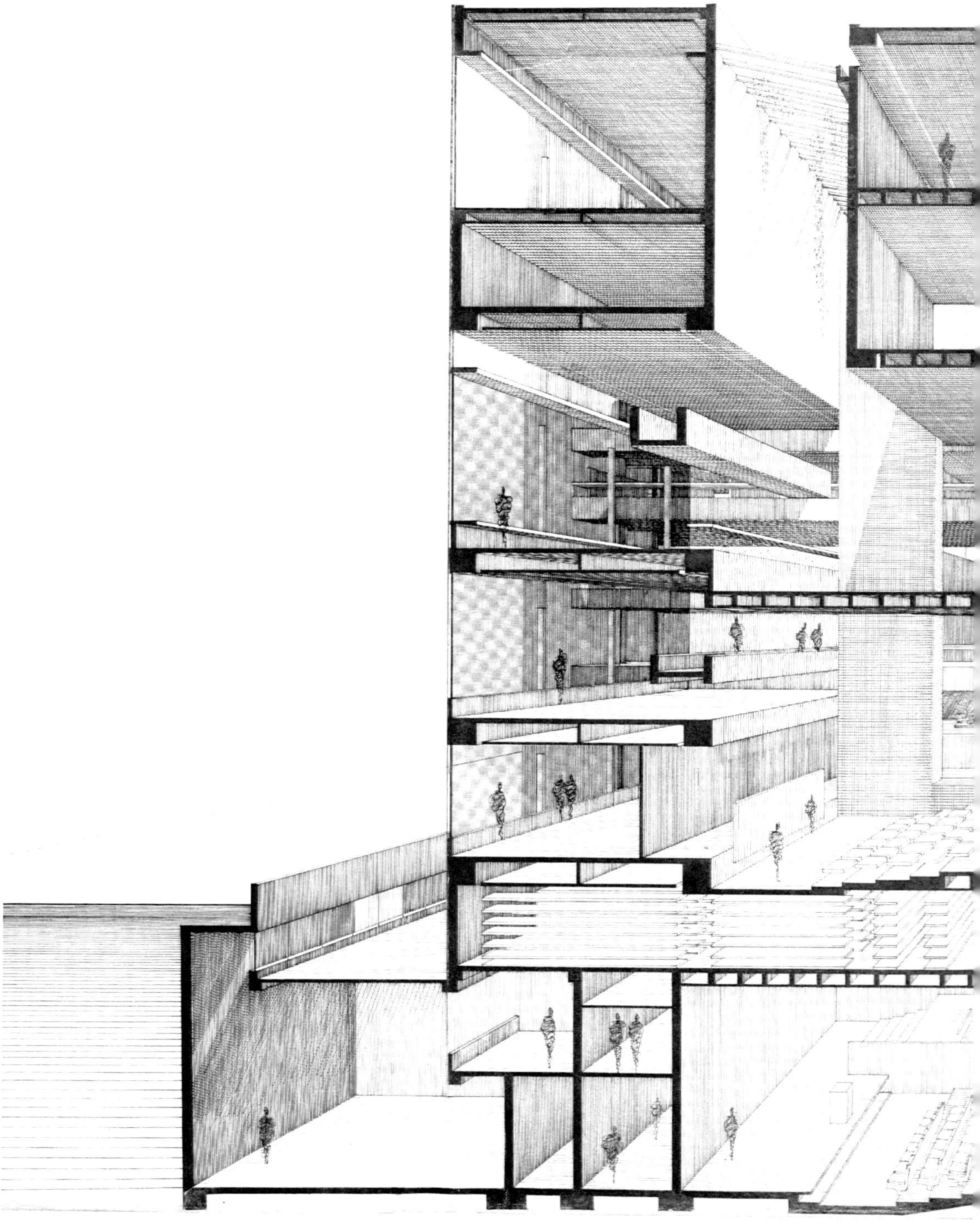

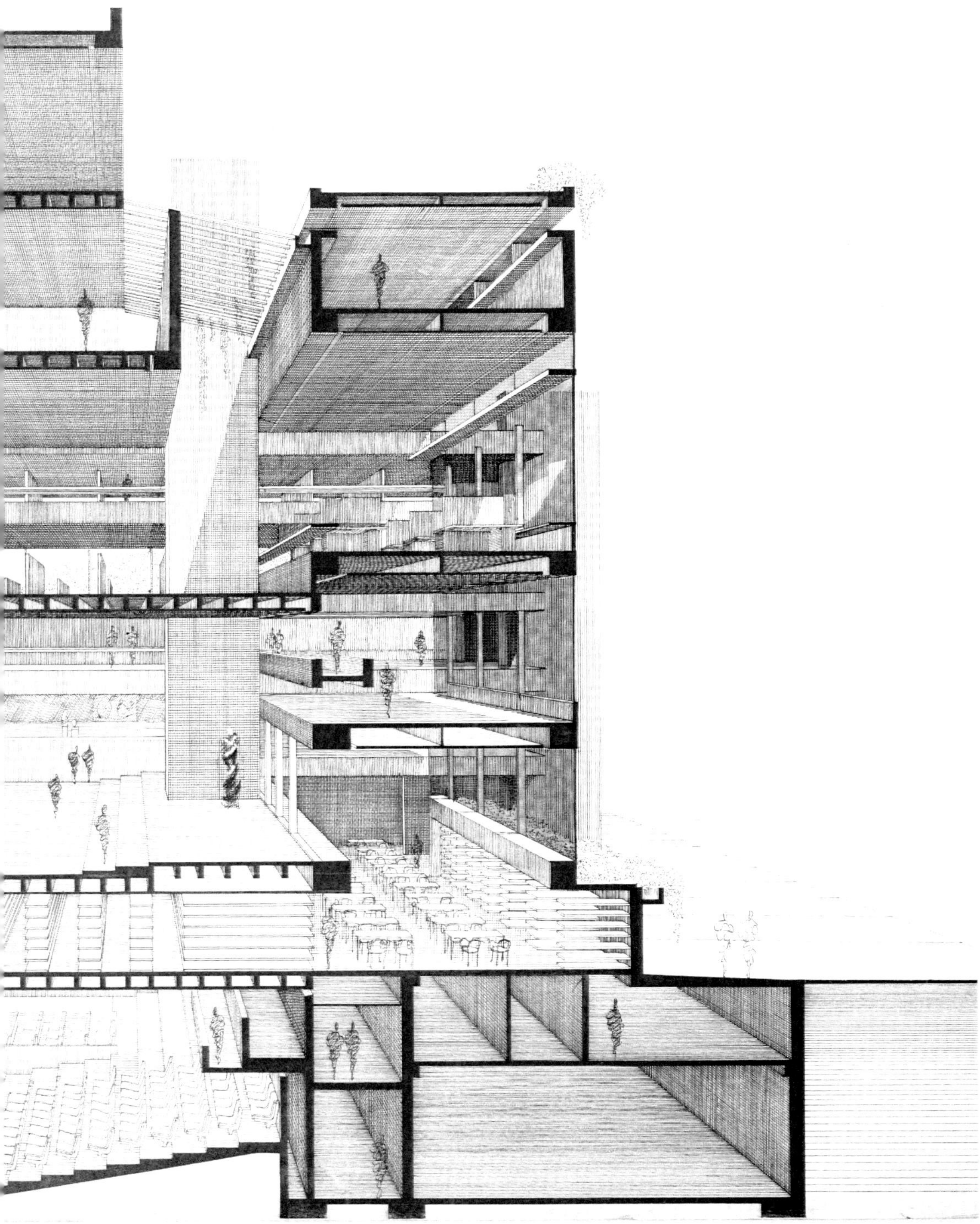

subjective qualities of the human body, mind, and emotions. One of the architect's most compelling signature traits, the perspective section can be used to trace the development of interior space in Rudolph's architecture and to explore the problems inherent in his attempts to make an architecture that would affect the psychology of its users.

Searching for a Distinctive Technique

Architectural drawing follows well-established conventions that would seem to allow little room for personal expression. And yet, Rudolph saw the medium as a means for expressing his ideas about architecture. The places where Rudolph trained acknowledged his skill at drawing from early on, but did not encourage practicing it as an expression of individuality, nor did they particularly endorse the perspective section. In the late 1930s, Rudolph received a conventional Beaux-Arts undergraduate education at Alabama Polytechnic (now Auburn University); helped architect Ralph Twitchell design Modernist houses in Sarasota, Florida, during a "gap year"; and matriculated at Harvard's Graduate School of Design (GSD) in fall 1941.

When the U.S. entered World War II in December 1941, Rudolph and most of his classmates joined the armed services. He enlisted in the Navy, took a maritime architecture course at MIT, and became a lieutenant supervising ship repair in the Brooklyn Navy Yard for the war's duration. Rudolph later said that those years were a time when ". . . I searched for a technique of drawing which would allow my personal vision to be suggested . . ."[3] The statement typifies how Rudolph used drawing to prove and produce evidence of his creativity, originality, and individuality, thus mythologizing these carefully constructed character traits, while giving very little credit to actual events or experiences that may have shaped his development.

One educational experience of this time that may have alerted Rudolph to the perspective section's potential was the course in maritime architecture he took at MIT. Textbooks in the discipline from this period often used the perspective section to explain the internal organization of ships. These drawings explained space, structure, and materials using just one image in a manner more economical and quicker for the eye to absorb, especially for large structures, than typical architectural representation, with its many plans and elevations **[Figure 8.2]**.[4] For Rudolph, perspective sections of ships would also have been appealing and familiar because of their regular appearances in the mass media. The perspective section was regularly used to explain the wondrous complexities of ocean liner interiors in advertising posters and in magazines, such as *Popular Science.* Ships and their imagery had also long appealed to the Modernist sensibility. Le Corbusier, of course, famously appropriated an ocean liner section to help explain the interior workings of his Unité d'habitation (Marseilles, France, 1946–1952).

The Harvard Box

After World War II ended, Rudolph was more eager to work than to complete his Harvard degree. He rejoined Twitchell's small firm in Sarasota, Florida, where vacationers were open to building Modernist holiday houses. While Twitchell secured clients and supervised construction, Rudolph concentrated on design, at first almost single-handedly producing all of the firm's drawings for building and publication in a manner notable for strong graphic and expressive qualities that conveyed the distinct contrast between sunlight and shadow in Florida. Rudolph returned to Harvard in 1947 where special consideration for veterans made it possible to complete his coursework and master's degree in only one semester.

One of Rudolph's GSD studio projects from 1947, a small, flat-roofed, rectangular, one-story "weekend house for an architect" shows how he accepted and yet questioned what he learned at Harvard. He sited it in Sarasota, and later revised it **[Figure 8.3]**. Rudolph's project for a rectangular house exemplified the "Harvard Box," a term students used to disparage the rote functionalist solutions favored

[3] Rudolph, "From Conception to Sketch to Rendering to Building," *Paul Rudolph Drawings* (Tokyo: A.D.A. Edita Tokyo Co., Ltd., 1972), 11.
[4] For a history of the relationship between maritime architecture and the architectural section focusing on seventeenth-century French practices, see Jacques Guillerme and Hélène Vérin. "The Archaeology of the Section," *Perspecta* 7 (1989): 226–57. Introductory textbooks on maritime architecture stressed the section. For two from the WWII period, see C.O. Liljegren, *Naval Architecture as Art and Science* (New York: Cornell Maritime Press, 1943), 5–12. And George C. Manning, *Manual of Ship Construction* (New York: D. Van Nostrand Company, Inc., 1942).

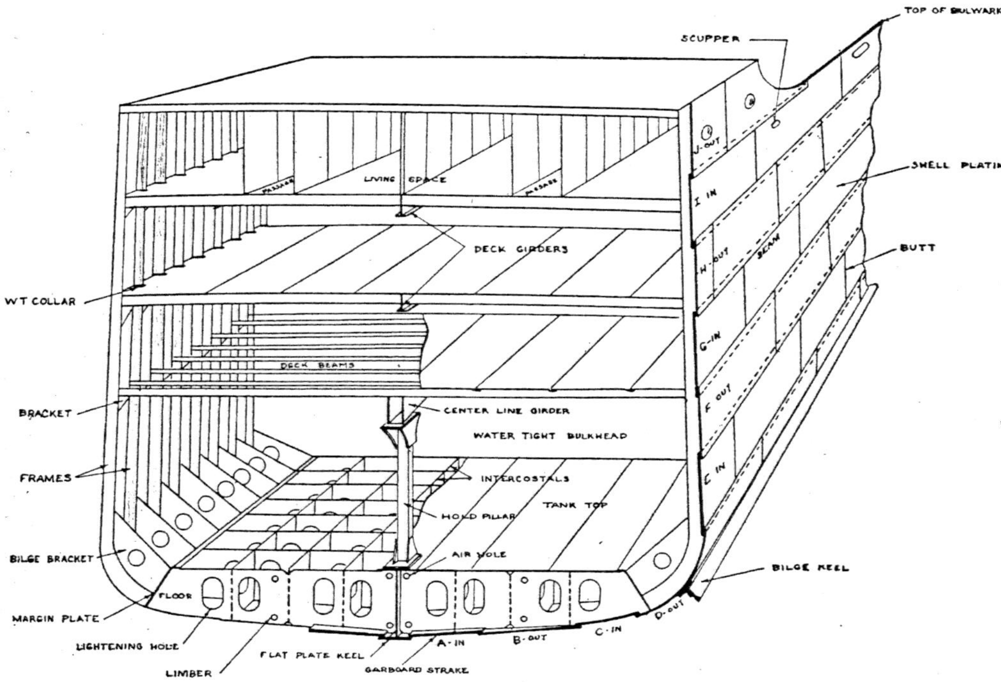

8.2
Perspective section from World War II era manual on maritime construction

by their instructors.[5] No matter what the program called for, the rectangular box was always the solution. A powerful force during the interwar years in Europe, functionalism emphasized the objective over the subjective and expressive, but many felt it had degenerated and become inhibiting as it was practiced in American architecture schools during the postwar years.[6] Gropius and colleagues close to him at the GSD stressed the functionalist approach in their teaching, emphasizing objectivity, science-based approaches, and teamwork, while discouraging overt expressions of individuality.

The Harvard Box was mandatory, even for Rudolph. But he enlivened his "weekend-house" rendition by departing from the typically utilitarian means of representation practiced at the GSD. Rudolph drew a skewed perspective view of his weekend house to reveal how it nearly floated above an artificial inlet. Showing that it was more than just a functional container, Rudolph nimbly engaged the house with the alternatingly dry, wet, and spongy Florida terrain under it, offering boats and inhabitants numerous opportunities to move between the structure and the water beneath it. Seen side-by-side, the perspective view is certainly more revealing and compelling than the accompanying diagram-like plans and elevations of the house. It suggests the increasingly expressive direction Rudolph's imagery and architecture would take over the next few years.

Opening up the Box

The Harvard weekend-house project of 1947 remained important for Rudolph. That same year, he revised it as a guest house for Mrs. Roberta Healy Finney (unbuilt project, Siesta Key, Florida, 1947). The Finney House became a model for his Florida houses

[5] For GSD pedagogy, see Jill Pearlman, *Inventing American Modernism: Joseph Hudnut, Walter Gropius, and the Bauhaus Legacy at Harvard* (Charlottesville, VA: University of Virginia Press, 2007). Also see, Anthony Alofsin, *Struggle for Modernism: Architecture, Landscape Architecture, and City Planning at Harvard* (New York and London: W.W. Norton & Company, 2002). Klaus Herdeg famously critiques the "Harvard Box" in his polemical book, *The Decorated Diagram: Harvard Architecture and the Failure of the Bauhaus Legacy* (Boston: MIT Press, 1983).

[6] Box-like solutions were endemic to American architecture schools in the 1940s and 1950s. In New Haven, students turned out Miesian-inflected "Yale Boxes," see Robert A.M. Stern and Jimmy Stamp, *Pedagogy and Place: 100 Years of Architecture Education at Yale* (New Haven and London: Yale University Press, 2016), 115.

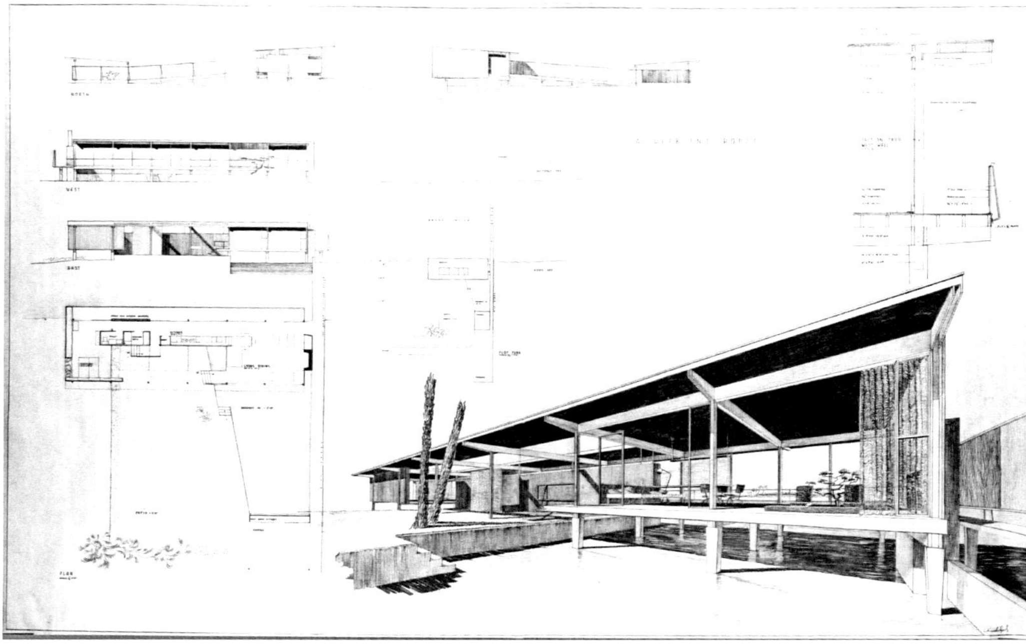

8.3
Paul Rudolph, Weekend House, project, 1947
Courtesy of the Frances Loeb Library, Harvard University Graduate School of Design

and a vehicle for his experiments with architectural representation. Rudolph's first known published use of the perspective section occurred when the Finney project appeared in *Interiors* magazine in 1950. For this section, Rudolph depicted a cut taken through the portion of the house raised above the inlet. The section could almost be mistaken for a depiction of a ship, barge, or dock rather than a conventional house. **[Figure 8.4]**

The house itself changed little from the original Harvard project, but the introduction of the section confirmed Rudolph's turn away from objectivity and functionalism. Its presence indicates a desire to engage the viewer, causing him or her to empathize with the building—or at least the image—in some way. While the functionalist plans and diagrams of the GSD imparted information in a matter-of-fact, objective manner, the perspective section rendered through the relatively simple means of one-point perspective very quickly pulls the eye of the viewer along the receding orthogonals, inwards and deep into the image. In this way, it helps the viewer to insert him or herself into the space, rather than distancing the viewer, as did the plan—a type of representation that requires an eye accustomed to the symbolism of its dashes signifying hidden beams, arcs denoting an opening door, or other such notations. It takes longer to read a plan than a perspective section. By following the receding orthogonal lines of the section, the viewer also experiences the house through Rudolph's viewpoint or subjectivity. Though they do not always realize it, viewers have similar experiences when watching films made by expert cinematographers.

Understanding that print media could help advance his career greatly, Rudolph crafted images for

8.4
Paul Rudolph, Finney House, perspective section, 1950

publication, like the perspective section, which were legible and eye-catching in order to appeal to prospective clients, fellow architects, and others. Wide-circulation magazines, such as *Vogue* and *House & Garden,* published Rudolph's Florida houses frequently, with inviting photographs by Ezra Stoller in which carefully selected objects such as lounge chairs and sunglasses evoked postwar leisure.

After leaving Twitchell to establish his own Sarasota office in 1952, Rudolph's work became more experimental, and he turned to the perspective section more frequently in order to explain projects with increasingly complex interiors. In his award-winning, unbuilt project for the Cohen Residence of 1952–1953 (Siesta Key, Florida), for example, a circular conversation platform floats in the middle of the double-height space at the center of the house **[Figure 8.5]**. In this section, it is evident how Rudolph considers the vertical dimension as much as the horizontal dimension, which the plan always emphasizes. This double-height space in the Cohen House is actually a screened area, like a giant porch, a porous space open to cooling breezes and the elements. Suggestive of new dimensions for Rudolph's architecture, it is ambiguously between indoors and outdoors. Ringed by balconies, it is also a prototype for similarly configured rooms in future buildings by Rudolph.

Once again, this image seems more like the depiction of a ship than a conventional house; the ground floor is almost flush with the watery surface of an adjacent canal visible on the far right. In just one example of how widely Rudolph's imagery circulated, drawings of the Cohen Residence appeared in several different American and European architectural journals during the 1950s,

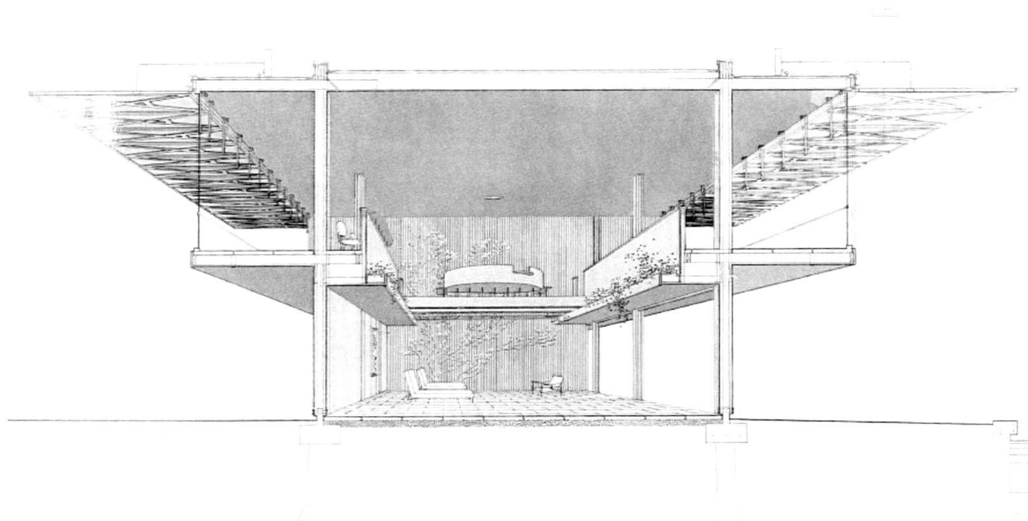

8.5
Paul Rudolph, Cohen Residence, Siesta Key, Florida, perspective section, 1952–1953

8.6
Kallmann, McKinnell, and Knowles, Boston City Hall, perspective section, 1961–1968

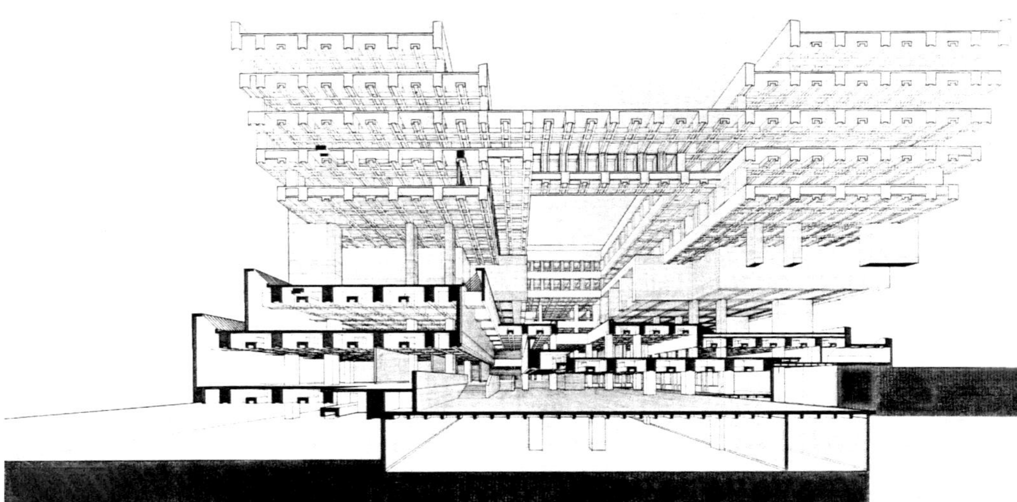

[7] For the Cohen House, see "House by Paul Rudolph," *California Arts and Architecture,* vol. 71 (September 1954): 14–15 and "Quatre Habitations en Floride, USA", *L'Architecture d'Aujourd'hui,* vol. 26 (November 1955): 34–35. The 1953 project won the Progressive Architecture Awards of 1954, "First Design Award: House, Siesta Key, Florida," *Progressive Architecture,* vol. 36 (January 1955): 6–67. Though it was a prize-winner, Rudolph built an entirely different project for the Cohen House in 1955. For images and an account of these different versions of the house, see Joseph King and Christopher Domin, *Paul Rudolph: The Florida Houses* (New York: Princeton Architectural Press, 2002), 173–77.

[8] Rudolph. "The Changing Philosophy of Architecture," *The Architectural Forum* 101 (July 1954): 120

[9] Rudolph, "Regionalism in Architecture," *Perspecta* 4 (1957): 16.

[10] Rudolph, "The Changing Philosophy of Architecture," 120.

ranging from *California Arts and Architecture* and *L'Architecture d'Aujourd'hui* to *Progressive Architecture,* which gave the house one of its yearly design awards in 1954.[7]

Humanizing Modernism

Rudolph's increasing use of the section coincides with his emergence in the mid-1950s as an outspoken critic of the postwar International Style who sought to create a more expressive architecture. A key word for the period, "expression," was employed by those who sought to temper Modernist abstraction with human emotions, resulting in an art and architecture based upon subjectivity, as in "Abstract Expressionism." Rudolph explained his standpoint in a series of well-received talks and articles during the 1950s. Decrying the current state of architecture, Rudolph said in 1954, "Modern architecture's range of expression is today from A to B."[8] In a direct rejoinder to the evenly illuminated and exposed glass curtain-walled buildings and interior spaces of the International Style, Rudolph wrote in 1957, "We need caves as well as gold-fish bowls."[9] This disarmingly simple dictum calling for a juxtaposition of opaque, darkened, enclosed spaces with transparent, bright, open ones became a basic precept for Rudolph's concept of interior spaces. The perspective section was the ideal means by which to represent these spatial juxtapositions and complex effects of light and shadow, and to consider how humans might react to them.

At the 1954 national conference of the American Institute of Architects, Rudolph called for spaces invested with "human" qualities which would strongly affect the body and the mind in a subjective way: "We need sequences of space which arouse one's curiosity, give a sense of anticipation, which beckon and impel us to rush forward to find that releasing space which dominates, which climaxes and acts as a magnet, and gives direction."[10] In Rudolph's description, spaces stimulate human moods and movement. Such positivist thinking reflected the particular thread of discourse about architectural "humanism" in the twentieth century that dated back to Geoffrey Scott's explanation of Renaissance architecture in his book, *The Architecture of Humanism* (1914), which achieved a new popularity in the 1950s.[11] Scott maintained that the humanism of Renaissance architecture was directly inspired by the human body, its emotions, and the genius of its individual designers, rather than functional requirements. Scott's thinking appealed to those like Rudolph, Eero Saarinen, and Philip Johnson who were intent on developing a dynamic architecture of form instead of function.[12] It would be expressive of their economically and politically powerful society.

Rudolph encountered other colleagues who admired Scott and thought similarly about architecture when he became a visiting critic at Yale in 1956. Architectural historian Vincent Scully used Scott to explain the ethos of architecture in late-1950s America, as the limitations imposed by functionalism and the International Style gave way to the "liberated and enriched" historically based forms of Saarinen, Johnson, and even Louis Kahn. Scully quoted Scott to define the body-centered, humanist architecture he advocated for an energetic postwar America, whose origins lay in Louis Sullivan and Frank Lloyd Wright. To describe Sullivan's buildings, Scully used this quote from the concluding chapter of Scott's book, where he said of Renaissance architecture: "The centre of that architecture was the human body: its method, to transcribe in stone the body's favorable states; and the moods of the spirit took visible shape along its borders, power and laughter, strength and terror and calm."[13]

All that Rudolph hoped that his architecture could achieve is expressed in these words. Rudolph took them to mean that the building should be a register of his own psychology, subjectivity, viewpoint, or genius, just like his perspective section drawings. His was the human body in Scott's description. But, as will be shown, there was a considerable difference between asking someone to see a building through Rudolph's viewpoint as expressed through a perspective section and asking them to use or inhabit a building so closely determined by his point of view.

[11] Geoffrey Scott, *The Architecture of Humanism: A Study in the History of Taste,* with an introduction by Henry Hope Reed Jr. (London: Constable and Company, 1914, 1999 edition). Rudolph quotes Scott in his article, "The Six Determinants of Architectural Form," *Architectural Record,* vol. 120 (October 1956): 186. Rudolph notes the book as an important influence in "Paul Rudolph: Drawings," *Architectural Forum* (June 1973): 51.

[12] Philip Johnson said Scott's *The Architecture of Humanism* was a "bible" for him. Philip Johnson, "Letter to Dr. Jurgen Joedicke," December 6, 1961. Published in John M. Jacobus, Jr., *Philip Johnson* (New York: George Braziller, 1962): 120.

[13] Scott, p. 177. Scully quotes this passage from Scott in Vincent Scully. "Modern Architecture: Toward a Redefinition of Style," *Perspecta* 4 (1957): 9. The quotation appears again in Vincent Scully,

Yale A&A

At the age of 39, in 1958, Rudolph reached the apogee of his career when he became the chairman of the Department of Architecture at Yale. His practice shifted towards the making of large-scale civic and academic buildings for a prosperous, powerful postwar America. He turned to the perspective section more frequently to explain their complexity. At this time, other architects also turned to the perspective section to explain the new generation of spatially complex, institutional buildings in concrete, which became known as Brutalism. Kallmann, McKinnell and Knowles memorably employed the perspective section to depict the interior spaces and structure of their famed Boston City Hall (1961–1968). Hazily rendered, compared to the hard lines of Rudolph's sections, the drawing was from a set of published renderings executed by the firm. Their atmospheric qualities softened the visual impact of the building's massive concrete forms for an architectural community and public still unsure about such monumentality.[14] **[Figure 8.6]**

Unlike many of his contemporaries, Rudolph rarely used professional renderers, preferring to produce drawings that truly represented his point of view. In his New Haven office, with the assistance of a staff of about ten full-time architects, Rudolph supervised the making of numerous drawings for presentation to clients and for publication. He received much help from skilled employees such as the British architect John Fowler, who well understood but questioned Rudolph's employment of the section, as shall be shown.[15] Despite his busy daily routine, making presentation drawings remained important to Rudolph. He was often intimately involved in making ones for his projects, frequently altering them when they were in production and executing some of his signature repetitive linework himself, a skill at which he excelled.

Rudolph also employed students from the Department of Architecture to execute the labor-intensive linework with the Rapidograph pen, such as Charles Gwathmey. The experience related to what they learned in Rudolph's Yale studios. He always required students to feature perspective sections in their final presentations. As a result, some, such as Norman Foster, one of Rudolph's most renowned students, frequently employed the perspective section to depict their own buildings. Foster later acknowledged that his teacher's imagery made a lifelong impression upon him.[16] By his published examples, Rudolph popularized the perspective section amongst architects during the 1960s, and drawings similar to his from across the world could be found in journals published from Japan to Germany. Following Rudolph's lead, professional architectural renderers of the late-twentieth century also popularized the perspective section, such as Paul Stevenson Oles, who was a Rudolph student from Yale.[17]

Soon after arriving at the University, Rudolph received the commission that would bring to fruition his experiments with the manipulation of interior space in order to stimulate psychological reactions. The Yale Art & Architecture Building (1958–1963) was intended to bring the various programs of the school together under one roof, including studio art, architecture, urban design, and the art history library.

The most striking image of its kind that he produced, Rudolph's widely published perspective section of the A&A Building depicted the complex interior with just one view that could be seen in a single glance.[18] **[Figure 8.1]** The drawing explained how the auditorium, library, exhibition gallery, and studio spaces were stacked on top of one another to take advantage of a constricted urban site. In a way that would have been difficult to illustrate even with many plans, the single drawing dramatically illustrated how the thirty-seven different levels of the building ranged from darkened "caves," like the basement auditorium, to dramatic "goldfish bowls," like the double-height drafting room. Exemplifying his volumetric approach to design, it demonstrates how Rudolph emphasized the vertical as much as the horizontal dimension in his architecture. Ringed by balconies, these double-height rooms are the fulfillment of the prototype suggested by the perspective section of Rudolph's unbuilt

Modern Architecture: The Architecture of Democracy/The Great Ages of World Architecture Series (New York: George Braziller, 1961), 45.

14 Gerhard Kallmann told the author (May 22, 2008) that the perspective section of Boston City Hall was one from a set of renderings completed in the firm's office after design work was completed to explain the structural system and interior spaces for a publication, though their haziness seems to obscure rather than reveal the building's qualities, "The New Boston City Hall," *Progressive Architecture,* v. 44 (April 1963): 137.

15 Rudolph and Fowler had frequent disagreements. Author's interview with Rudolph office employee, William de Cossy, June 22, 2007.

16 Norman Foster, "Norman Foster on Paul Rudolph," *Architects on Architects,* edited by Susan Gray (New York: McGraw-Hill, 2002), 29. Foster said much the same in an interview with the author, January 21, 2002.

Cohen House **[Figure 8.5]**. The perspective section shows how the rooms related to one another. Both in the drawing and as actually achieved in the built structure, the chambers are connected visually by long diagonal vistas, making it possible to see through the body of the building—thus linking different activities and functions together: from designing, to exhibiting works, to library research—and outside to the city streets, reminding students of the importance of the urban context, something Rudolph emphasized in his teaching. Despite the heaviness of the concrete walls, there is flexibility here, suggestive of dialogues between the inhabitants and the multiple ways in which the interiors related to one another and the campus and city.

In keeping with his thinking about how light and shadow affected emotions, Rudolph used the perspective section to depict how sunlight penetrated deep into the building through multilevel shafts topped by skylights. He showed how the A&A's corrugated concrete walls cast shifting plays of light and shadow, represented by cross-hatching and many parallel vertical lines. Rudolph later hinted at how his signature linework might have inspired the corrugated concrete treatment of the walls.[19] The contrast between light and shadow gave the drawing a somber quality, imparting a sense of atmosphere and emotion.

In what became still another of his signature touches, Rudolph himself drew the distinctive spiraling human figures which populate the drawing to illustrate scale and to show how he imagined the building affecting the inhabitants. As quickly drawn as a doodle, each figure is a register of the immediate energy of Rudolph's hand as the pen touches paper. Each maintains its balance on just one tiny

8.7
Paul Rudolph, scale human figure, c. 1961

[17] Helmut Jacoby, *New Techniques in Architectural Rendering* (New York: Praeger, 1971), 64. Himself a leading renderer who knew Rudolph well, Jacoby describes Oles's work and provides examples of his perspective sections, 26, 42–45. The book is a catalogue of works by leading renderers of the day, many of whom used the perspective section in a manner similar to Rudolph. For examples, see: Donald D. Hanson, 57; and David Bité, who also worked for Rudolph, 112–117.

[18] The perspective section of the Yale A&A first appeared in print soon after the December 1962 groundbreaking: "Yale's New Art and Architecture Building," *Architectural Record*, vol. 131 (January 1962): 16–17. The original of the image depicted here is in the collection of Manuscripts and Archives, Yale University Library.

[19] Rudolph, "From Conception to Sketch to Rendering to Building,"

point amidst the building's many levels, platforms, and chasms, buffeted by the waves of emotion Rudolph imagines the building emitting. **[Figure 8.7]** Further evidence of how Rudolph thought that buildings affected the body and mind appears in colorful sketches he began producing of his own buildings in the 1960s, culminating many years later in a series analysing the plan of Mies van der Rohe's German or Barcelona Pavilion (Barcelona, Spain, 1929; reconstructed, 1986). Freely rendered compared to the perspective section's standardized format, Rudolph attempted in these studies to analyze movement, light and even reflections by drawing irregular lines in colored pencil, their different hues suggesting varying degrees of intensity.

Not long after the A&A Building was completed to almost universal acclaim, John Fowler wrote a trenchant review of it suggesting that his employer had become overly reliant upon the perspective section. Fowler thought the section had driven the composition of the building almost as much as the program. He wrote, "Rudolph works very quickly, almost impetuously. His architecture becomes a process of assembling incidents of 'excitement.' His excellent drawings perform the function of bringing these together. Conceivably there is no other contemporary architect who relies on perspective drawings as he does, and his buildings even begin to acquire their characteristics."[20] Rudolph believed he could articulate his subjectivity as a designer through the perspective section, but he may have become overly reliant upon it, just as his GSD instructors had relied too often upon the "Harvard Box." Architectural drawing, speech, and handwriting are established conventions that to some degree define the thinking of designers, speakers, and writers as much as they articulate their utterances; this is true too of today's designers who use software they did not program to design their buildings. Does the perspective section reveal anything really personal about Rudolph, or did it become for him a rote and formalist manipulation of conventions?

Reflecting the viewpoint of fellow Britons who thought that ethics should outweigh aesthetics—namely Reyner Banham—Fowler concluded that the A&A Building was a superficial answer to the problem of creating such a complex building.[21] For Fowler, the building was an overly grandiose, formalist exercise that neglected basic functional needs. Rudolph's repeated use of the section was a symptom of his increasing formalism, a problem for Rudolph and all of postwar Modernism.

Published in spring 1964, Fowler's review reflected growing disenchantment at Yale with the A&A and Rudolph. The students and many faculty found Rudolph's "gold-fish bowls" too hot and too bright, his caves dark and claustrophobic rather than comforting, and the complex relationships between his spaces bewildering. The building was about him, not them. Their growing discontent challenged Rudolph's authority at Yale, one of several factors that led him to resign by 1965 to pursue what he anticipated would be a flourishing practice in Manhattan. This was not to be. By the mid-1970s, Rudolph experienced an almost complete reversal of fortune: fire gutted his Yale A&A Building in 1969, his Modernism became the target of postmodernist critiques, and a troubled economy caused commissions to fall off for the type of large-scale, publicly funded institutional buildings in concrete that had become his specialty.

Reckoning with the Rendering

Withdrawing from architectural discourse as his reputation declined, Rudolph turned inwards during the 1970s. He still made complex, compelling drawings, some of which attest to the almost completely interior turn that he took both personally and professionally. The perspective section of his remarkable Manhattan penthouse (1988) depicts a fantastically intricate array of caves, gold-fish bowls, double-height rooms, and terraces linked by staircases and transparent Plexiglas bridges **[Figure 8.8]**. Carrying the qualities of the section into the actual built penthouse, these Plexiglas bridges functioned like cuts in the floors which made it possible to peer through the body of the house, seeing the different levels below as though

Paul Rudolph Drawings (Tokyo: A.D.A. Edita Tokyo Co., Ltd., 1972), 7.

[20] John Fowler, "Art and Architecture Building, Yale, USA," *Architectural Design,* vol. 34, (April 1964): 160.

[21] Reyner Banham criticized Rudolph's A&A Building and also saw it as wholly a manifestation of Rudolph's drawing techniques. Reyner Banham, "Convenient Benches and Handy Hooks: Functional Considerations in the Criticism of the Art of Architecture," in Marcus Whiffen, ed., *The History, Theory and Criticism of Architecture, Papers from the 1964 AIA-ACSA Teacher Seminar* (Cambridge: MIT Press, 1965): 91–106.

looking into a perspective section. The penthouse is the work by Rudolph where the drawing and the completed building bear the closest resemblance to one another. The built penthouse expressed Rudolph's own subjectivity, but it also stimulated an entire range of varied reactions from those who encountered it that Rudolph could not anticipate or control. Rudolph's architecture makes situations that produce multiple unpredictable, emotional reactions. His penthouse captivated some, and disconcerted others. Rudolph enjoyed drily recounting how the penthouse's Plexiglas bridges caused a visitor susceptible to vertigo to faint.[22]

Such an anecdote might lead one to conclude that Rudolph remained unaware or heedless of how buildings formulated from his viewpoint affected users other than himself. Rudolph was, in fact, cognizant by this time of the limitations of his design methods, especially his reliance upon drawings. He knew that his drawings could not anticipate the reactions of users. In his 1972 monograph of drawings published at a troubled period for him of self-doubt and reflection, just three years after the immolation of his A&A Building and on the eve of the postmodernism that would soon take him to task, he mused ruefully about the complicated relationship between architecture, its image, and its reception: "The psychological impact of the architect's design will not be truly known until it is built and, even then, its meaning will vary for individuals and will also vary with the passage of time. Renderings seldom convey the psychological meaning, the building's true essence."[23]

Rudolph's many signatures—the parallel line work, the corrugated concrete, the perspective sections, and the wiry human figures which populate them—helped promote his carefully constructed genius, but they also became registers of his agony (itself a quality often seen as characteristic of genius) about making architecture. These signatures also reveal the greater dilemmas of postwar Modernism's attempts to humanize itself by emphasizing individuality, creativity, and emotion. Despite their strong physical presence and many signature notes, Rudolph and his architecture are not the stable, knowable subjects they might initially seem to be. Tracing the perspective section through Rudolph's work provokes questions about making, looking, inhabiting, and feeling that raise discussions about him and his architecture to the ontological level.

[22] Joseph Giovannini, "If There's a Heaven, It Should Expect Changes," *The New York Times,* Thursday, August 14, 1997, C1, C10.
[23] Paul Rudolph, "From Conception to Sketch to Rendering to Building," *Paul Rudolph Drawings* (Tokyo: A.D.A. Edita Tokyo, Ltd, 1972), p. 11.

8.8 [next spread]
Paul Rudolph, 23 Beekman Place Residence, New York City, perspective section, 1967

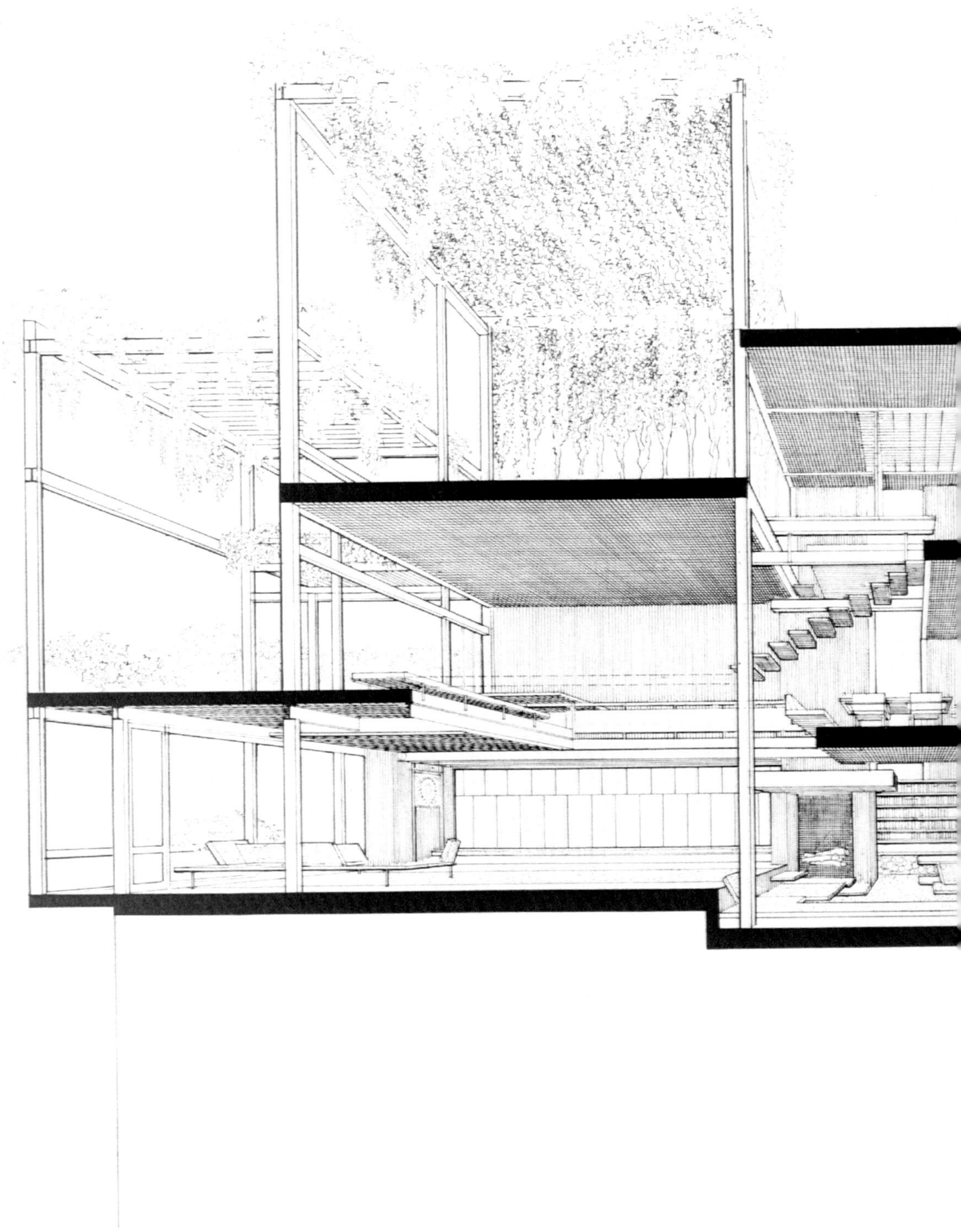

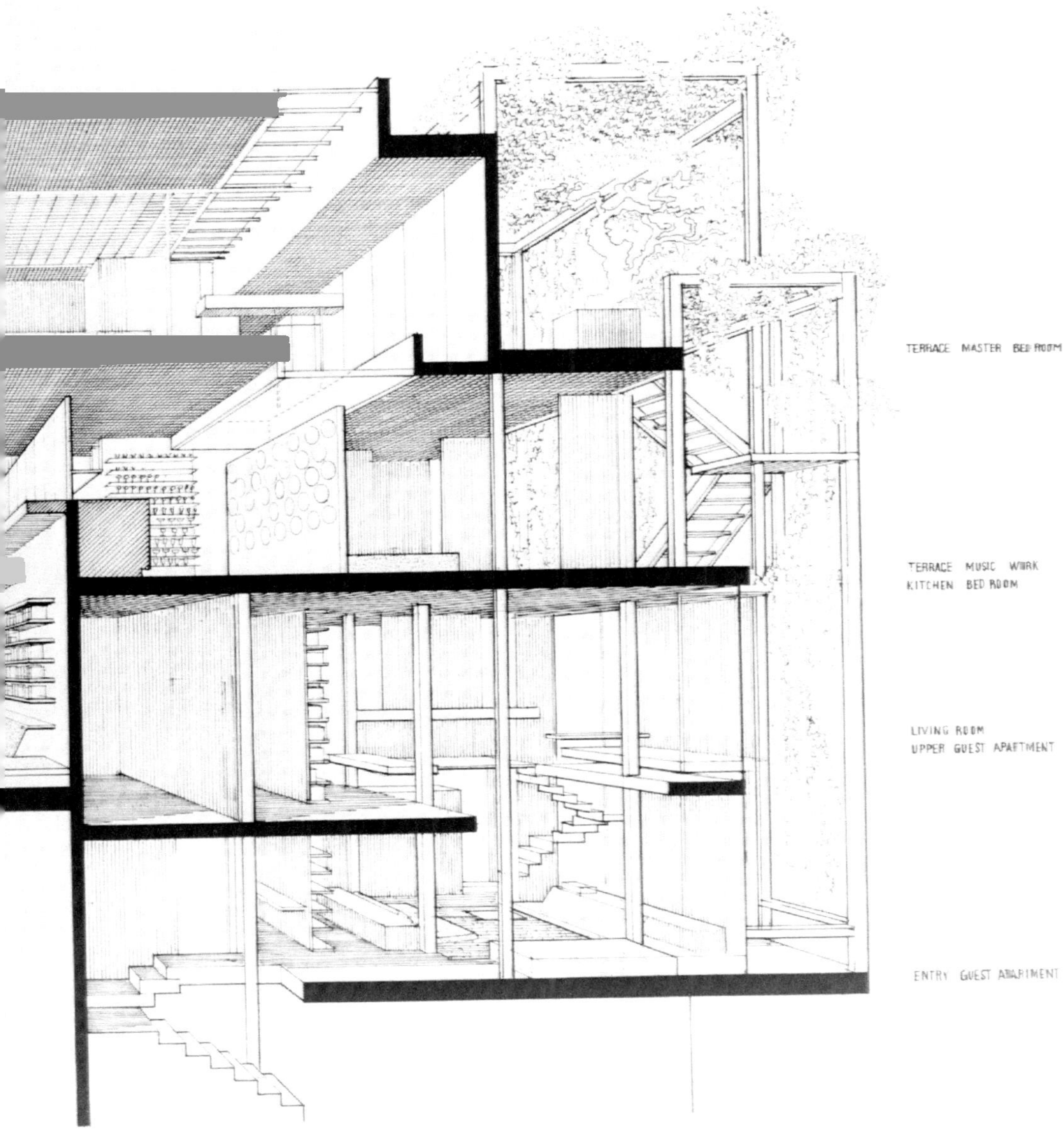
TERRACE MASTER BED ROOM
TERRACE MUSIC WORK
KITCHEN BED ROOM
LIVING ROOM
UPPER GUEST APARTMENT
ENTRY GUEST APARTMENT

DISCOURSE

Brut or not Brut? Paul Rudolph and the Anglo-American Axis

Louis Martin

As an architect and educator, Paul Rudolph played a role in the architectural discourse of the 1960s that can be better understood through a close examination of the exchanges between the design cultures of England and America. In 1970, Peter Eisenman wrote about the "complex relationship between England and the U.S."[1] He explained that, in the 1950s, "England was [for an American student like him] a place of debate, of ideas—a kind of intellectual refuge of the Modern Movement."[2] He saw in the Architectural Association and Cambridge University two centers of intellectual debate, homes of small, yet effective, polemical groups. But more than schools, it was certainly the British architectural press that nourished what Eisenman called "the American romance with English intellectual attitudes."[3] Periodicals such as *The Architectural Review* and *Architectural Design* disseminated images and published criticism that generated new trends. Of these, the New Brutalism was the most exciting.

But the view from Britain was quite different.[4] For instance, Colin St John Wilson (1922–2007), the first-year Master at Cambridge, saw America as a sort of intellectual no-man's-land. Wilson, who was invited by Paul Rudolph to teach at Yale in 1961, wrote in 1965:

"In America today, there is no public forum for the exchange of ideas, no group gathered around a common idea (and therefore no rebel groups), no discussion that is more than one man deep, no magazine that attempts to focus upon the state of current polemic. This is the starvation of thought."[5]

Judging by this excerpt, polemics was undoubtedly a favorite sport of British architects.

A review of the British Modern Movement in architecture written by John Summerson (1904–1992) in 1957 confirms this impression. Summerson conceded that the English Moderns of the 1930s made only a very modest contribution to the European movement. But he acknowledged the existence, in the late 1950s, of a real school of Modern design in Great Britain. He wrote that there was, in the British school, an agreement:

". . . to be radical, to be continuously critical of results and to go back again and again to the programme and wrestle with its implications till it yields an answer which has the stamp of reality. This radicalism is the great thing in English architecture today. Once lose it (sic) and 'English modern' becomes just so much provincial back-wash from the Channel and the Atlantic. Furthermore, it is only a thoroughly radical and realistic attitude which will maintain the architect in his role of leadership."[6]

Summerson certainly had in mind the new generation banding behind the New Brutalism, "the first native art movement in Britain," according to Reyner Banham (1922–1988).[7] As early as 1955, Banham indicated that what characterized the New Brutalism was precisely its brutality, its *je-m'en-foutisme,* its bloody-mindedness. The strength of British architectural Brutalism resided in its inelоquence, its anti-arty detailing: that distinguished the Smithsons' school at Hunstanton **[Figure 9.1, 9.2]** from Louis Kahn's Yale Art Center **[Figure 9.3, 9.4]**. According to Banham, Brutalism was at once principles and slogan. Its aesthetic principles were rather general if not vague, but the ethic of its slogan adhered ruthlessly to one of the basic moral imperatives of the Modern movement: honesty of structure and materials. Moreover, contact with Brutalist architecture tended to drive one to hard judgment of non-Brutalist architecture. The gap between the aesthetic principles and the ethic of Brutalism was bridged by the concept of "image." For Banham, the word *image* meant something visually valuable, but not in the classical sense. For Thomas Aquinas, beauty was that, which seen, pleased. In contrast, a Brutalist image was that, which seen, affected the emotions, a situation that could subsume the pleasure caused by beauty. The Brutalist image was radically anti-academic, anti-beauty, anti-art. Banham concluded: "What pleased St. Thomas was an abstract quality, beauty—what moves a new Brutalist is the thing in itself, in its totality and with all its overtones of human associations." Brutalist architecture was apprehended as a memorable image: that visual quality was what distinguished Brutalism from

[1] Peter D. Eisenman, "Building in Meaning: Review of Meaning in Architecture," *Architectural Forum* 133 (July–August 1970): 88, 90.
[2] Ibid.
[3] Peter D. Eisenman, "Book Review: Ordinariness and Light by Alison and Peter Smithson," *Architectural Forum* 134 (May 1971): 76, 80.
[4] As Eisenman explained, "To an English architect of the late '50s and early '60s, American architecture was considered with polite embarrassment and an irony about the financial resources Americans had available to implement their technology." Cf. Eisenman, "Building in Meaning," op. cit.
[5] Colin St John Wilson, "Open Letter to an American Student" *Architectural Design,* 35:3 (March 1965): AD6–AD7.
[6] John Summerson, "Introduction" to Trevor Dannatt, *Modern Architecture in Britain* (London: Batsford, 1959).
[7] Reyner Banham, "The New Brutalism," *The Architectural Review,* 708 (December 1955): 357.

9.1–9.2
Alison and Peter Smithson, Hunstanton Secondary Modern School, Hunstanton, England, 1950–1954
Reginald Hugo de Burgh Galwey © RIBA Library Photographs Collection

9.3
Louis I. Kahn, Yale University Art Gallery, New Haven, Connecticut, entrance, 1953

9.4
Louis I. Kahn, Yale University Art Gallery, New Haven, Connecticut, courtyard, 1953

routine functionalism.[8] Brutalism was thus instrumental in the promotion of the idea that radicalism was a measure of an architect's leadership.

Paul Rudolph manifested sympathy for English criticism when he was named chairman of Yale's Architecture department in February 1958.[9] In a text on architectural education, he argued that criticism might improve design, but he also noted that there were no critics in the USA comparable to those in England.[10] He asserted, polemically, that American cab drivers were better architectural critics than many architects. He also expressed his desire to conduct a radical criticism of the tenets of Modern architecture.[11] If he accepted to teach at Yale, Rudolph added, it was because he believed action had outstripped theory; to pierce the unknown, theory now had to overtake action.[12]

Retrospectively, Rudolph's longing for a theory seems odd. In the few texts he published, he wished to distance himself from the International Style, but he never developed, in writing at least, a transmittable theory. Rudolph was trapped in the double bind of his generation: he had to pay homage to the masters either by imitating their architectural forms or by imitating their individual creative freedom. In the manifesto he published in *Perspecta* 7 in 1961, Rudolph expressed clearly that he chose individualism.[13]

Perspecta 7 was conceived by editor James Baker as a symposium intended to assess the current state of American architecture. Five critics were invited to comment on a group of five architects, which included Rudolph, who were considered "responsible" for what American architecture was and was not.[14] Three critics were British and none of them said much about Rudolph.[15] While James Gowan argued that Rudolph's recent works failed to integrate structure and form,[16] Colin St John Wilson and Peter Collins did not even mention his name.[17]

Yet, Collins had exposed his views on Rudolph in an earlier text titled, "After Frank Lloyd Wright," published in *The Manchester Guardian* in the fall of 1960.[18] Written some time after Rudolph lectured on his work at McGill University, the article was republished in *Progressive Architecture* in August 1961 under the title, "Whither Paul Rudolph?" **[Figure 9.5]** The intention of this reprint was to prompt a reply from Reyner Banham.[19]

Collins maintained with verve that Rudolph was "forced by Madison Avenue to be a Form-Giver" and therefore "to be a leader of fashion." The real problem was that Rudolph confessed he had no fixed direction. For Collins, Rudolph's lack of consistent design principles explained why his buildings seemed unrelated to the work of other architects, and even unrelated to one another "in character, materials, or structural systems."

Collins argued that Rudolph's "indecision was exacerbated by the fact that, though temperamentally a disciple of Le Corbusier, he received

[8] Ibid. Looking at the recent projects by the Smithsons, Banham noticed a shift towards aformal images in projects like Golden Lane and Sheffield. He suggested that the unity of these images was no longer realized by geometry but by topological relationships.
[9] Robert A. M. Stern, "Yale 1950–1965," *Oppositions,* no. 4, (October 1974): 46.
[10] Paul Rudolph, "The Awesome Moment," *Journal of Architectural Education,* 13:2 (Autumn 1958): 50–51. This issue of the JAE reports the proceeding of an AIA-ACSA Seminar titled "The Teaching of Architecture."
[11] Rudolph wrote: "The last decade has thrown glaring light on the omissions, thinness, paucity of ideas, naïveté with regard to symbols, lack of creativeness and expressiveness of architectural theories as they were developed by the 1920s." Ibid. The same quotation was found in a longer text that Rudolph apparently read in the Forum program organized by Henry-Russell Hitchcock for The Voice of America. See: Paul Rudolph, "Architectural Education in U.S.A." *Zodiac* 8 (1961): [162]–65.
[12] It is not clear if Rudolph intended, with this opposition of theory and action, to refute Gerhardt Kallmann of Columbia University who saw the emergence of "Action Architecture" in America as a pendant of English Brutalism. G.M. Kallmann, "The 'Action' Architecture of a New Generation," *Architectural Forum* 11:4 (October 1959):132–137, 244. In his talk at the 1958 AIA-ACSA seminar, Kallmann mentioned that whether it was called "action," "brutalist," or "concrete," the harsh new aesthetics in architecture existed in many countries. G.M. Kallmann, "Vital Impulse," *Journal of Architectural Education,* op. cit., 38–41. Rudolph was perhaps inspired by John Summerson's "Case for a Theory of Architecture," a discourse given at the Royal Institute of British Architects (RIBA) in 1957, in which the influential English historian denounced the lack of an adequate theory "as a means of introducing students to the principles of modern design." John Summerson, "The Case for a Theory of Modern Architecture," *RIBA Journal,* 64, (June 1957): 307–310.
[13] Paul Rudolph, "Rudolph," *Perspecta* 7 (1961): 51–64.
[14] James Baker, "Editor's note," *Perspecta* 7, op. cit.: 1.
[15] The British presence at Yale culminated apparently in the academic year 1961–1962. Robert Stern points out that Rudolph imported "a certain amount of outside talent, often from Europe." Many of Rudolph's guests, like James Stirling, Colin St John Wilson, Alison and Peter Smithson, Ralph Erskine, and Serge Chermayeff had received their architectural education in Britain. Stern also mentions the presence in the 1961–1962 masters class of "a remarkable group of English students, including Eldred Evans, Norman Foster, and Richard Rogers." He reports that the English criticized the forced monumentality prevalent at the school and adds, "for many, the arrival of the English critics at the school was a breath of fresh air; for others it was reversion to weak, diagrammatic design or to a form of militant anti-intellectualism." For M.J. Long, who was a student at

his graduate training at Harvard University under Gropius." Rudolph, Collins maintained, was in the process of reacting against the discipline of the Bauhaus in the same way Gropius himself had reacted against the academic system fifty years earlier. Rudolph's latest projects illustrated his "painful metamorphosis from Bauhausian chrysalis to Le Corbusian butterfly." Rudolph's recent design for the nondenominational chapel at the Tuskegee Institute **[Figure 9.6]** was paradigmatic: Collins saw in the drawings a direct influence of Le Corbusier's chapel at Ronchamp and in Rudolph's intention to create an "inviolable asylum" an analogue to the "fortress of faith" of La Tourette. While, only a few years before, Rudolph's Jewett Arts Center at Wellesley College had been designed to harmonize with the existing campus, the concrete Tuskegee Chapel pretended to refer to the Institute's first structures but rejected outright the founder's demand that every building be of brick.

Collins reported that, when asked whether he believed in encouraging his students to explore the way he did it himself, or whether on the contrary he expected that in due course he would have worked out some coherent doctrine that he could teach authoritatively, Rudolph replied evasively that the professions of teacher and architect were entirely distinct. This, Collins concluded, could only mean that Rudolph taught no doctrine at all and thus sided with Le Corbusier, who believed in the unfettered genius of the plastic artist. Such a position was totally irreconcilable with Gropius's insistence that architecture had to be taught systematically because it was simply the art of building.

A few months later, in March, 1962, Rudolph complained to Collins in an unpublished two-page letter.[20] He was furious that Collins interpreted casual remarks of his as if they were the stated policy of Yale's School of Architecture. He wrote that, if he really thought as Collins indicated in his article, he "should resign his post at Yale, and would indeed do so." He added that he regretted having lectured at McGill and announced that he would never do so again. Finally, he concluded that he thought the article was unfair and vicious.

Eighteen months later, Yale invited Nikolaus Pevsner (1902–1983) to give an address at the inauguration of Rudolph's Art and Architecture Building **[Figure 9.7, 9.8]**. A German refugee who settled in England during the 1930s, Pevsner had become famous in the English-speaking world for his book, *Pioneers of Modern Design* (1936), in which he traced the origins of Gropius's Modern factory style of the 1910s back to William Morris and the English Arts and Crafts Movement. Editor of the prestigious *Architectural Review* during World War II, he was seen in England as both a spokesman of the Modern movement, and an expert of English historical architecture.[21] In a talk given at the Royal Institute of British Architects (RIBA) in 1961, Pevsner had condemned the imitation of historical forms in recent architecture, which

Yale at the time, the English critics "were never anti-intellectual; on the contrary, they were highly articulate and historically conscious." Stern again.: 47–48, 51.
[16] According to Gowan, Rudolph's early houses placed a very strong emphasis on structure and in some cases too much. His recent buildings at Yale University and Wellesley College failed to integrate structure and form. James Gowan, "Notes on American Architecture," *Perspecta* 7, op. cit.: 77–82.
[17] St John Wilson criticized the diagrammatic structural form of Saarinen's MIT auditorium, but he praised Aalto's MIT dormitory and Kahn's model for the Richards Medical Research Laboratories at the University of Pennsylvania. Colin St John Wilson, "Open and Closed," *Perspecta* 7, op. cit., 97–102. Peter Collins associated the biographical method in art history with the promotion of individualistic values such as *avant-gardisme,* novelty, and originality. He argued that this attitude, which treated architecture as an art of personal expression, was alien to the idea that new buildings could harmonize with their surroundings. P. Collins, "The Form Givers," *Perspecta* 7, op. cit.: 91–96.
[18] Collins, "After Frank Lloyd Wright," *The Manchester Guardian,* Thursday, 10 November 1960. An architect from Leeds, Peter Collins taught architectural history at Yale for a year in 1955. He was hired by McGill University in 1956. In 1959, he published a well-received book titled, *Concrete: The Vision of a New Architecture,* which examined the work of Auguste Perret and his predecessors. He was a regular contributor to *The Architectural Review* and *The Manchester Guardian.* Annmarie Adams, "Collins, Peter," *The Canadian Encyclopedia* http://www.thecanadianencyclopedia.com/index.cfm?PgNm=TCE&Params=A1ARTA0009713
[19] As a matter of fact, Collins wrote his polemical critique of Paul Rudolph for *Canadian Architect,* which commissioned it but refused to publish it. In a letter to editor Jan Rowan dated 13 January 1961, Collins submitted it for publication to *Progressive Architecture,* with the frank intention of prompting a reply from Reyner Banham. Since the piece had already been published in *The Manchester Guardian,* Rowan asked Collins to rework the text; Collins changed only the opening paragraph. *Progressive Architecture* published the essay under the title "Whither Paul Rudolph?" in August 1961. These documents are kept in the Collins archive deposited at the Canadian Architecture Collection at McGill University, CAC 64-009-019.
[20] These letters were found in the Collins archive, CAC 64-009-019.
[21] Over the years, Pevsner produced an inventory of all significant buildings in England, a work totaling 46 tomes. Thesis advisor of Reyner Banham, he had infuriated the younger generation during the 1950s in celebrating the Englishness of English Art. Reyner Banham, "The Revenge of the Picturesque: English Architectural Polemics, 1945–1965," in *Concerning Architecture: Essays on Architectural Writers and Writings presented to Nikolaus Pevsner,* ed. John Summerson (London: Allen Lane, 1968), 265–273

9.5
Peter Collins, "Whither Paul Rudolph?," ***Progressive Architecture,*** **August, 1961**

Whither Paul Rudolph?

BY PETER COLLINS

One of the more famous mavericks of the modern movement is discussed in this article by McGill University's Associate Professor of Architecture. The author analyzes Rudolph's work and speculates on his possible future development. The original version of the article appeared in The Guardian *(Manchester, England); it has since been somewhat modified by the author for presentation to P/A readers.*

Now that Frank Lloyd Wright no longer dominates the architectural scene, Paul Rudolph is probably the popular press's ideal choice for the role of American Form-Giver of the Space Age, since he was actually born and educated in the United States, and in appearance has all that appeal which we now associate with candidates for the Presidency. His boyish smile, his Ivy League haircut, and his air of quiet determination all produce a confidence-inspiring idea of conformity and good citizenship, whilst his gift for impressive but noncommittal utterances might well be the envy of the most experienced senator. ("The important thing about Ronchamp," he recently remarked, "is that it speaks to many kinds of people, as a chapel should.")

Yet his air of conformity is deceptive, for he is a bohemian and a revolutionary at heart, and leaped to fame ten years ago by producing one of the most ingenious and original summer cottages ever to be constructed in a land positively infested with summer cottages: a single-story house measuring 22 ft by 36 ft, built on such extraordinarily Giedionesque principles of suspension that it was immediately published in the more sensational architectural magazines. He now publicly derides this structure for its illogicality, but continues to astound the bourgeoisie with the novelty of even more enterprising architectural shapes.

The variety of these shapes must have been particularly disconcerting to the art historian because they lack that one quality on which the latter's bread and butter depends—namely, classifiability. Not only have they the appearance of being unrelated to the work of other architects; they do not even seem related to one another in character, materials, or structural systems. On what principles, it is frequently rhetorically asked, are his designs based?

Paul Rudolph justifies the apparent inconsequence of his work by frankly explaining that he has as yet no fixed principles, and asserts that he is still searching for an architecture that will correspond to his own personality, and reflect with complete integrity his, as yet incoherent, sensibility as to what architecture should be. At first this may seem very modest, but it is tinged with an architectural arrogance peculiar to [illegible] age. "Avant moi le déluge," might be his motto. He designs as if no architectural vocabulary existed, and clearly intends to reject the 19th-Century idea that architectural forms develop by a cooperative evolutionary process. He does this, I am convinced, not because he really wishes to, but because of the inescapable pressure of publicity that has been built up around him. He is a classic product of those advertising techniques which, as J. K. Galbraith has pointed out, are now sapping the morale of North American society. On the strength of one or two modest, even though brilliant, little buildings, he has been fêted by the professional press, showered with important commissions (including a United States embassy), and ultimately raised to the chairmanship of one of the most influential schools of architecture on the continent. Every project that comes from his office is now widely publicized, minutely examined by architects and students, and prepared for inclusion in any histories of modern architecture that may be currently in the press. He can no longer afford to design anything

9.6
Paul Rudolph, Tuskegee Chapel, Tuskegee Institute, Tuskegee, Alabama, perspective drawing, c. 1960

he denounced as a resurgence of historicism and a retreat from the Modern style.[22]

Considering that Rudolph publicly distanced himself from Gropius and the International Style, the invitation was provocative and Pevsner did not hide his embarrassment at judging Rudolph's building.[23] For him, the A&A was the work of an individual, just like Peter Wight's Street Hall had been a century before **[Figure 9.9]**; but Street Hall was provincial, while the A&A was a work of international stature. For Pevsner, the problem was that such works could not be imitated, while the style of the 1930s could be with impunity because it was an "exacting style." But he warned the students that imitating an artist-architect like Paul Rudolph would be catastrophic because, being primarily concerned with self-expression, such a great individualist was inimitable.

Pevsner concluded in noticing that the return to individualism in the 1940s and 1950s marked a decisive change. Feeling outdated, he welcomed the idea that Rudolph would help students develop their own provocative styles. He concluded with the observation that the A&A was a rare instance in which the client and the architect were the same person. Consequently, the building could not be failed for lack of partnership between client and architect.

With this diplomatic assessment, Pevsner avoided engaging in the controversy over the legitimacy of individualism in architectural education and thus stayed cautiously away from the painful polemics started by Collins.[24]

Reyner Banham certainly knew these events when he wrote his paper for the American Institute of Architects/Association of Collegiate Schools of Architecture (AIA-ACSA) Teacher Seminar titled, "History, Theory, and Criticism of Architecture," organized at the Cranbrook Academy of Art in 1964.[25] On this occasion, Peter Collins spoke on the necessity of a consistent theory for architectural design based on historical precedents. Banham, who spoke on criticism, argued instead that a theory of the French kind, as promoted by Collins, had become obsolete. Moreover, he considered that contemporary theory was vacuous and empty of formal content and devices. In focusing on general rules, theory forgot those particular reasons "which cause buildings to be created and cause buildings to be the precise way they are."[26] He indicated that John Summerson "in a famous paper at RIBA on the absence of any theory of Modern architecture, spoke of the "programme" as being the generator of architectural form in the Modern movement."[27] Whether the architect accepted the brief wholly or rejected it outright, the programme remained his basic term of reference, and was therefore the basic term of reference for any discussion of a building. Banham conceived criticism as a description looking for "the consistent working out of a personal response to the commission."

To illustrate his point, Banham compared Rudolph's Art and Architecture Building at Yale **[Figure 9.7, 9.8]** and Stirling and Gowan's Engineering Block at Leicester University **[Figure 9.10]**. The contrast revealed two opposite approaches. In the first case, the architect was to a certain extent his own client, and after numerous modifications the building ended up being exactly like the drawing. Banham concluded: "it is a building *about draftsmanship* . . . it is a building *for* draftsmanship and a building conceived *in terms of* draftsmanship." In the second case, the job was conceived in terms of engineering, and for economic reasons the conception was fixed very quickly and industrial materials were used. Stirling and Gowan used these restrictions to strengthen the symbolic expression of the building. Interestingly, Banham excluded these two buildings from his official history of Brutalism published in 1966.[28] Although the Leicester Engineering Building's dramatic play of volumes kept something of the aggressive informality of early Brutalism, Banham claimed the work could not be included, for its style no longer depended on

[22] Nikolaus Pevsner, "Modern Architecture and the Historian or the Return of Historicism," *RIBA Journal,* (April 1961): 230–240.
[23] Pevsner, "Address Given at the Inauguration of the New Art and Architecture Building at Yale University, November 9, 1963," *The Journal of the Society of Architectural Historians* 26 (1), 1967: 4–7.
[24] The reader will be interested to know that Pevsner added the following note at the end of his text when it was published in 1967: "Paul Rudolph has left Yale, and settled down in practice, leaving a building to unforeseen successors, tailored by him to his needs, desires, and perhaps foibles exclusively."
[25] Reyner Banham, "Convenient Benches and Handy Hooks: Functional Considerations in the Criticism of the Art of Architecture," in *The History, Theory, and Criticism of Architecture: Papers from the 1964 AIA-ACSA Teacher Seminar* (Cambridge, Mass.: The MIT Press, 1965), 91–106.
[26] Ibid.
[27] Ibid.
[28] Banham, *The New Brutalism : Ethic or Aesthetics?* (New York: Reinhold Publishing Corporation, 1966), 196.

9.7
Paul Rudolph, Yale Art and Architecture Building, Yale University, New Haven, Connecticut, 1958-1963

9.8
Paul Rudolph, Yale Art and Architecture Building, Yale University, New Haven, Connecticut, 1958-1963

9.9
Peter Wright, Street Hall, Yale University, New Haven, Connecticut, 1864

9.10
Stirling and Gowan, Engineering Laboratories, Leicester University, United Kingdom, 1963

9.11
Paul Rudolph, Married Student Housing, Yale University, New Haven, Connecticut, 1962

Le Corbusier.[29] And, among the buildings of Paul Rudolph, it was not the Art and Architecture Building but the Yale Married Student Housing (1962) that Banham considered Brutalist **[Figure 9.11, 9.12]**.[30] Because Rudolph chose deliberately the image of an Italian hill town to group the housing units, this cluster belonged to the few Brutalist realizations concerned with the problem of the total built environment.

Retrospectively, Banham's method of stylistic classification, which played the memorable image against honesty of structure and materials, seems dubious.[31] On the one hand, he excluded the A&A Building from Brutalism because its surface was "artfully coarse," but he never discussed its image. On the other hand, he praised the image of the Housing project but never examined its construction. Perhaps Banham never saw the buildings completed.[32] Curiously, he did not mention that Rudolph designed two projects for the Married Student Housing. The first was to be built of exposed concrete blocks with "Dox" concrete floors. But to lower the cost, Rudolph designed a second project, which was actually built of wood frames with brick veneer.[33] The facades incorporated concrete strips signaling the positions of the internal wooden floors and roof. The construction details of the built project had none of the structural honesty of a Brutalist canon like Ham Common by Stirling and Gowan, where brick actually supported the exposed concrete floors **[Figure 9.13]**.

That Banham left these details out caused no harm to the thesis of his book.[34] His goal was to express his profound disappointment with the new directions of British Brutalist architects. He judged that they did not break with the classical architectural tradition and never embraced the technological tradition that would create an *"architecture autre."* Banham acknowledged that American architects like Philip Johnson, John Johansen, and Rudolph were quicker than he was "to see that the Brutalists were really their allies," not his. Although the ethical stand of Brutalism was established on the "idea that the relationships of the parts and materials of a building are a working morality," the Brutalists never abandoned the aesthetic framework that restricted, Banham believed, the "White Architecture" of the 1930s. Moreover, recent buildings like the Economist cluster by the Smithsons showed that the ethic of Brutalism proved to be "backward-looking . . . like every reformist trend in architecture." Overall, Banham concluded that it was "very clear that the biggest and most important fact about the British contribution to Brutalism [was] that it [was] all over."

In spite of Banham's proclamation, the Brutalist ethic did not vanish overnight. It survived, metamorphosed, in the critique Robert Venturi and Denise Scott Brown developed in *Learning from Las Vegas.* Although a large part of the book denounced the heroic aesthetics of Brutalism, this critique was based on a polemical analysis of images. Denise Scott Brown explained in an essay titled "Learning from Brutalism" that she was deeply influenced by the Smithsons when she was a student at the Architectural Association in London during the 1950s.[35] She shared the New Brutalists' sensibility for what Peter Smithson called "active socio-plastics," that is the "delight in places and things other architects considered ugly." She also shared their belief that beauty could emerge from designing in a straightforward and unsentimental way for community life. Later, during her studies at the University of Pennsylvania, Scott Brown discovered the work of American sociologist Herbert Gans, in which she found "a similar philosophy (minus the aesthetics)." So, in her work, the Brutalist fascination for found objects and Pop imagery was combined with a new notion: the split between high and low culture in American society described by Gans.

[29] "In many ways, Stirling and Gowan's laboratory-block for Leicester University comes nearer to Brutalism in the emotional sense of a rough, tough building, and in the dramatic space-play of its sectional organization it carries something still of the aggressive informality of the mood of the middle fifties. But stylistic dependence on any building by Le Corbusier is something it does not show at all." Ibid., 134.

[30] Ibid., 130.

[31] In his review of Banham's book, Robin Boyd pointed out that Banham's selection was "by no means arbitrary but extremely personal." According to Boyd, "Paul Rudolph's Yale Art and Architecture Building, with its internal dead-drop gangway, would have had an honoured place. Instead it is mentioned in a way to suggest it was blackballed." This type of exclusion, Boyd wrote ironically, indicated the "finesse of [Banham's] argument." R. Boyd, "The Sad End of New Brutalism," *Architectural Review* 845, July 1967: 9–11.

[32] Banham based his analysis of the Married Graduate Student Housing on the article, "Married Student Dormitories for Yale Planned Like an Italian Hill Town," *Architectural Record,* March 1961, 142–146, which showed drawings of the preliminary project, but he published photographs of the second project, the one built at Yale, to illustrate his analysis. Rudolph's Housing complex was finished when Banham visited Yale at the end of spring 1962; Marshall Burchard, "A New Urban Pattern," *Architectural Forum,* March 1962: 98–100. But Banham did not mention Rudolph's project in his denunciation of Eero Saarinen's Morse and Stiles dormitories. Reyner Banham, "Morse and Stiles," *New Stateman,* July 13, 1962; reprinted in part in *Architectural Forum* 117:12, December 1962: 110–111.

[33] "Rudolph," *Perspecta* 7, op. cit., 52.

[34] Banham, *The New Brutalism...*, op. cit., 134–135.

[35] Denise Scott Brown, "Learning from Brutalism," in *The Independent Group: Postwar Britain and the Aesthetics of Plenty,* David Rob-

Therefore, it is not a coincidence if the theory of ugly and ordinary architecture was based on a critique of the image. From the start, the authors wrote, "We shall emphasize image—image over process or form..."[36] This is a clear indication of their Brutalist heritage. And in their comparison of their Guild House with Rudolph's Crawford Manor, they judged precisely the image of these buildings.[37] They asserted:

"... it is the contrast in the *images* of these buildings in relation to their systems of construction that we want to emphasize. The system of construction and program of Guild House is ordinary and conventional and looks it; the system of construction and program of Crawford Manor is ordinary and conventional but doesn't look it."[38]

Their critique of Rudolph's aesthetic thus reiterated the Brutalist ethical valuation of the honesty of structure and materials. Yet, after they revealed the "lack of correspondence between substance and image" in Crawford Manor, the authors made the following clarification: "We criticize Crawford Manor not for 'dishonesty' but for irrelevance today." The irrelevance of Crawford Manor's aesthetic was its exclusivism: as all works of the Late Modern style, the critics maintained, Crawford Manor impoverished itself by rejecting denotative ornament. The expressionist image of Crawford Manor suggested "the reformist-progressive social and industrial aims that [Modern architecture] could seldom achieve in reality."

Something happened to Brutalism after it crossed the Atlantic: Scott Brown no longer appreciated the "image" through Banham's vague phenomenological model in which the sight of architecture affected emotions, but through the lenses of semiology in which architecture was equated to a language of signs transmitting information. From the ethical point of view, Scott Brown argued that she kept finding help in sociology while the Smithsons "abandoned socio-plastics in favour of Late Modern structural expressionism," a lesser creed in her opinion.[39] From the aesthetic point of view, the coarse construction of Le Corbusier's late projects was superseded by a fascination for Pop imagery in the mid-1960s. While Banham realized he was wrong in believing that the Brutalists were "on the threshold of an utterly uninhibited functionalism, free, even, of the machine aesthetics,"[40] he predicted that a Pop architecture would emerge in 1966.[41] Thoroughly saturated with the Dadaist sensibility of the British Independent Group, Banham could see in the image of an American hamburger bar a truly liberating potential. While Venturi's *Complexity and Contradiction in Architecture* could be seen as a peculiar manifestation of Banham's prophecy, the authors of *Learning from Las Vegas* never embraced the English romance with American popular culture. Inoculated with the split of high and low culture, their semiological analysis of American suburbia looked at commercial architecture with scholarly irony rather than avant-garde radicalism. In the process, Pop imagery lost its millennial overtones and became "dumb and ordinary."[42]

This review shows that the English critics never engaged in a real dialogue with Paul Rudolph. They used his work as a counter-example in their discussion of issues that were quite foreign to the architect's intentions. Ultimately, their writings reflect their own concerns, not Rudolph's.

The New Brutalism: ethic or aesthetic? Banham asked. Completely caught in this predicament, the reception of Paul Rudolph's architecture by English critics illustrates how Brutalist ethical polemics undermined, finally, all Brutalist and non-Brutalist aesthetic experiments.

bins, ed., (Cambridge, Mass., and London, England: The MIT Press, 1990), 203–06. (Publication accompanying the exhibition.)

36 Robert Venturi and Denise Scott Brown, "Ugly and Ordinary Architecture or the Decorated Shed," *Architectural Forum,* November 1971: 64–67. The whole quotation reads as follows: "We shall emphasize image—image over process or form—in asserting that architecture depends in its perception and creation on past experience and emotional association, and that these symbolic and representational elements may often be contradictory to the form, structure, and program with which they combine in the same building."

37 The authors warned the reader that their critique was limited: "Lastly, please don't criticize us for primarily analyzing image: we are doing so simply because image is pertinent to our argument, not because we wish to deny an interest in or the importance of process, program, and structure or, indeed, social issues, in architecture or in these two buildings," Ibid.

38 Ibid.

39 Scott Brown, "Learning from Brutalism," op.cit.

40 Banham, *The New Brutalism...*, op. cit., 135.

41 Reyner Banham, "The Spec-Builders: Towards a Pop Architecture," *Architectural Review* 132:785, July 1962: 43–6. Banham wrote: "Since it is believed in some circles that any revolution in the pure arts must, of some historical necessity, be followed by an equivalent upset in architecture, it is anticipated that the cordon sanitaire between Pop Art and architecture is about to be breached like a metropolitan green belt, and a Pop Architecture emerge about 1966."

42 This, as Peter Eisenman once pointed out, was a major difference between the ordinariness the Smithsons discovered while visiting Mies's buildings in Chicago and the ordinariness Venturi and Scott Brown found in Las Vegas. Eisenman, "Book Review: Ordinariness and Light...", op. cit.

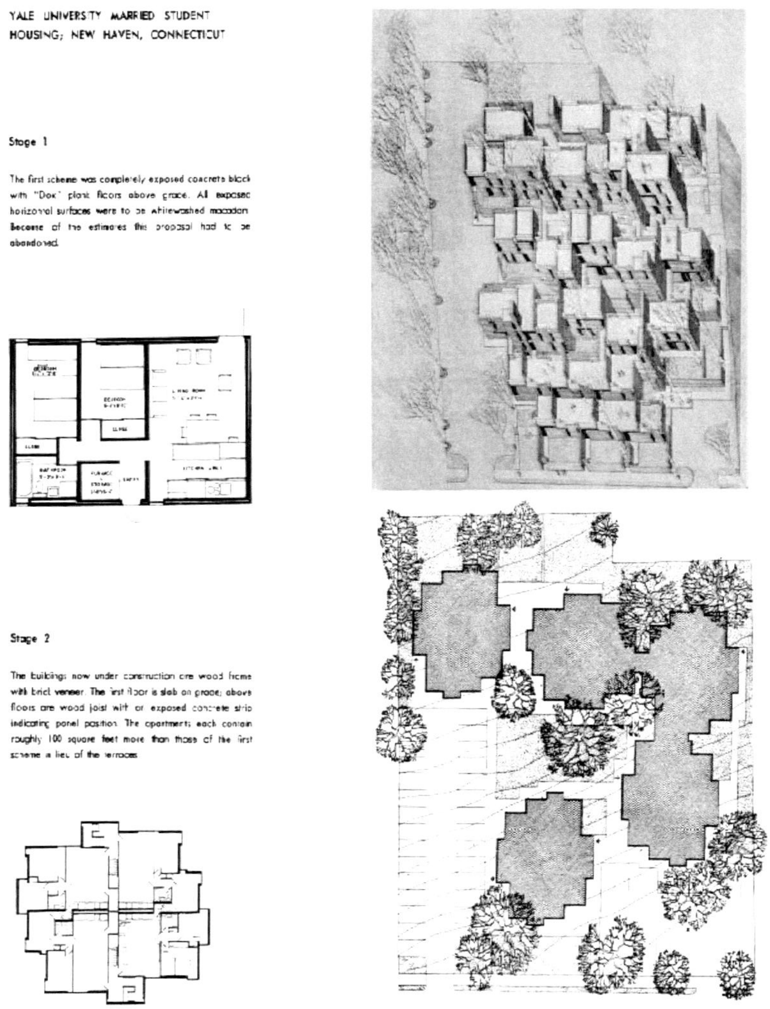

9.12
Paul Rudolph, Married Student Housing, Yale University, New Haven, Connecticut, 1962

9.13
Stirling and Gowan, Ham Common Flats, London, United Kingdom, 1955–1958 Colin Westwood © RIBA Library Photographs

9.14 [next spread]
Paul Rudolph, Married Student Housing, Yale University, New Haven, Connecticut, section, 1962

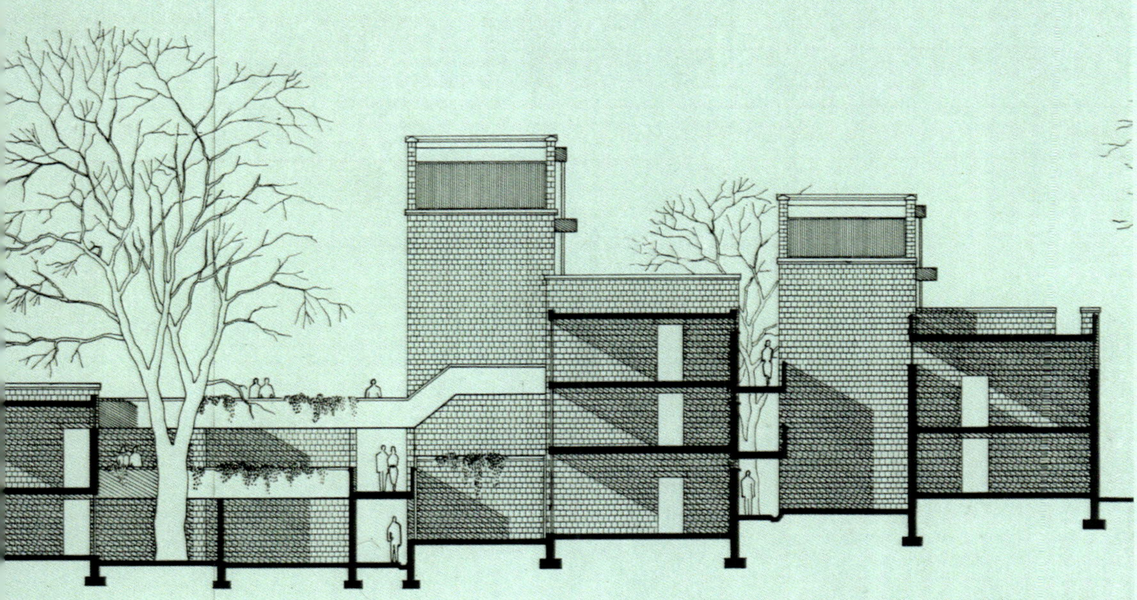

Heroes and Jesters

Emmanuel Petit

10.1
Robert Venturi and Denise Scott Brown, "Ugly and Ordinary Architecture, or the Decorated Shed," 1971

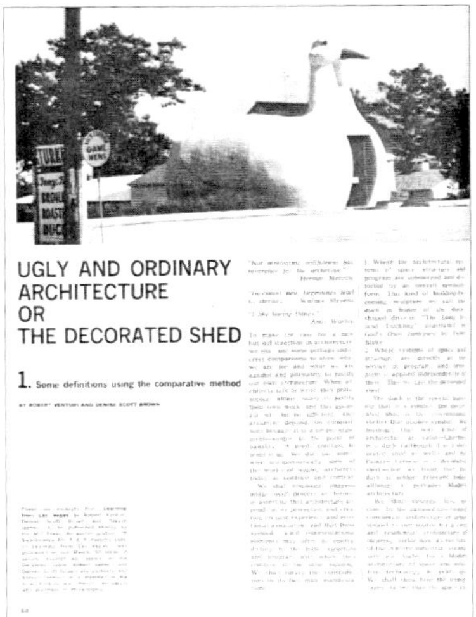
UGLY AND ORDINARY ARCHITECTURE OR THE DECORATED SHED

1. Some definitions using the comparative method

10.2
Alison and Peter Smithson, *The Heroic Period of Modern Architecture*, 1965

The most potent moments for historiography come into view when factual events intersect with the persuasive rhetoric of certain individuals who describe these events. Often, the protagonists of such moments are categorized as heroes; conventionally, the hero possesses commonly accepted virtues and beliefs to be looked up to. He is an agent of change, whereas the deeds and thoughts in the realm of the ordinary do not usually pass the threshold of history-writing, and simply drop out of the picture of history: They are considered status quo. With Paul Rudolph, a fascinating reversal of the normal terminology of historiography seems to have occurred. Such was the intriguing strategy of Robert Venturi and Denise Scott Brown, when they offered Rudolph an ironic—but piercing—kind of compliment in their text published in *Architectural Forum* in 1971, entitled "Ugly and Ordinary Architecture, or the Decorated Shed," which was reprinted a year later in their book, *Learning From Las Vegas* **[Figure 10.1]**. They described Rudolph's Crawford Manor Housing for the Elderly in New Haven as "heroic and original architecture," in contrast to their own Guild House in Philadelphia, which is "ugly and ordinary." Here, the alleged heroes (the architecture and its creator) were no longer perceived as the agents of historical change, but relegated to the old, elitist regime, which had been superseded by the vitality of the "ordinary." In January 1970, Ada Louise Huxtable announced in the headlines of one of her texts in *The New York Times* that "Heroics are Out, Ordinary is In"[1]; apparently, some modifications had been made to the ethics of heroism in architecture and elsewhere, and, despite himself, Paul Rudolph occupied a very important inflection point of history between two extreme versions of the hero in architecture.

The Venturis' claim proved to be effective because Alison and Peter Smithson had guest edited an issue of *Architectural Design* in 1965, entitled "The Heroic Period of Modern Architecture"—a period that had seen its demise a generation prior to their text **[Figure 10.2]**:

[1] Ada Louise Huxtable, "Heroics are Out, Ordinary Is In," *The New York Times*, January 18, 1970, Section 2: 27.

[2] Alison and Peter Smithson, "Prelude to the Heroic Period of Modern Architecture," *Architectural Design* (December 1965); later republished as *The Heroic Period of Modern Architecture* (London: Thames & Hudson, 1981), 5; [my emphases].

[3] Sibyl Moholy-Nagy, introduction to *The Architecture of Paul Rudolph* (London: Thames & Hudson, 1970).

In the period just before and just after the First World War, a new idea of architecture came into being. In an amazingly short time it mastered its necessary techniques and produced buildings which were as completely realized as any in the previous history of architecture. "The period ended when absolute conviction in the movement died, around 1929."[2]

This statement about the end of the heroic period came in handy for Venturi and Scott Brown to explain the belatedness of Rudolph, and certainly influenced their choice of "compliment" when they called Rudolph's architecture "heroic." Also, the same year as Huxtable's article, Sibyl Moholy-Nagy claimed the following in an early monograph on Rudolph, to which she contributed an introduction: "Rudolph's production during the past 25 years is probably the most versatile of the new wave, but it is not an isolated exception, as Louis Sullivan's and Frank Lloyd Wright's concepts had been in their time. It, rather, represents the logical conclusion of an historical genesis that took almost 200 years to complete."[3] Rudolph is portrayed as a figure at the end of a tradition—the last man standing in a time of heroes, which had lasted two centuries and was now coming to an end. For Moholy-Nagy, Rudolph participated in an historical *Aufhebung,* and seemed to embody the "world-historical" *Geist* of a period that both culminated and ended with him. At the same time, she acknowledged a hierarchy of heroes, so to speak, where Sullivan and Wright were deemed more individualistic and more liberated than Rudolph had ever been.

It is well known that Rudolph was almost ignored by the academic press starting in the early seventies; while one can agree with Robert Bruegmann's suggestion that the polemic of *Learning From Las Vegas* was a symptom, not the cause of the decline of Rudolph's reputation, there is no doubt that Venturi and Scott Brown were able to encapsulate a general societal tendency into a striking rhetoric revolving around the predicament of heroism in the late '60s.[4] In this quarrel of the ancients and the moderns, the ancients were the moderns, and the moderns wanted to partake in an older, and more stable, humanist tradition. This inversion could be ascribed to a kind of nonchalant *jeu de mot* on my part, but *only if we did not know that the fallen hero is a favorite trope of postmodernism.* Hence, Venturi and Scott Brown's designation of Rudolph's architecture as heroic is far more than a casual aside or anecdote of history; their rhetoric already contained an idea that would become so fundamental for postmodernism's relationship to the past, including its recent, i.e. "modern," past: distancing (or "swerving"—if one chooses to use the term Harold Bloom coined in his *The Anxiety of Influence,* published in 1973, the year after *Learning From Las Vegas*). And no event could have been more compelling to symbolize the fall of a hero (like the ambitious Icarus) than the then recent incineration of Rudolph's most remarkable oeuvre, the Art and Architecture Building in 1969, no matter what the cause of the fire was in the end **[Figure 10.3]**. There could have been no better springboard for Venturi's body of thought and career than to declare the tragic fallenness of the Modernist hero, Paul Rudolph, whose assistant, Venturi, had been at Yale. Vincent Scully had handed Venturi the combat shout for this historical battle in Scully's foreword to *Complexity and Contradiction* (1966): Venturi was to be the anti-hero, the one who replied to a hero's "steel-toothed smile" (=Le Corbusier's) with the "shrug of a shoulder."[5] The tragic generation of heroes, from Le Corbusier to Rudolph, was to be followed by a more lenient one, which self-consciously accepted the relative and temporary nature of their architectural theories. Two decades after *Complexity and Contradiction,* Scully confirmed that Venturi's buildings took up ". . . their roles in a gentle comedy of citizenship rather than in a melodrama of pseudoheroic aggression"[6]; part of the latter category were some of Rudolph's buildings, notably the Yale Art and Architecture building, which Scully considered "an unforgivable building . . . [where] the materials—with the hammered surface—are very questionable. It's sad, though, [Scully claimed] because it culminated that sort of heroic period in our culture. I think the A&A Building and Becton [Engineering and Applied

[4] Robert Bruegmann, introduction to Roberto de Alba, *Paul Rudolph: The Late Work* (New York: Princeton Architectural Press, 2003).

[5] See Vincent Scully, introduction to Robert Venturi's *Complexity and Contradiction* (New York: The Museum of Modern Art & Chicago: the Graham Foundation for Advanced Studies in the Fine Arts, first published in 1966), 1998 edition. The quote reads: ". . . Venturi is so consistently anti-heroic, compulsively qualifying his recommendations with an implied irony at every turn. Le Corbusier used irony too, but his was as sharp as a steel-toothed smile. Venturi shrugs his shoulders ruefully and moves on."

[6] Scully, "Robert Venturi's Gentle Architecture," *The Architecture of Robert Venturi,* Christopher Mead, ed. (Albuquerque: University of New Mexico Press, 1989), 8.

Science Center] are two of remarkably few failures of Yale's Modern buildings . . ."[7] Venturi promptly accepted the unusual historical role of the anti-hero, and made of Rudolph a worthy nemesis.

In his generation of architects, Venturi was not the only one to use the ruse of designating fallen heroes in order to establish new paradigms; the Japanese architect Arata Isozaki staged a rebellion against the positivism of his teacher, the Corbusian Kenzo Tange, and exploited Japanese death iconography as well as the images of the devastation of Hiroshima and Nagasaki in an exhibition to indicate that the heroes of progress and modernization tended to forget that their creative efforts will inevitably be overcome by history; instead of ignoring and disregarding this fact, it should be seen as part of the complexity and poetry of every life cycle, which always includes the death of ideas and convictions. Isozaki's installation, *Electric Labyrinth,* which he prepared for the Milan Triennale, was destroyed alongside the other contributors' installations during the inaugural press opening on May 30, 1968, by protesting artists, architects, and intellectuals from the Milan University **[Figure 10.4]**.

10.3
Yale Art and Architecture Building, Yale University, New Haven, Connecticut, aftermath of fire, 1969

The fire in the A&A Building, on the one hand, could only be perceived by the Modernist Rudolph as an unspecific yet deep criticism of his personal worldview, and be even personally vexing to him; Peter Blake recalled in 1977 that ". . . there is no question at all that the building has been deeply hurt—and so has its architect. He did not visit it until five years after that fire. And he will not visit it now that the university's management has finished it off."[8] On the other hand, the destruction of Isozaki's exhibition in Milan a year earlier was in a way predictable, and only a confirmation of Isozaki's theory: everybody builds on the ruins of previous generations, and will be overcome by the next generation; he was no exception to this.

10.4
Arata Isozaki, *Electric Labyrinth* exhibition, Milan Triennale, 1968

There is no doubt that the terms of heroism, from Wright to Rudolph, and from Rudolph to Venturi, had changed. In each case, the story of heroism of

[7] "Vincent Scully: On Architecture and its Integral Landscape," *Yale Bulletin & Calendar,* December 3, 2004, vol. 33, no. 13.
[8] Peter Blake, *Form Follows Fiasco: Why Modern Architecture Hasn't Worked,* (New York: Little, Brown & Co., 1977), 18.

10.5
Aldo Rossi, "This is long ago" sketch (from Aldo Rossi, *The Architecture of the City,* 1966)

10.6
Gary Cooper in *The Fountainhead* (Film directed by King Vidor, 1949)

American architecture was a declaration of independence from European cultural domination; this was the case with Wright, a bit with Rudolph, and a lot with Venturi. It is the case that around the late sixties, and seventies, recovering from the disillusionments of Fascist heroism, Europe still celebrated the absurd hero of Existentialism, described foremost in Albert Camus's recounting of the myth of Sisyphus during WWII; although this is something to be explored in detail, for it seems that the relentlessly repetitive nature of Aldo Rossi's archetypes in Italy, or Oswald Mathias Ungers's morphological *mises-en-abime* in Germany, were still rooted in the cyclical-historical, tragic, theatrical, but genuine consciousness of Sisyphus, for whom persistence for the collective survival of humanity—not individual overcoming—was the highest virtue **[Figure 10.5]**. Nevertheless, the American story is a different one. The extreme individualism of Wright, which Moholy-Nagy pointed out in the above quote[9], owed a lot to the notion of the *infinitude of private man,* which poet and philosopher Ralph Waldo Emerson had made fundamental to the credo of American Transcendentalism, mainly with his essay "The American Scholar" from 1837.[10] And, almost predictably, and like the Scottish essayist, satirist, and historian Thomas Carlyle, whom he admired, Emerson also wrote an essay titled "Heroism," in 1841, that can be considered a foundational philosophy of the American hero in which the self-confidence and positivism of nineteenth-century America shone through. From Emerson's observations, we can extract the following:

"The hero is a mind of such balance that no disturbances can shake his will, but pleasantly, and, as it were, merrily, he advances to his own music. . . . There is somewhat (sic!) not philosophical in heroism . . . it has pride; it is the extreme of individual nature. Nevertheless, we must profoundly revere it. . . . Heroism feels and never reasons, and therefore is always right. . . . Heroism works in contradiction to the voice of mankind. . . . Heroism is an obedience

[9] Moholy-Nagy, introduction to *The Architecture of Paul Rudolph* (London: Thames & Hudson, 1970).

[10] "The American Scholar" was a speech given by Ralph Waldo Emerson in 1837 to the Phi Beta Kappa Society in Cambridge, Massachusetts. He was invited to speak as a result of his groundbreaking work *Nature,* published a year earlier, in which he established a new way for America's historically young society to look at the world. The American culture was still heavily influenced by Europe 60 years after declaring independence, and Emerson was, for the first time in the country's history, providing a roadmap on how to escape from underneath that veil and build a new American identity.

[11] Ralph Waldo Emerson, Essay VIII: "Heroism," in *Essays* (n.p., 1841).

[12] In his text, "Burnham, Sullivan, Roark, and the Myth of the Heroic Architect," Ross Miller explains: "While visionaries like Louis Sullivan (1856–1924) and Frank Lloyd Wright (1867–1959) were thought to be Rand's models for Roark, it was Daniel Burnham whose career and attitude towards the profession completed a century-long process of myth-making that put the architect at the center of critical and social attention. . . . Burnham combined the brilliance of a visionary with a businessman's will to get things done; Burnham appropriated the

to a secret impulse of an individual's character . . . for every heroic act measures itself by its contempt of some external good. . . . Its jest is the littleness of common life."[11]

This is not the place to elaborate on the parallels between Emerson's heroic individualism and Wright's convictions, but the caricature made of the latter in Ayn Rand's *Fountainhead* (1943) can figure as an effective reminder of the archetype of the modern American hero.[12] **[Figure 10.6]** The actor Gary Cooper was a more than appropriate choice to play the role of the stoic, dogmatic, and passionate individualist Howard Roark in the film of 1949; Cooper had become one of America's biggest celebrities when he starred in *Sergeant York* in 1941, the biographical film about the real-life war hero Alvin York, who became the legendary, most-decorated American soldier of World War I. The transfer of the ideological gravitas from one film to the other, from war to architecture, was implicit but clear. With a heavy-handed moralism, the story of the *Fountainhead* opens with Roark being thrown out of architecture school, with the dean's warning sounding in his ears: ". . . do you want to stand alone in the whole wide world? There's no place for originality in architecture."[13]

In a just slightly more subdued manner, the precepts of Emerson's American individualism, and the caricature made of it in the *Fountainhead,* can still be seen in Rudolph's architecture and his writings. If Emerson observed that "there is somewhat (sic!) not philosophical in heroism,"[14] Rudolph remarked in an interview that "you have to be a little bit stupid to be an architect . . . [because] you have to be opinionated."[15] Elsewhere, he remarks: "The architect must be uniquely prejudiced. If his work is to ring with conviction, he will be completely committed to his particular way of seeing the universe. It is only then that every man sees his particular truth. Only a few find themselves in such a way."[16] Where Emerson urged us to "Build . . . your own world. As fast as you conform your life to the pure idea in your mind, that will unfold its great proportions,"[17] Rudolph stated that "[W]e need the men in whom love overflows the channel of personal expression, fires the imagination of hundreds, and provides a world of perceptions and sensations of their own, extraordinarily insultingly different from anyone else's."[18] And Emerson's trust in the creative infinitude of the individual is echoed in Rudolph; Nikolaus Pevsner underlined this in his speech at the A&A's inauguration, when he critiqued the 1940s and '50s return to individualism in architecture, and admonished the students against mimicking what ultimately he thought lacked discipline; Pevsner declared: "But woe to him who imitates Paul Rudolph, who imitates Saarinen, Philip Johnson (I mean Philip the Second), or Yamasaki. The result would be a catastrophe. The great individualist, the artist-architect, who is primarily concerned with self-expression, is inimitable."[19] Where Emerson declared that "every heroic act measures itself by its contempt of some external good . . . ,"[20] Rudolph saw architectural design as the exalted task of an individual creator able to rise above the banality and pettiness of the everyday with his art, and to will a world with his self-reliant, creative force. In 1961, Rudolph wrote:

"We must understand that after all the building committees, the conflicting interests, the budget considerations and *the limitations of his fellow man* have been taken into consideration, that his [the architect's] responsibility has just begun. He must understand that in the exhilarating, awesome moment when he takes a pencil in hand, and holds it poised above a white sheet of paper, that he has suspended there all that will ever be. The creative act is all that matters."[21]

Very much in line with the myth of the heroic artist, Rudolph's statement replicated many a decree of contemporary Abstract Expressionism in art; the spontaneous, subconscious, emotionally intense, abstract, gestural process was to reveal a formal truth, where the *image* was the outcome but not the guiding energy of the act of creation. In addition, the artistic search was conceived as a solipsistic

visionary heroic mode—as first expressed by Thomas Jefferson (and later by Sullivan)—and grafted it onto the dominant business ethic of the day." *The Art Institute of Chicago Museum Studies,* vol. 13, no. 2: 87.

[13] Quoted in Demetrios Matheou, "Ayn Rand: Architecture's Only Hero" [film review], *RIBA Journal* (November 1998), vol. 105, no. 11: 24–25.

[14] Emerson, "Heroism."

[15] George Goodwin interview with Paul Rudolph, sound recording on audiotape, 7 January 1993.

[16] Rudolph, *Perspecta* 7 (1961).

[17] Emerson, "The American Scholar," concluding sentences of essay.

[18] Rudolph, "To Enrich Our Architecture," *Journal of Architectural Education* (Spring 1958), vol. 13, no. 1: 56.

[19] Address given by Nikolaus Pevsner at the inauguration of the new Art & Architecture Building at Yale University, 6.

[20] Emerson, "Heroism."

[21] Rudolph, "The Architectural Education in U.S.A.," *Zodiac* 8 (1961): 162–165, quoted in Robert A.M. Stern, "Yale 1950–1965": 47, in: Stern, *Architects on Architects,* Paul Goldberger, ed. (New York: McGraw-Hill, 2002), 184; [my emphasis].

enterprise of a character who had a privileged access to the laws of spatial relationships: "Insofar as he is an artist, Rudolph claimed, the architect must inevitably be subject to the same rule as any other artist, that of personal expression. Here he is alone, despite his many roles."[22]

Towards the end of the sixties, Venturi and Scott Brown's world was a different one. While Rudolph continued to refer to "space" as the central, and almost exclusive, concern of architecture, the Venturis set out to develop an interest in architectural iconography strongly influenced by Pop Art and its appropriation of the imagery of the commercial vernacular, advertising, and mass media. And something happened to the understanding of heroism in the decade in which Pop Art developed. Artists like Roy Lichtenstein searched for their hero in a very different place: his hero existed *as an image,* and was heroic because the social protocols of communication (i.e., mass media and mass culture) had made him into an idol. His was not a war hero, nor the originator of new ideas, nor even a particularly creative individualist, but the result of the cult of the image that everybody could not only aspire to, but actually identify with. In particular, Lichtenstein saw the poignant satirical potential in the banality of the comic strip hero and the superficiality of everyday realism **[Figure 10.7]**. How much his parody of heroism was preparatory of a culturally, politically, and socially rebellious time headed towards a crisis of institutional

[22] Rudolph, "Acceptance Speech" of the Arnold W. Brunner Memorial Prize, *American Academy of Arts and Letters,* second series, no. 9, 1959.

10.7 [opposite page]
Roy Lichtenstein, *In the Car,* 1963
© Estate of Roy Lichtenstein

10.8
Protest in Beinecke Plaza at Yale with students scaling *Lipstick (Ascending) on Caterpillar Tracks* by Claes Oldenburg, 1969

authority is well known; let us just recall that Claes Oldenburg mounted his first public sculpture at Yale in the spring of 1969, and hoped that his *Lipstick (Ascending) on Caterpillar Tracks* would send a more tender message (of what to do with phallic power) to a nation engaged in a tough war in Vietnam. In this degenerating conflict, the meaning and sense of heroism in the United States was on the way to being altered forever, and many had lost their blind trust in the ideology of "big systems," whose single-mindedness was now considered morally naive. The *Lipstick's* blown-up scale seemed to reproduce the glorious monumentality of Rudolph's A&A Building, Saarinen's Stiles & Morse Colleges or Bunshaft's Beinecke Library, but with a radically different intention: that of mocking it **[Figure 10.8]**.

From Pop Art, Venturi, Scott Brown, and Steven Izenour deduced an attitude that questioned what they identified as authoritarianism within architecture; yet the architect who was sensitive to the pluralism of ethical aspirations and aesthetic taste, could no longer subscribe to the same top-down approach. For this to happen, a new type of (non-heroic) architect needed to be found. In *Learning From Las Vegas,* the authors explained that,

". . . people's architecture as the people want it (and not as some architect decides Man needs it) does not stand much chance [until it] is acceptable to the decision makers. Helping this to happen is a non-reprehensible part of the role of the high-design architect; it provides, together with moral subversion through irony and the use of a joke to get to seriousness, the weapons of artists of non-authoritarian temperament in social situations that do not agree with them. *The architect becomes a jester.*"[23]

The Venturis hoped that a realignment of architecture with the communicatory potential of the *image* could do away with the narrow-mindedness of architects' professional monologues, and provide the conditions for architecture to embrace a pluralist society. This step of deliberate and diplomatic superficiality, of course, remained unacceptable to Rudolph, who continued to declare that he was ". . . not at all interested in cartoons of architecture; they are purely an image. . . . As far as I am concerned, [Rudolph explained], the idea of the image being "it" results in caricatures."[24]

At Yale, the Venturis received ideological support for their inclusivist approach from Rudolph's successor as chairman in 1965, Charles Moore. Like the Venturis, Moore saw architecture as a field that had to do away with hermeticism and redefine itself as a public art. As a consequence, Moore suggested that architecture should adopt certain techniques of public rhetoric, including the use of casual asides, of the polemical overstatement, and of the cliché metaphor. In other words, the allegedly objective discourse of the author had to contain a self-aware reminder of the presence of the speaker's *subjectivity.* In his later project for the Piazza d'Italia (1978) in New Orleans, Moore demonstrated how architecture could address the question of the public image and identity of a community. In order to prove his point about the involvement of the architect in this process of public diplomacy, he inserted a bas-relief medallion of his self-portrait in the urban stage set **[Figure 10.9]**. Like the architecture, its architect was turned into a satirical image, which preempted any criticism of authoritarianism. This was Moore's way to signal his doubt vis-à-vis the lonesome quest of the hero-architect and his monumental architecture. Whereas Moore could fundamentally agree with the role of Venturi's jester-architect as a facilitator of social communication, he thought that the latter still adhered to certain heroic instincts of Rudolph and others. A year after *Learning From Las Vegas* appeared, Moore explained that in Venturi's recent writings,

". . . the whole opportunity for expression is taken as a burden, and it becomes a dreary need to be profound and serious and meaningful—and all of that is to be done with the "ordinary." I am interested in getting the freedom from seriousness to mess around, so as to allow a chance to have something exciting and unexpected and wonderful happen. I'm really very heavily distressed by this sanctification of ordinary that begins to make it as difficult to kick as the elegances of the Johnsons and Rudolphs. I attempt to deal with things that are not so ponderous that they can't be lifted, and to keep a certain silliness afloat so that results can also come out of circumstance and out of accident."[25]

Based on the existing literature on Rudolph, it is almost a reflex of revisionist historiography to

10.9
Bas-relief self portrait of Charles Moore, Piazza d'Italia, New Orleans, Louisiana, 1978

[23] Robert Venturi, Denise Scott Brown, Steven Izenour, *Learning From Las Vegas: The Forgotten Symbolism of Architectural Form,* revisited edition (Cambridge, Mass.: The MIT Press, 1977), 161; originally published in 1972 as *Learning From Las Vegas;* [my emphasis].
[24] Rudolph, "Excerpts from a Conversation," *Perspecta* 22, 1986: 102–107; in *Paul Rudolph: Writings on Architecture* (New Haven: Yale School of Architecture and Yale University Press, 2008), 133.
[25] "Interview with John Wesley Cook and Heinrich Klotz," Charles W. Moore, *You Have to Pay for the Public Life* (Cambridge, Mass.: The MIT Press, 2001), 197; originally published in John W. Cook and Heinrich Klotz, *Conversations with Architects* (New York: Praeger, 1973), 200–201.

explain why the two stances of the hero and the jester, which were once seen as opposite, were not so very different after all. It has been argued that Rudolph and the Venturis shared a commitment to define urban spaces of differential character and were influenced by their respective journeys to Europe; that both had a specific interest in using "history" as an imaginative resource; that each of them adorned their buildings with fragmentary allusions and denotations of a quasi-semantic nature; and that both theorized the value of "cliché," the local, and the vernacular. While all of this may be the case, one should not be blinded by an excess of scholarly nuance and forget that the decline of Rudolph's reputation transcended the particular quarrel between Rudolph and the Venturis. This episode is just one of the more polemical narratives that marks a true shift of episteme at this moment in historical time. Rudolph continued his abstract quest for spatial complexity, not least in his buildings in Southeast Asia **[Figure 10.10]**. Only a few architects (one of the most illustrious examples was James Stirling) consciously embraced the shift of consciousness that can be witnessed between the mid-sixties and late seventies. While Rudolph still believed that he could single-handedly engender the geometric, sculptural, and monumental world, the social dimension of the jester-architect was better schooled for survival in the emerging cultural milieu of a simultaneously ideological and enlightened 60s and 70s; the jester was supposed to know how to use a healthy dose of cynicism, wit, and humor to contribute his expertise to the communal problem of the human habitat. The fact that Rudolph became obsolete for academia, even though he continued to conceive spatially highly intricate and fascinating buildings, shows that the architectural discussion has discriminated between the relevant ideas and philosophies which constitute the keystone of architecture, and of which Rudolph had produced many up to a certain critical point, somewhere in the second half of the 1960s.

10.10
Paul Rudolph, Bond Centre, Hong Kong, drawing of the base, 1984–1988

10.11 [next spread]
Paul Rudolph, Yale Art and Architecture Building, Yale University, New Haven, Connecticut, view of interior, 1958–1963

Space as Ritual

Eeva-Liisa Pelkonen

11.1
Paul Rudolph in architecture studio of Yale Art and Architecture Building, New Haven, Connecticut, 1958–1963

Sometime in late 1964 or early 1965, Paul Rudolph posed for a photograph in which he overlooks the fourth-floor studio of the recently opened Yale Art and Architecture Building **[Figure 11.1]**. In the space below him clean-cut young men wearing dress shirts and ties work at drafting boards, oblivious to the architect's presence. Rudolph stares intently at the camera, yet as he rests his arms on a low bush-hammered concrete wall in the foreground, our attention is drawn to his hands. They are huge.

The photographer is no longer known, but he or she must have known something about the issues surrounding Rudolph's architecture during the early part of his career: space as a key architectural element and a belief in a strong psychophysical dimension of architectural experience.

These ideas can be traced at least in part to Henri Focillon, the renowned French art historian who taught at Yale University's Department of the History of Art between 1934–1940, and whose 1934 book *La vie des formes* (published in English as *The Life of Forms in Art* in 1948) was widely read by Yale students and faculty during Rudolph's tenure as the chairman of the School of Architecture from 1957 to 1965.[1]

Focillon's thesis can be summed up as follows: art is an integral part of life. Its forms do not represent anything, but rather evolve as part of our engagement with the world. Art's significance is measured in its ability to enhance and enrich life. Space is one of Focillon's key concepts. In the chapter, "Forms in the Realm of Space," he discusses how the "space of life" and the "space of art" converge. Space, like life, is for Focillon a "plastic and changing material."[2] What follows is a discussion about how such a deeply psychophysical and symbolic understanding of spatial experience informed Rudolph's architecture.

[1] I owe this information to Alexander Purves, who studied under Rudolph.

[2] Henri Focillon, *The Life of Forms in Art,* trans. Charles Beecher Hogan and George Kubler (New York: Zone Books, 1992), 65. Orig. *La vie des formes* (Paris: Presses Universitaires de France, 1934).

11.2
Cover, *Progressive Architecture,*
February 1964

11.3
Fourth-floor studios at the Yale Art and Architecture Building, Yale University, New Haven, Connecticut, 1969

Space

The left side of the photograph of Rudolph captures his own ability to create spatial drama and dynamism. Our eyes drift from desk to desk, then through the building and out to the city. The pinwheeling plan has turned the central space into a vortex of creativity, with Rudolph acting as the wizard behind the scenes.

Almost as soon as the A&A Building opened, space became its most celebrated and contested aspect. *Progressive Architecture's* February 1964 cover story is telling: both the building's fate and the architect's reputation hinged on the question of whether architectural space should exercise psychological power over the viewer or simply fulfill a function **[Figure 11.2]**. The magazine's editorial sums up the questions raised by the building as follows: "Can the building, despite its functional challenges, be considered a tremendous architectural success because it excites the imagination, stimulates the senses, and makes one wonder at man's ingenuity in the manipulation of masses, the shaping of spaces, and the use of light and color?"[3] The question reveals that architectural criticism at the time hinged between the Modernist dogma of "form follows function" and the interest in the experiential, including imaginary, aspects of architecture.[4]

The primacy of space over function gained new meaning only four years into the building's existence when art and architecture students—no longer dressed in white shirts or clean shaven—started to change the building's interior by putting up their own structures within Rudolph's carefully constructed spatial vertigo. A photograph from 1967 is a stark contrast to the one taken only three years earlier: ad hoc enclosures and their hippie inhabitants occupy the double-height fourth-floor studio space of the A&A Building previously occupied by the more orderly scene presided over by Rudolph **[Figure 11.3]**. There is no sign of Charles Moore, who took over from Rudolph in 1965.

It might come as a surprise that the radical art and architecture students of the late 1960s, who would be expected to appreciate the almost psychedelic intensity of the building, actually despised the building, and accused its architect of arrogance at the expense of functional needs.[5] The art students, for example, were unable to work on big canvases in their eight-foot-high studios on the sixth and seventh floors. The building was vandalized and covered with graffiti, and when it mysteriously burst into flame on June 14, 1969, the architecture students were suspected of arson. Many believed that the building was at least in part the cause of such aberrant behavior and anger.[6] Rudolph's intense spaces had triggered a bad trip.

One could argue that such acts substantiated Focillon's argument that the space of art can and should have power over the viewer and that architecture is a symbolic art form that acts on our senses in a very primordial way. To be sure, if measured only by the way the building affected its occupants, the building was a great success; it triggered strong emotions, albeit not necessarily the kind the architect had anticipated.

The idea that Rudolph's architecture had such a powerful effect on its users had been established early in his career, as many critics noted his focus on creating spatial experiences over simply providing for functional concerns. The title of an article on Rudolph's unbuilt project for the Sigma Alpha Epsilon Fraternity House (1952, unbuilt) at the University of Miami, published in *Architectural Forum* in 1953, is telling: "Formal Buildings for Formal Rituals."[7] Significantly, the article replaced the term *function,* which was then becoming a code word for everything that was wrong with Modern architecture, with the word *ritual,* suggesting that

[3] Jan C. Rowan, *Progressive Architecture* (February 1964): 107. Her comments led to a multi-spread article on the Art and Architecture Building.

[4] Philip Johnson's "The Seven Crutches of Modern Architecture" was originally delivered as a lecture at Harvard University in 1954 and published in *Perspecta* 3 (1955): 40–44. In it Johnson talks about a "crutch of utility." In my article "Eero Saarinen's Search for (Communicative) Form," I discuss Saarinen's reception, which was similarly centered around this question of image and expression versus functional and structural form. See Eeva-Liisa Pelkonen and Donald Albrecht, eds., *Eero Saarinen: Shaping the Future* (New Haven: Yale University Press, 2006).

[5] I owe this information to Turner Brooks, who experienced these events as an architecture student.

[6] See, for example, Ellen Perry Berkeley, "Architecture on the Campus: Yale; A Building as a Teacher," *Architectural Forum,* vol. 127 (July–August 1967): 47–63. Berkeley contrasts photographs of the building at its prime with images of the state of affairs three years later and tries to find reasons for the students' acts.

[7] "Formal Buildings for Formal Rituals," n.a., *Architectural Record* (August 1953): 117.

Rudolph's functional building, rather than simply fulfilling the fraternity's needs, would engage the user of its spaces both physically and psychologically. The key argument was that architecture's task is not only to fulfill functional needs but also to construct spatial and visual experiences that have the power to transform one's state of mind. The article also noted how Rudolph crafted his spaces by "careful and imaginative detailing to hold the spectator's interest at close quarters."[8]

Two exhibitions that Rudolph designed in the early 1950s provided a laboratory to experiment with such spatial techniques. The first of these was for the *Good Design* exhibitions, curated by Edgar Kaufman Jr., which took place in 1952, first at the Merchandise Mart in Chicago and then at the Museum of Modern Art (MoMA) in New York. For both installations, Rudolph, working with the lighting designer Richard Kelly, used varying degrees of opaque and transparent walls made of plastic cords, woven cane, and Cocoon (a plastic spray developed for military use) and Kelly's ambient lighting to create highly dramatic contrasts between dark and light areas of the exhibition. An isometric drawing shows the subtle spatial alterations between the dimly lit, spatially compressed areas and the light, open spaces **[Figure 11.4]**. Significantly, only the space between the enclosing walls of the exhibition area is highlighted; it seems to have a palpable material quality. In his book, *Display* (1953), the architect George Nelson celebrated Rudolph's "flair for the dramatic" when discussing Rudolph's exhibition design, while Rudolph himself is quoted about his desire to provide "psychological contrast"[9] in order to keep the visitor psychologically attuned throughout the visit. Nelson also notes how the exhibition consists of "almost nothing"; the focus is on sculpting space with light and human activity.

The success of *Good Design* led to the commission to design the blockbuster exhibition, *The Family of Man,* at MoMA in 1955. Curated by Edward Steichen, the exhibition contained some 2,000 photographs selected from the hundreds of thousands of images submitted by people from all over the world to convey the idea of universal humanity in the aftermath of World War II. Rudolph's installation created a kind of "image space" in which the eye was invited to wander from photograph to photograph, making connections, drawing analogies, and creating narratives without ever settling into a single story line. **[Figure 11.5, 11.6]** The design endorsed various ways of looking at the images by alternately exploding the space with transparent walls and then compressing space with curtains to make intimate nooks and force close-up views. As in the *Good Design* installation, lighting was used in *The Family of Man* to choreograph the movement of the body and the eye in order to charge the already emotionally laden images with an atmospheric intensity that resonated with the theme of the exhibition. Rather than communicate information, the exhibition installation helped to manipulate emotions according to the needs of the subject matter of the exhibit. One can imagine the emotional intensity of wandering among photographs of people from around the world, all of them gazing back at you. It must have felt like merging oneself with humanity at large.

For Rudolph, the psychophysical role of architecture was ultimately to calibrate man's relationship with the world. In 1955, referring to the Walker Guest House (1952–1953) on Sanibel Island, Florida, he wrote, "We need 'caves' as well as 'gold-fish bowls'. . . . Thus if you desire to retire from the world you have a cave, but when you feel good there is the joy of an open pavilion."[10] **[Figure 11.7]** He assumed that people psychologically alternated between being extroverted and introverted and that these characteristics could be translated into primordial architectural models. Architecture's role was not simply to accommodate these states of being, but also to activate and control them; architecture could spur people to tune in or tune out of the world around them.

Another photograph by Elliott Erwitt from 1962, this one of Rudolph's New Haven house as seen from outside during a cocktail party, is suggestive of Rudolph's desire to use architecture as an

[8] Ibid.
[9] George Nelson, *Display* (New York: Whitney Publications, 1953), 134.
[10] Paul Rudolph, "Regionalism in Architecture," *Perspecta* (1957): 12–19. Reprinted in Paul Rudolph, *Writings on Architecture* (New Haven: Yale School of Architecture, 2009), 36.

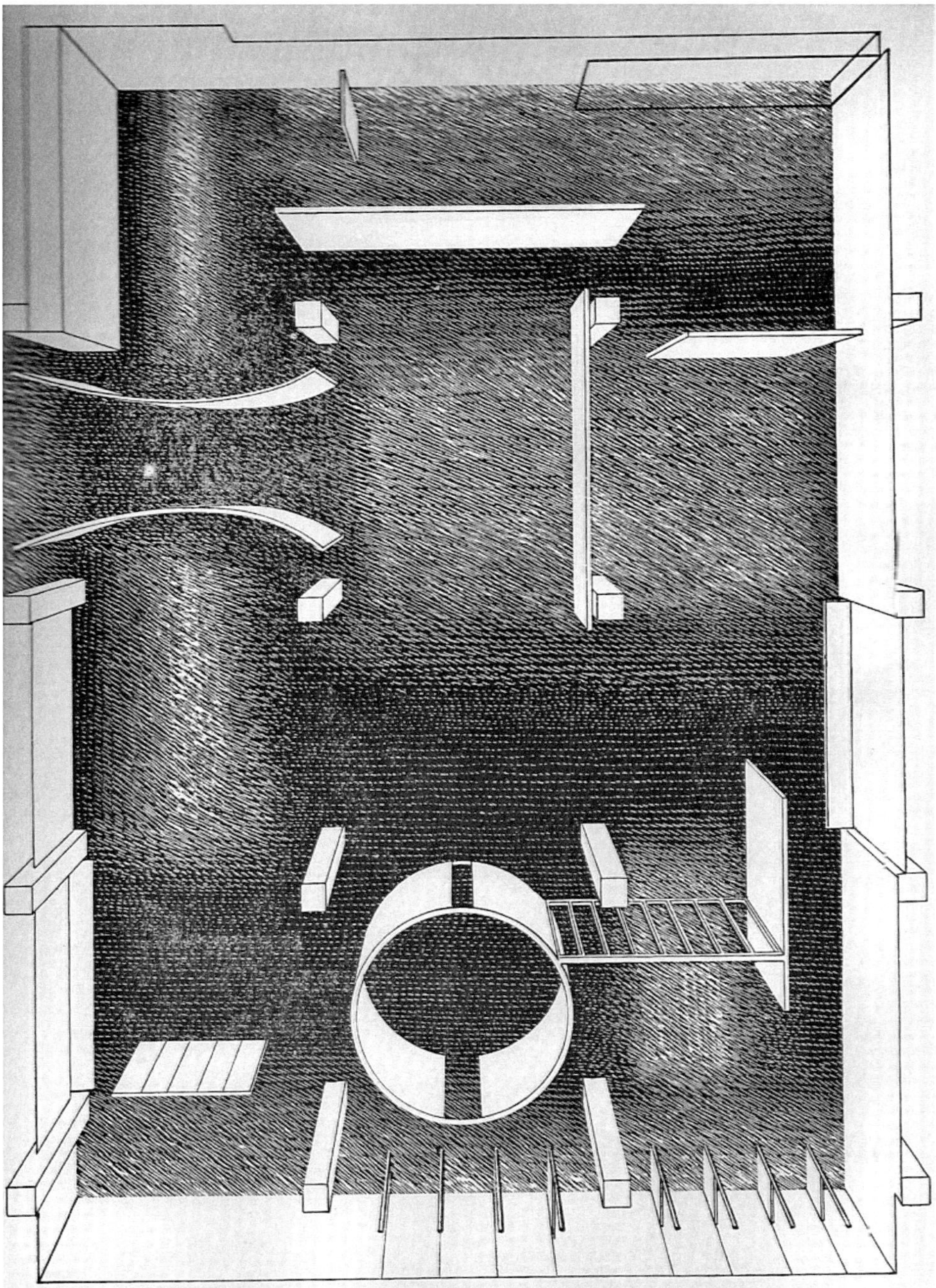

11.4
Paul Rudolph, *Good Design* exhibition, Museum of Modern Art, plan perspective with shading (Richard Kelly, lighting designer), 1952

11.5
Paul Rudolph, installation for *The Family of Man* exhibition, 1955 (Edward Steichen, curator) © Ezra Stoller/Esto

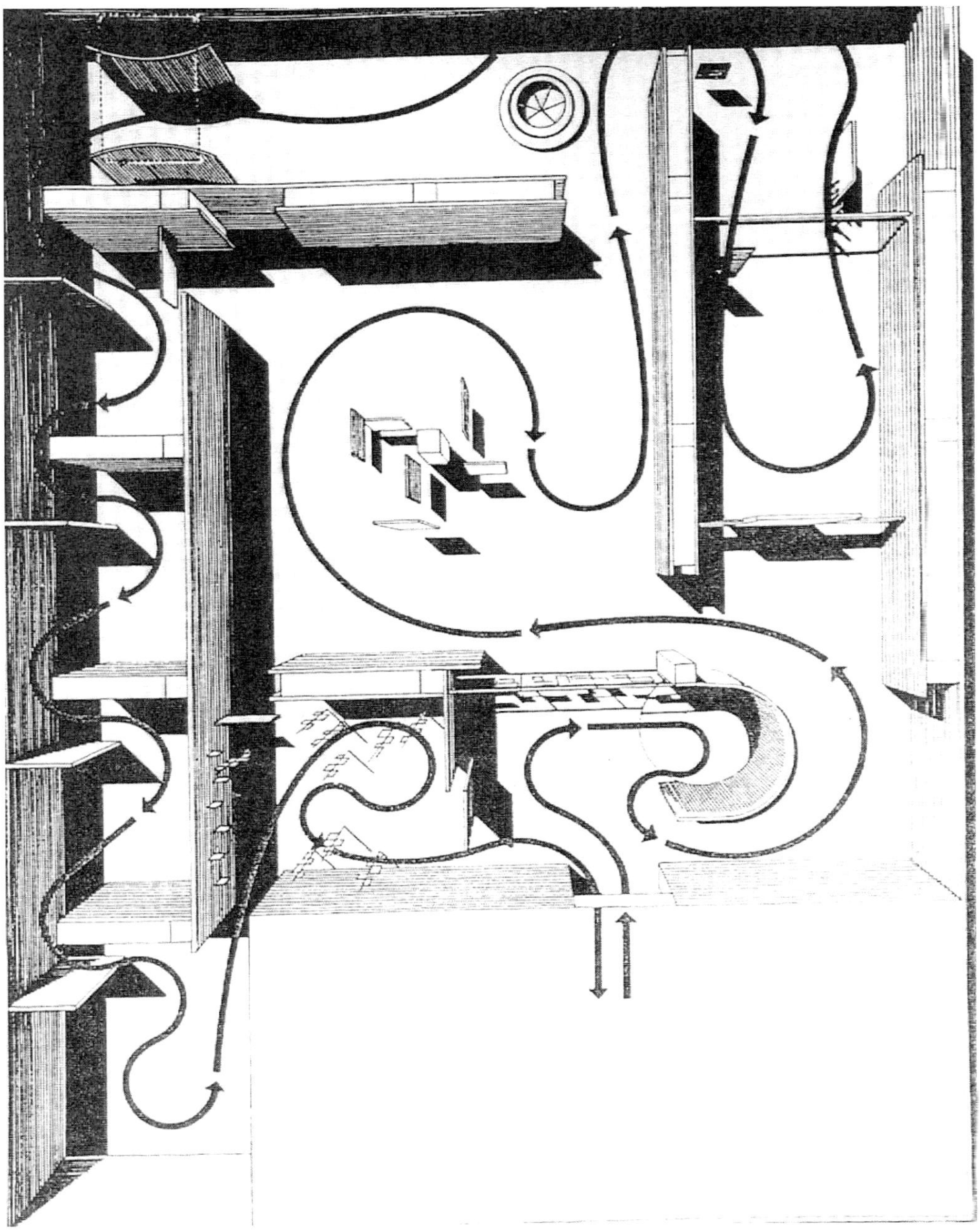

11.6
Paul Rudolph, installation for *The Family of Man* exhibition, Museum of Modern Art, plan perspective with circulation arrows, 1955

11.7
Paul Rudolph, Walker Guest House, Sanibel Island, Florida, 1952–1953

11.8
Image from "Paul Rudolph. How one of the great young architects lives and works," Paul Rudolph Residence, New Haven, Connecticut, 1962

interface between man and the world **[Figure 11.8]**. The glass surface that mediates the relationship between inside and outside produces constantly flickering images from without and within on its surface, as if displaying the human interaction at the heart of Rudolph's spatial imagination. Here activity crafts space.

Surfaces and Patterns

Rudolph's use of space to mediate man's relationship to the world was complemented by his careful use of materials, texture, and light to amplify both visual and haptic sensations. Many contemporary critics drew attention to the heightened visual aspects of Rudolph's play of planes and surfaces. Writing in *Architectural Review's* special issue devoted to American architecture in 1957, critic John Knox Shear focused on the frontal, planar view of the Walker Guest House, calling attention to how "its fine, spare frame is carefully scaled: the total structure—in plan or profile—presents a simple retainable image; its voids and solids produce a rich play of light and shadows."[11] Shear's words echo Le Corbusier's famous dictum in *Toward an Architecture:* "Architecture is the masterly, correct, and magnificent play of masses brought together in light,"[12] which famously reduced architecture to an optical phenomenon. In addition, Le Corbusier codified different types of forms and patterns with different sensations, such as "equilibrium" and "diversity." The Swiss architect famously preferred the former, embodied in Platonic solids, but Rudolph clearly preferred the latter, seen in the various types of patterns and lines that marked his buildings.

[11] John Knox Shear, "One Hundred Years of Significant Buildings," *Architectural Forum* (February 1957): 204.
[12] Le Corbusier, *Toward an Architecture,* trans. John Goodman (Los Angeles: Getty Research Institute, 2007), 31.

11.9
Paul Rudolph, Blue Cross/Blue Shield Building, Boston, Massachusetts, 1957–1960

A review of Rudolph's Blue Shield/Blue Cross Building in Boston, titled "Pattern with Purpose," celebrated the architect's ability to combine structure and decoration in a "patterned structure."[13] **[Figure 11.9]**. With the visual still the primary way of experiencing buildings, the eye was invited to take pleasure in the dynamic pattern created by the extruded steel structure covered with a precast concrete veneer, which cast shifting shadows across the facade. To add to the display of dynamic surface effects, white quartz added to the concrete created a shimmering effect.[14]

Rudolph's shift from the thin membranes of the early projects to the use of concrete in the late 1950s had attracted attention, not least because it was in stark contrast to the abstract white surface of International Style Modernism. Henry-Russell Hitchcock who with Philip Johnson helped to coin the term with the *Modern Architecture: International Exhibition* presentation in 1932, noted upon completion of the A&A Building how "Rudolph's exterior is one of the most boldly plastic that the postwar years have produced."[15] Rudolph considered the A&A's concrete to be "at once expressive of concrete and human rather than machinelike, warm rather than cold, in its boldly sensuous character."[16] The plasticity of the surface did not—and still does not—simply produce different moods but became an animated entity in itself, able to arouse emotional responses, as if a living thing.

The Architect and His Hands

When making sense of the strong psychophysical dimension of Rudolph's buildings, critics could

[13] "Pattern with Purpose," n.a., *Architectural Forum* (August 1958): 110–113.
[14] For more information about the building see Timothy M. Rohan, "Challenging the Curtain Wall; Paul Rudolph's Blue Cross and Blue Shield Building," *Journal of Architectural Historians*, vol. 66, no. 1 (March 2007): 84–109.

[15] Henry-Russell Hitchcock, "Connecticut, U.S.A. in 1963," *Zodiac* 13 (1964): 14.
[16] Ibid.

not resist making links between the architect, his psyche, and the character of his buildings. To be sure, Rudolph himself was as famous as his buildings. His rise into the architectural elite was phenomenally rapid. Not only was he building by his early thirties, by his late thirties he was world-famous. He was thirty-six when he received first prize in the Young Architect Competition in the 1954 São Paulo Biennial for the Walker Guest House. Throughout the 1950s Rudolph's work was often published in tandem with the slightly older group of architects considered the leading American "form-givers" of the era: Eero Saarinen (1910–1961), Gordon Bunshaft (1909–1990), Louis Kahn (1901–1974), and Harry Weese (1915–1998), when American architecture was the envy of the world. In 1953, *Architectural Review* reported that Rudolph was "on the threshold of a world reputation." He was barely forty when he was appointed chairman of architecture at Yale in 1958.

Around 1957, magazines and books began to publish photographs of Rudolph drawing. While Eero Saarinen, his mentor and, for a brief time, employer, was often photographed with his perpetual pipe, Rudolph's main prop was the pencil. In one photo he bends over a drawing table so that his face is only inches away from his paper. Rudolph was already famous as a draftsman, and his projects, when published, were often accompanied by his stunning drawings **[Figure 11.10]**. Vincent Scully was the first to theorize this aspect of Rudolph's architecture, seeing the link between the spatial and material ambience and the act of drawing, which for him provided the link to the architect's psyche. Scully writes in his customary psychologizing tone:

"Whoever uses the building is caught up in human complexity—in the curiously intimate scale of personal drama—in that insatiable will and unappeasable anxiety.

One senses the fast-drawing pencil with its compulsively neat, parallel linear shadings, which studied each nook and cranny time after time, proliferating forms, breaking them down, recombining."

Scully continues to consider the building with its multitude of levels, nooks, and crannies "as complicated as any human soul, as dark and tortuous in some places, as surprisingly generous in many others, lighted from unexpected sources, a never-ending wonder to explore."

Rudolph, according to Scully, did not merely represent his ideas in a drawing, but his hand and the pencil acted as a seismograph that registered the movements of his mind on the paper as lines.[17] Here, Rudolph comes across as the ultimate modern man, hypersensitive to the world around him.

His ode to Rudolph's drawings was based on an idea of hand-mind coordination as reflective of the ideal harmony between man and the world. Hands mediate that relationship through creative work. Similarly, in the *The Life of Forms in Art,* Focillon discusses the emphasis placed on hands in painting and the way they have been treated as windows to the human soul. He celebrates the creative act conducted by hands as an unmediated registration of the movements of the mind, writing, "Through his hands man establishes contact with the austerity of thought. They quarry its rough mass. Upon it they impose form, outline and, in the very act of writing, style."[18] Focillon's account of the creative act comes close to Scully's praise of Rudolph's drawing; the hand has an ability to guide the thought, helping us to see and to think before we can even put the idea into words.

Rudolph was not the only architect shown drawing in the 1950s. For example, Le Corbusier's hands are shown drawing in his book, *Creation is a Patient Search,* published in 1960, and Alvar Aalto is sketching in a photograph published in a 1957 issue of the Italian magazine, *Zodiac.* Here, too, the creative act conducted by hands was a sign of a truly sensitive human being, which in the context of postwar Europe can be interpreted as something that became valued as a sign of individual freedom after years of totalitarianism.

The most defining moments of Rudolph's career occurred in the 1950s and 1960s, at the same time that the notion of the individual creator as the

[17] Vincent Scully, "Art and Architecture Building Yale University," *The Architectural Review,* vol. 807 (May 1964): 332.
[18] Focillon, *The Life of Forms in Art,* 157.

promise of a truly authentic human existence began incrementally to become less and less believable. A photograph of Rudolph drawing, circa 1960, seems to capture this shift; it is rather intense and hardly communicates ease with the world. Rudolph's nose is only a few inches from the paper, the lines a bit too frantic. In another photograph, from 1966, Rudolph's hands are no longer drawing but rather clutching the corrugated wall surface. Instead of calling for a response from the viewer, these portraits communicated a sense of closure; all that is left is the architect and his building, which was no longer communicating with its audience.

Rudolph was only fifty years old when the A&A Building caught fire in 1969. Suddenly, he and his building were considered out of sync with their time, even though for a decade prior Rudolph had been presumably completely in sync with the minute movements of the human psyche.

Coda

The A&A Building, renamed Paul Rudolph Hall in 2008, continues today to intrigue and engage its viewers with its grand and intimate spaces. Before its restoration was completed in 2008, it appeared as a beautiful ruin with traces of life and time everywhere: spray paint, food stains, cracked concrete. The events of the past are now part of the collective memory of the building. After years of being blocked off, the numerous vistas into the city through multiple spaces, as well as experience of simultaneous activities that go on in and around the building, can once again be enjoyed. To be sure, if the ability to create spatial dynamism and celebrate human life was at the crux of Rudolph's architecture, the building remains an architectural tour de force.

11.10 [above]
Paul Rudolph, Yale Art and Architecture Building, Yale University, perspectival rendering, 1962
© The Museum of Modern Art/Licensed by SCALA/ Art Resource, NY

11.11 [next spread]
Paul Rudolph, Oriental Masonic Gardens, New Haven, Connecticut, second floor plan, 1968–1971

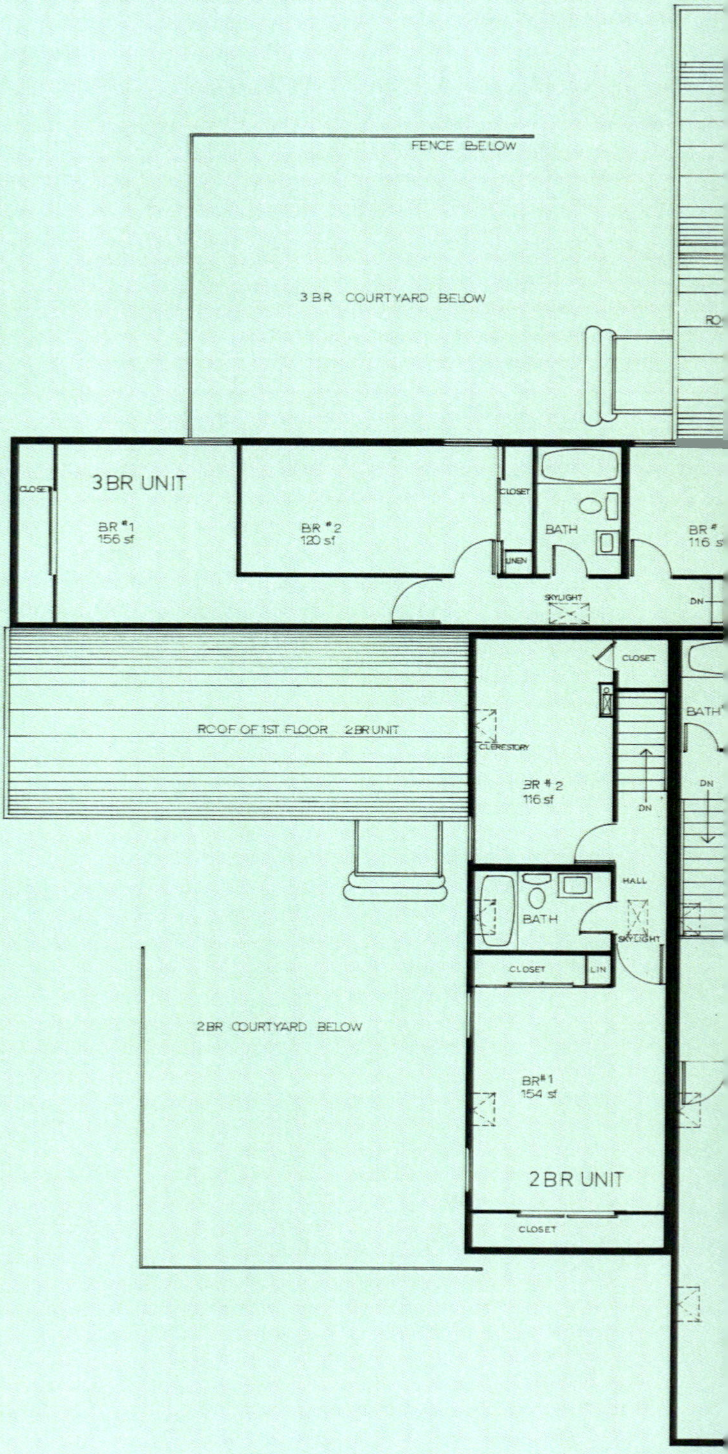
FENCE BELOW
3 BR COURTYARD BELOW
3BR UNIT
CLOSET
BR #1
156 sf
BR #2
120 sf
CLOSET
LINEN
BATH
SKYLIGHT
DN
ROOF OF 1ST FLOOR 2BR UNIT
CLOSET
CLERESTORY
BR #2
116 sf
DN
HALL
BATH
SKYLIGHT
CLOSET
LIN
2BR COURTYARD BELOW
BR #1
154 sf
2BR UNIT
CLOSET

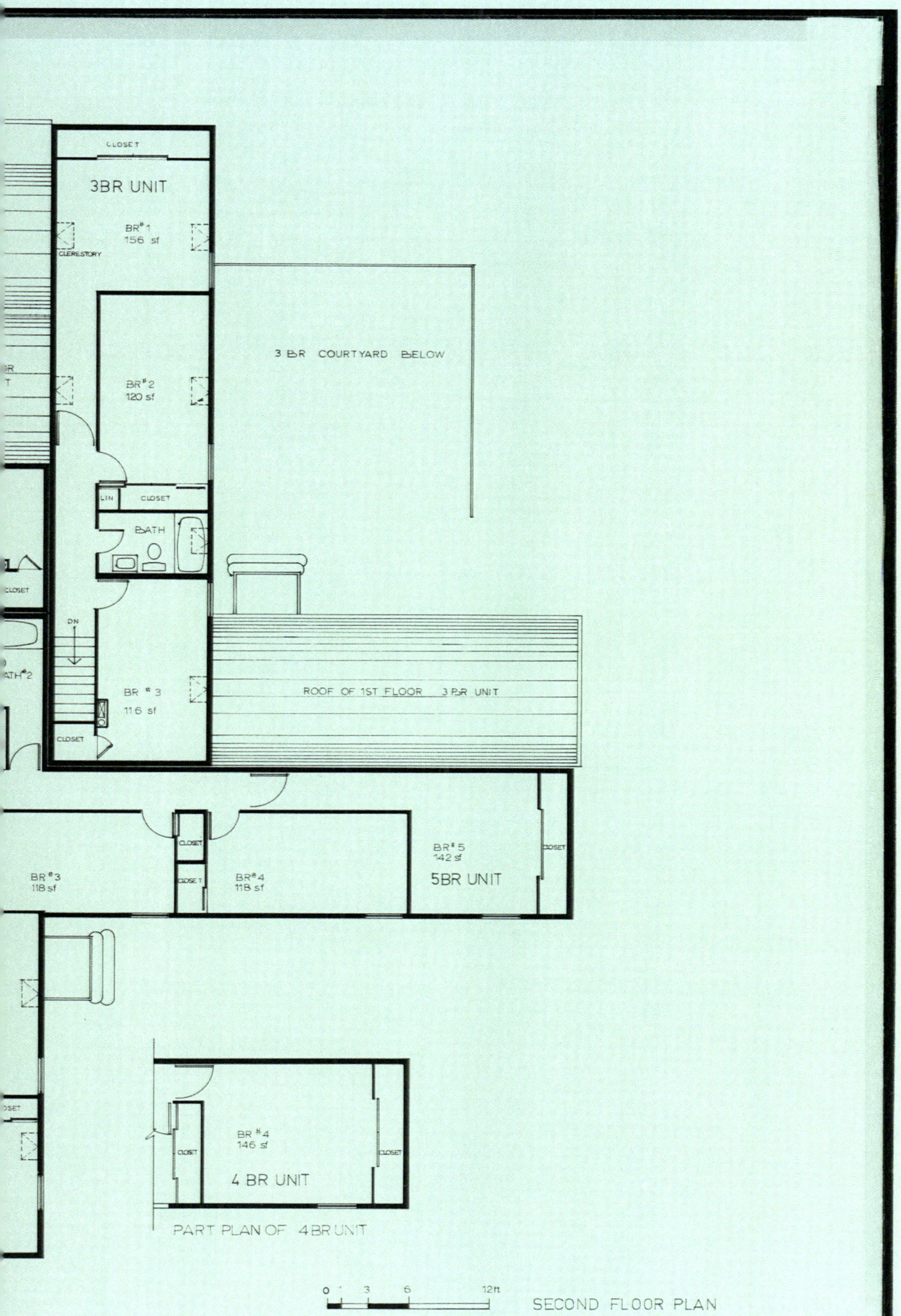

SECOND FLOOR PLAN

AUTHORS

Kazi K. Ashraf is an architect and architectural historian. After having taught at the University of Hawaii at Manoa, University of Pennsylvania, Temple University and Pratt Institute, Ashraf currently directs the Bengal Institute for Architecture, Landscapes and Settlements, in Dhaka, Bangladesh. Ashraf's publications include: *Locations: Anthology of Architecture and Urbanism* (2016), *Architecture and Asceticism in India* (University of Hawaii Press, 2013); *An Architect in Bangladesh: Conversations with Muzharul Islam* (LOKA, 2014); *Designing Dhaka: A Manifesto for a Better City* (LOKA, 2012); and a special issue of *Architectural Design "Made in India"* (2007) that received the Pierre Vago Journalism Award. He has also contributed to *The Architectural Review, Architectural Design, Topos, Journal of Architectural Education*, and other publications.

Lizabeth Cohen is the Dean of the Radcliffe Institute for Advanced Study and the Howard Mumford Jones Professor of American Studies in the Department of History, both at Harvard University. Among her many publications, she is the author of *Making a New Deal: Industrial Workers in America, 1919–1939* (Cambridge, 1990; 2nd edition 2008; Canto Classic 2015), *A Consumers' Republic: The Politics of Mass Consumption in Postwar America* (Knopf 2003), and *Saving America's Cities: Ed Logue and the Struggle to Renew Urban America in the Suburban Age* (Farrar, Straus & Giroux, 2019), to which this essay is related. She is a member of the American Academy of Arts and Sciences.

Brian D. Goldstein is assistant professor of architectural history at Swarthmore College. He was previously assistant professor at the University of New Mexico and an A.W. Mellon Postdoctoral Fellow at the University of Wisconsin–Madison. He is the author of *The Roots of Urban Renaissance: Gentrification and the Struggle Over Harlem* (Harvard University Press, 2017). His writing has also appeared in the *Journal of American History, Journal of Urban History*, and in the edited collections *Affordable Housing in New York* (Princeton University Press, 2016) and *Summer in the City: John Lindsay, New York, and the American Dream* (Johns Hopkins University Press, 2014).

Pat Kirkham is Professor of Design History at the University of Kingston, UK, in the Department of Art, Design, and Architecture, and Professor Emerita at Bard Graduate Center: Decorative Arts, Design History, Material Culture, New York. She has written widely on design, gender, and film. Her many publications include *Charles and Ray Eames: Designers of The Twentieth Century* (MIT Press, 1995); *The Gendered Object* (Manchester University Press: ed. and contributing author, 1996), *Women Designers in the USA 1900-1000: Diversity and Difference* (Yale University Press: ed. and contributing author, 2000); *Saul Bass: A Life in Design and Film* (LKP, 2011), *Eva Zeisel* (Chronicle Books: ed. and contributing author,

2013). She is currently co-curating an exhibition on William Morris and the British Arts and Crafts Movement and completing a book on working on the Eameses and Hollywood.

Sylvia Lavin is an architectural historian, critic, and curator who works across a wide spectrum of historical periods. She is known for her simultaneous engagement with academic scholarship and contemporary architectural practice. She published her first books, *Quatremère de Quincy and the Invention of a Modern Language of Architecture* and *Form Follows Libido: Architecture and Richard Neutra in a Psychoanalytic Culture,* in 1992 and 2005. Her most recent books include, *Kissing Architecture,* published by Princeton University Press and *Flash in the Pan,* an AA publication. Ms. Lavin is currently working on *The Duck and the Document,* an exhibition on the history of Postmodernism and on *Exhibition Models/Super Models,* a double installation for the Chicago Architecture Biennial and the Princeton University School of Architecture Gallery. Previous exhibitions include, *Everything Loose Will Land,* an examination of architecture and the arts in Los Angeles in the 1970s. She is Professor and Director of the Critical Studies Program in the Department of Architecture and Urban Design at UCLA.

Réjean Legault is associate professor at the École de Design of the Université du Québec à Montréal. Among his contributions to architectural research, he established the Visiting Scholars Program at the Canadian Centre for Architecture and directed its Study Centre. His own research, lectures, and publications focus on the historiography of modern architecture, the relationship between materials and architectural modernity, postwar tectonics, and the idea of Brutalism in architecture. He is the editor of *Anxious Modernisms: Experimentation in Postwar Architectural Culture* (with Sarah Williams Goldhagen, 2000), and the author of numerous journal articles, volume chapters, and exhibition catalog contributions.

Louis Martin is associate professor in the Department of Art History at the Université du Québec à Montréal. He is the editor of *On Architecture: Melvin Charney, A Critical Anthology* (MQUP, 2013). He received his Ph.D. in Architecture from Princeton University in 2002, with his doctoral dissertation entitled *The Search for a Theory in Architecture: Anglo-American Debates, 1957-1976.* He is currently editing the book *Papineau, Gérin-Lajoie, Le Blanc: An Architecture for Modern Québec.* Martin is the author of essays published in *Log, Assemblage,* the *Journal of the Society of Architectural Historians, Casabella, ARQ, Les cahiers de la recherche architecturale et urbaine,* and *Exposé,* among others. He is a member of LEAP *(Laboratoire d'étude de l'architecture potentielle).*

Eric Paul Mumford is Rebecca and John Voyles Professor of Architecture in the Sam Fox School of Design & Visual Arts at Washington University in St. Louis. He is the author of a textbook, *Designing the Modern City: Urbanism since 1850*, forthcoming from Yale University Press, and *The CIAM Discourse on Urbanism, 1928–1960* (MIT Press, 2000); *Modern Architecture in St. Louis* (Washington University, 2004); and *Defining Urban Design: CIAM Architects and the Formation of a Discipline, 1937–1969* (Yale University Press, 2009), along with several edited books and many scholarly articles. He is currently also an advisor to the exhibition, *Transformative Visions: Landscape, Art, and Design*, at the Kemper Museum of Art, Washington University.

Ken Tadashi Oshima is professor of architecture at the University of Washington, Seattle and has served as President of the Society of Architectural Historians from 2016–2018. Oshima's publications include *Kiyonori Kikutake: Between Land and Sea* (Lars Müller, 2016), *Architecturalized Asia* (University of Hong Kong Press, 2013), *International Architecture in Interwar Japan: Constructing Kokusai Kenchiku* (University of Washington Press, 2009), and *Arata Isozaki* (Phaidon, 2009). He curated the exhibitions *Tectonic Visions Between Land and Sea: Works of Kiyonori Kikutake* (Harvard GSD, 2012), *SANAA: Beyond Borders* (Henry Art Gallery 2007–2008), and was co-curator of *Frank Lloyd Wright at 150: Unpacking the Archive* (MoMA, 2017) and *"Crafting a Modern World: The Architecture and Design of Antonin and Noémi Raymond"* (University of Pennsylvania, University of California-Santa Barbara, Kamakura Museum of Modern Art, 2006–2007).

Eeva-Liisa Pelkonen is an associate professor at Yale School of Architecture, where she teaches design, history and theory. Her scholarly work deals with the genesis and meaning of form in various geographic and historical contexts. She is the author of three books: *Achtung Architektur! Image and Phantasm in Contemporary Austrian Architecture* (MIT Press/Graham Foundation, 1996), *Alvar Aalto: Architecture, Modernity and Geopolitics* (Yale University Press, 2009), and *Kevin Roche: Architecture as an Environment* (Yale University Press, 2011), and a co-editor with Donald Albrecht of *Eero Saarinen: Shaping the Future* (Yale University Press, 2006), as well as with Carson Chan and David Andrew Tasman of *Exhibiting Architecture: A Paradox?* (Yale School of Architecture and Actar, 2015).

Emmanuel Petit is currently a visiting professor at the École Polytechnique Fédérale in Lausanne, Switzerland, and taught architectural design and theory at Yale School of Architecture, Harvard Graduate School of Design, MIT, and The Bartlett School of Architecture as associate professor and visiting associate professor. He is the author of *Irony, or The Self-Critical Opacity of Postmodern Architecture* (Yale University Press, 2013), and editor of *Reckoning with Colin Rowe* (Routledge, 2015), of *Schlepping Through Ambivalence: Writings on An American Architectural Condition* (Yale University Press, 2011), and of *Philip Johnson: The Constancy of Change* (Yale University Press, 2009). He is founding partner of EPISTEME architecture with Ralitza Petit, and partner at JEAN PETIT ARCHITECTES S.A.

Timothy M. Rohan is associate professor in the Department of the History of Art and Architecture at the University of Massachusetts Amherst. He is the author of *The Architecture of Paul Rudolph* (Yale University Press, 2014), organizer of "Reassessing Rudolph: Architecture and Reputation" conference at Yale (January 23–24, 2009), and editor of this volume of essays first given at that conference. He also curated an exhibition at the Yale School of Architecture (2008–2009) about Rudolph's New Haven projects in conjunction with the rededication of Rudolph's Yale Art and Architecture Building (1958–1963) as Rudolph Hall. Rohan is the author of articles published in the J*ournal of the Society of Architectural Historians, Casabella, Art in America*, and other publications.

Tom Tredway is an assistant professor in the Department of Design at California State University, Long Beach. His publications include contributions to *Biography, Identity and the Modern Interior* (Ashgate, 2013), *Eva Zeisel: Life, Design, and Beauty* (Chronicle, 2013), and *History of Design: Decorative Arts and Material Culture, 1400-2000* (Bard Graduate Center and Yale University Press, 2013).

Image Credits

Every reasonable attempt has been made to identify owners of copyright. Errors or omissions will be corrected in subsequent editions.

Peter Aaron © Otto: 4.9, 4.10

Tazrin Ahmed: 3.5

Architecture and Urbanism 49.1 (1975): 1.7

"Pattern with a Purpose," n.a. *Architecture Forum* (August 1958): 11.9

Kazi Ashraf: 3.1, 3.6, 3.7, 3.10, 3.11

Harry Benson: 4.8

Roy Berkeley: 11.3

Bharat Kala Bhaban: 3.4

Peter Bray: 1.12

Reginald Hugo de Burgh Galwey © RIBA Library Photographs Collection: 9.1, 9.2

Jean Paul Carlhian: 9.7

Clare Floyd DeVries: 10.9

Elliott Erwitt © Magnum Photos: 11.8

Lionel Freedman: 9.4

Oberto Gili: 7.1, 7.2, 7.3

Brian D. Goldstein: 1.3

Pino Guidolotti © Serralves: 10.4

Saif Ul Haque: 3.2

Frances Loeb Library, Harvard University Graduate School of Design: 8.3

Journal Bay State Architecture: 5.10

Journal Concrete Products: 5.8, 5.9

Library of Congress, Prints and Photographs Division: 0.1, 1.1, 1.4, 1.5, 1.11, 1.13, 2.2, 2.4, 2.7, 3.9, 4.2, 4.4, 4.11, 5.2, 5.5, 5.7, 5.11, 6.1, 6.2, 6.3, 6.5, 6.6, 6.7, 6.8, 7.4, 7.5, 7.6, 7.7, 7.8, 8.4, 8.5, 8.8, 9.6, 9.11, 9.14, 10.10, 10.11, 11.1, 11.2, 11.11

Library of Congress, The Paul Rudolph Archive, Prints and Photographs Division: 1.8, 1.9, 1.10, 3.8

Roy Lichtenstein © Estate of Roy Lichtenstein 10.7

Laurence Lowry: 2.1

George C. Manning, *Manual of Ship Construction* (New York: D. Van Nostrand Company, Inc., 1942): 8.2

Massachusetts Institute of Technology, Courtesy of MIT Libraries, Rotch Visual Collections, Photo by G.E. Kidder Smith: 6.9

Eric Mumford: 2.6, 2.8

The Museum of Modern Art © Licensed by SCALA/Art Resource, NY: 11.10

George Nelson, *Display* (1953): 11.4, 11.6

Scott Norsworthy: 5.3

Bob Perron: 5.6

Perspecta 7 (1961): 9.12

Progressive Architecture, (August 1961): 9.5, (April 1963): 8.6

James Righter: 6.10, 6.11, 6.12, 10.8

Alison and Peter Smithson, *The Heroic Period of Modern Architecture* (London: Thames and Hudson, 1965): 10.2

Ezra Stoller © Esto: 1.6, 4.1, 4.3, 4.5, 4.6, 4.7, 5.1, 5.4, 6.4, 9.8, 9.9, 11.5, 11.7

Manfredo Tafuri, *Architecture and Utopia: Design and Capitalist Development* (Cambridge: MIT Press, 1979): 10.5

Ralph Taylor: 1.2

Stanley Tigerman: 3.3

Robert Venturi, Denise Scott Brown, and Steven Izenour, *Learning from Las Vegas: The Forgotten Symbolism of Architectural Form* (Cambridge, Mass: MIT Press, 1977): 10.1

Warner Brothers, *The Fountainhead* (1949): 10.6

Colin Westwood © RIBA Library Photographs Collection: 9.13

Wikimedia Commons: 2.3, 2.5, 9.3, 9.10

Yale University Manuscripts and Archives, School of Architecture, Yale University, memorabilia, c. 1913–2011 (inclusive): 8.1, 8.7

Yale University Manuscripts and Archives, Yale University buildings and grounds photo-graphs, 1716–2004 (inclusive), Manuscripts & Archives Yale University: 10.3

Acknowledgements

There are many people I would like to thank for their valuable support in completing this book, especially Robert A. M. Stern, former dean of the Yale School of Architecture, who initiated its concept by asking me to organize the symposium, "Reassessing Rudolph: Architecture and Reputation," in 2009. Dean Deborah Berke of the Yale School of Architecture made it possible to complete the publication.

I would especially like to thank all of the authors who contributed dedicated scholarship to create their essays. To complete the book production, I would like to thank Nina Rappaport, Publications Director at Yale School of Architecture, as well as Cynthia Davidson and Ann Holcomb, who copy edited the manuscript.

Numerous people assisted with the images, including Erica Stoller of Esto and Yale University Manuscripts and Archives. Special thanks go to Amy Kessler who designed and organized the book, from its layout to research on the images and obtaining the permissions.

Timothy M. Rohan